Study Guide

SO-DOQ-769

Financial Accounting
An Introduction to Concepts, Methods, and Uses
ELEVENTH EDITION

Clyde P. Stickney

Dartmouth College

Roman L. Weil

University of Chicago

Prepared by

LeBrone Harris

University of South Florida

James Moon

Illinois State University

COPYRIGHT © 2006
Thomson South-Western, a part of The Thomson Corporation. Thomson, the Star logo, and South-Western are trademarks used herein under license.

Printed in the United States of America
1 2 3 4 5 08 07 06 05

ISBN: 0-324-22678-0

For permission to use material from this text or product, submit a request online at http://www.thomsonrights.com.

For more information about our products, contact us at:

Thomson Learning Academic Resource Center

1-800-423-0563

Thomson Higher Education
5191 Natorp Boulevard
Mason, OH 45040
USA

THOMSON
™
SOUTH-WESTERN

Australia · Canada · Mexico · Singapore · Spain · United Kingdom · United States

Introduction to Business Activities and Overview of Financial Statements and the Reporting Process

Chapter Highlights

1. Firms prepare financial statements for various external users-owners, lenders, regulators, and employees. The statements attempt to present in a meaningful way the results of a firm's business activities.

2. Companies establish goals or targets that are the end results toward which the energies of the firm are directed. The company's strategies are the means for achieving the company's goals.

3. Financing activities involve obtaining funds from two principal sources: owners and creditors. For a corporation, owners receive shares of common stock to provide evidence of ownership. The firm need not repay the owners at a particular future date. Instead the owners receive distributions, called dividends, when the firm decides to pay them. Creditors provide funds and require that the firm repay the funds, usually with interest, at a specific date.

4. Funds obtained from owners and creditors are invested in various items needed to carry out the firm's business activities. The funds are invested in various resources in order to generate earnings.

5. Firms communicate the results of their business activities through the annual report to shareholders. Included in the annual report are a letter from the chairperson of the firm's board of directors and from its chief executive officer, a management discussion and analysis section in which a firm's management discusses reasons for changes in profitability and risk during the past year, and the firm's financial statements and supplementary information.

6. The balance sheet presents a snapshot, at a moment in time, of the investing and financing activities of a firm. The balance sheet presents a listing of a firm's assets, liabilities, and shareholders' equity.

7. Assets are economic resources that have the potential or ability to provide future services or benefits to the firm.

8. Liabilities are creditors' claims on the assets of a firm and show the sources of the funds the firm uses to acquire the assets. Typically, liabilities require that a specific amount be paid on a specified date.

9. Shareholders' equity is the owners' claim on the assets of the firm. The owners' claim is called a residual interest because owners have a claim on all assets of the firm in excess of those required to meet creditors' claims.

10. Shareholders' equity is generally comprised of two parts: contributed capital and retained earnings. The funds invested by shareholders make up contributed capital. Retained earnings represent the earnings realized by a firm since its formation in excess of dividends distributed to shareholders.

11. The relative mix of assets reflects a firm's investment decisions, and the relative mix of liabilities plus shareholders' equity reflects a firm's financing decisions. Therefore, Assets = Liabilities + Shareholders' Equity
    or   Investing = Financing
                Resources = Sources of Resources
                Resources = Claims on Resources

12. The balance sheet presents an overall view of a company's financial position as of a given date and classifies assets and liabilities as being either current or noncurrent.

13. Current assets include cash and assets that are expected to be turned into cash, or sold, or consumed within approximately one year from the date of the balance sheet. Current liabilities represent obligations that are expected to be paid within one year.

14. Noncurrent assets are typically held and used for several years. Noncurrent liabilities and shareholders' equity are a firm's longer-term sources of funds.

15. Assets, liabilities, and shareholders' equity items might have balance sheet values measured on one of two bases: (a) a historical valuation, or (b) a current valuation.

16. A historical valuation reflects the acquisition cost of assets or the amounts of funds originally obtained from creditors or owners. A current valuation reflects the current cost of acquiring assets or the current market value of creditors' and owners' claims on a firm.

17. The income statement presents the results of the operating activities of a firm for a period of time. Net income or earnings is the difference between revenues and expenses.

18. Revenues are a measure of the inflows of assets (or reductions in liabilities) from selling goods and providing services to customers. Expenses are a measure of the outflows of assets (or increases in liabilities) used in generating revenue. Net income results when revenues exceed expenses. When expenses for a period exceed revenues, a firm incurs a net loss.

19. The income statement links the beginning and ending balance sheets through the Retained Earnings account. The amount of net income helps explain the change in retained earnings between the beginning and end of the period.

20. The statement of cash flows reports the net cash flow relating to operating, investing, and financing activities for a period of time. The statement explains the change in cash between the beginning and end of the period and details the major investing and financing activities of the period.

2

21. For most firms, a primary source of cash is the firm's operating activities. The excess of cash received from customers over the amount of cash paid to suppliers, employees, and others is the amount of cash provided by the firm's operating activities.

22. Investing activities include selling existing noncurrent assets and the acquisition of noncurrent assets.

23. Financing activities include new financing (issuing bonds or common stock) and using cash to pay dividends and to retire old financing.

24. Every set of published financial statements is supplemented by explanatory notes. These notes indicate the accounting methods used by the firm and also disclose additional information which elaborates on items presented in the three principal statements. To fully understand a firm's balance sheet, income statement, and statement of cash flows, a careful reading of the notes is required.

25. A certified public accountant, upon the examination of a client's accounting records and procedures, expresses an opinion on the fairness of the client's financial statements.

26. The opinion usually contains three paragraphs. The first paragraph indicates the financial presentations covered by the opinion and indicates that the responsibility for the financial statements rests with management. The second paragraph affirms that auditing standards and practices generally accepted by the accounting profession have been followed by the auditor unless otherwise noted and described. The opinion expressed by the auditor in the third paragraph regarding the financial statement's fair presentation of financial position and results of operations may be unqualified or qualified.

27. Most opinions are unqualified. The auditor describes no exceptions or qualifications to its opinion that the financial statements are fairly presented in conformity with generally accepted accounting principles.

28. If an auditor cannot express an opinion as to the fairness of the financial statements as a whole, the auditor must issue either a disclaimer of opinion or an adverse opinion.

29. One issue that faces the accounting profession is: Who should have the authority for establishing acceptable accounting standards? A governmental body could develop accounting standards and use its legislative power to enforce them. A private sector body would more likely incorporate viewpoints of various preparer and user groups in developing accounting standards but would lack the power to enforce the accounting standards.

30. Another issue faced by the accounting profession is: Should standard-setters require uniformity in accounting method across firms or should firms be allowed flexibility in selecting accounting methods?

31. A third issue concerns the type of accounting standards that standard-setting bodies should adopt. One approach is to specify general principles for a particular reporting topic and permit firms and their independent auditors to make judgements as to the application of those general principles to the particular circumstances. A second approach is a detailed rules-based approach which attempts to constrain opportunistic actions by management by closing perceived loopholes in reporting standards.

32. Employees of a firm conduct internal audits (a) to assess the capability of the firm's accounting system to accumulate, measure, and synthesize transactional data properly and (b) to assess the operational effectiveness of the firm's accounting system. External audits by independent auditors assess whether the financial statements "present fairly the financial position...and the results of operations and cash flows... in conformity with generally accepted accounting principles."

33. Financial statements should serve as reliable signals of value changes of firms so that investors, security analysts, and other users can make wise economic decisions. Minimizing intentional management bias through appropriately applied accounting standards and effective, independent audits enhances the reliability of the financial statements.

34. The Securities and Exchange Commission (SEC) has the legal authority to set acceptable accounting methods, or standards, in the United States. The SEC has delegated most of the responsibility for establishing such standards to the Financial Accounting Standards Board (FASB).

35. The FASB issues its major pronouncements in the form of Statements of Financial Accounting Standards. These pronouncements are referred to as generally accepted accounting principles (GAAP). For some financial reporting topics, the FASB requires the use of a uniform accounting method by all firms. In other cases, firms enjoy some freedom to select from a limited set of alternative methods. The current standard-setting approach lies somewhere between uniformity and flexibility, tilting toward uniformity.

36. The FASB has developed a conceptual framework to use as a guide for setting accounting standards. One of the components of the conceptual framework is a statement of the objectives of financial reporting. The seven objectives are:

    a. Provide information useful for making investment and credit decisions.
    b. Provide information to help investors and creditors assess the amount, timing, and uncertainty of cash flows.
    c. Provide information about economic resources and claims on those resources.
    d. Provide information about a firm's operating performance.
    e. Provide information about how a firm obtains and uses cash.
    f. Provide information for assessing management's stewardship responsibility to owners.
    g. Provide explanatory and interpretative information to help users understand the financial information provided.

4

37. The Public Company Accounting Oversight Board (PCAOB) has responsibility for monitoring the quality of audits and the financial reporting process. The Sarbanes-Oxley Act which set up the PCAOB requires the PCAOB to register firms conducting independent audits, establish or adopt acceptable auditing, quality control, and independence standards, and provide for periodic "audits" of the auditors.

38. The globalization of capital markets in recent years has increased the need for comparable and understandable financial statements across countries. The International Accounting Standards Board (IASB) has played an important role in developing acceptable accounting principles worldwide.

Questions and Exercises

True/False. For each of the following statements, place a T or F in the space provided to indicate whether the statement is true or false.

_____ 1. An important part of an annual report is the report's management discussion and analysis section. This section is devoted to a discussion of the firm's new product offerings.

_____ 2. The Financial Accounting Standards Board (FASB) has responsibility for monitoring the quality of audits and the financial reporting process.

_____ 3. The International Accounting Standards Board (IASB) has the legal authority to set acceptable accounting standards for European countries.

_____ 4. A firm's balance sheet reports the company's financial position while its income statement reports the firm's profitability.

_____ 5. Paying dividends to shareholders would be reported in a firm's statement of cash flows as an investing activity.

_____ 6. Noncurrent assets provide firms with long-term productive capacity.

_____ 7. Contributed capital represents the earnings realized by a firm since its formation in excess of dividends distributed to stockholders.

_____ 8. Acquisition of noncurrent assets is an activity that would result in an inflow of cash for a firm.

_____ 9. One of the objectives of accounting is to help investors and creditors assess the amount, timing, and uncertainty of cash flows.

_____ 10. Financial accounting is concerned with the preparation of reports that provide information to users external to the firm.

_____ 11. Shareholders' equity is the owners' claim on the assets of the firm.

_____ 12. A disclaimer of opinion or an adverse opinion occurs when the auditor believes an opinion cannot be expressed as to the fairness of the financial statements as a whole.

_____ 13. The balance sheet presents the results of earnings activity over time.

_____ 14. Financial reporting should provide useful information for making rational investment and credit decisions.

_____ 15. Issuing bonds or common stock are examples of investing activities that would result in an inflow of cash for a firm.

_____ 16. The Securities and Exchange Commission has the legal authority to establish accounting standards and issues its pronouncements in the form of Statements of Financial Accounting Standards.

_____ 17. The first paragraph of the auditor's opinion indicates the financial presentations covered by the opinion and indicates that the responsibility for the financial statements rests with management.

_____ 18. The income statement attempts to present an overall view of a firm's financial position at a given date.

_____ 19. Current liabilities include liabilities that are expected to be paid within one year.

_____ 20. "Generally accepted accounting principles" are the accounting methods and procedures used by firms in preparing their financial statements.

_____ 21. The statement of cash flows provides information about the operating, financing, and investing activities of a firm.

_____ 22. The terms net income, earnings, and profits are synonymous and are defined as the difference between revenues and expenses for a period.

_____ 23. Retained earnings represents the sum of all prior earnings of the firm in excess of dividends.

_____ 24. Most auditors' opinions are qualified because of uncertainties regarding the valuation of assets or outstanding litigation.

_____ 25. The two sources of any firm's assets are the firm's creditors and owners.

Matching.
From the list of terms below, select that term which is most closely associated with each of the descriptive phrases or statements that follows and place the letter for that term in the space provided.

a.	Assets	p.	MD&A
b.	Balance Sheet	q.	Net Income
c.	Contributed Capital	r.	Net Loss
d.	Disclaimer of Opinion or Adverse Opinion	s.	Operating Activities
e.	Dividends	t.	PCAOB
f.	Expenses	u.	Retained Earnings
g.	FASB	v.	Revenues

h. Financing Activities

i. Goals

j. Historical Valuation

k. IASB

l. Income Statement

m. Internal Audits

n. Investing Activities

o. Liabilities

w. Sarbanes-Oxley Act of 2002

x. SEC

y. Shareholders's Equity

z. Statement of Cash Flows

aa. Statement of Financial Accounting Standards

bb. Strategy

cc. Unqualified Opinion

_____ 1. Issuing long term debt is an example of this kind of activity.

_____ 2. These audits are conducted by a firm's employees and do not add as much credibility to the firm's financial statements as an independent audit provides.

_____ 3. This group has responsibility for monitoring the quality of audits and the financial reporting process.

_____ 4. Major pronouncements issued by the Financial Accounting Standards Board.

_____ 5. This legislation established the Public Company Accounting Oversight Board.

_____ 6. This financial statement presents an overall view of a company's financial position as of a given date.

_____ 7. This financial statement presents the results of earnings activity over time.

_____ 8. Such an opinion states that the statements "present fairly the financial position...and the results of operations and cash flows ...in conformity with generally accepted accounting principles."

_____ 9. Economic resources that have the potential or ability to provide future services or benefits to the firm.

_____ 10. Inflows of assets (or reductions in liabilities) from selling goods and providing services to customers.

_____ 11. This should be a primary source of cash for most firms.

_____ 12. The excess of expenses over revenues for a period.

_____ 13. Owners' claim on the assets of the company. The owners' claim is called a residual interest.

_____ 14. Reflects the acquisition cost of assets or the amounts of funds originally obtained from creditors or owners.

_____ 15. This item represents the earnings, or profits, realized by the firm since its formation in excess of dividends distributed to shareholders.

_____ 16. Such an opinion is given when the auditor feels an opinion cannot be expressed as to the fairness of the financial statements as a whole.

_____ 17. The excess of revenues over expenses for a period.

_____ 18. Represents a measure of the assets provided by the original shareholder in exchange for an ownership interest in the firm.

_____ 19. Outflows of assets (or increases in liabilities) used up in generating revenue.

_____ 20. This financial statement reports the net cash flows relating to operating, investing, and financing activities for a period of time.

_____ 21. Creditors' claims on the resources of the company.

_____ 22. Although it has no legal authority, this organization has played a role in developing acceptable accounting principles worldwide.

_____ 23. This organization is an agency of the federal government and has the legal authority to set acceptable accounting standards in the United States.

_____ 24. This private-sector group has been given the responsibility to establish acceptable accounting standards in the United States.

_____ 25. Refers to the targets, or end results, toward which the firm directs its energies.

_____ 26. Distributions paid to owners of a firm.

_____ 27. Purchasing land, building, and equipment which provide a firm with the capacity to manufacture and sell its product is an example of this kind of activity.

_____ 28. Refers to a letter from the firm's management summarizing the activities of the past year and assessing the firm's prospects for the coming year. This letter appears in the annual report to shareholders.

_____ 29. A firm might choose to emphasize cost control and strive to be the low-cost producer in its industry as a way of reaching its goals or targets.

Multiple Choice. Choose the best answer for each of the following questions and enter the identifying letter in the space provided.

_____ 1. Which of the following has the legal authority to establish acceptable accounting methods, or standards, in the United States?

    a. FASB
    b. SEC
    c. IASB
    d. PCAOB

_____ 2. Which of the following would not appear on a balance sheet?

    a. Merchandise Inventory
    b. Accounts Payable
    c. Common Stock
    d. Dividends

_____ 3. Which of the following would not appear on a balance sheet?

    a. Retained Earnings.
    b. Bonds Payable.
    c. Cost of Goods Sold.
    d. Accounts Receivable.

_____ 4. Which of the following transactions of the Filipp Company does not result in an outflow of cash?

    a. Purchased a tract of land.
    b. Paid dividends to shareholders.
    c. Reacquired some of the company's common stock.
    d. Long-term debt was issued.

_____ 5. Which of the following is not a current asset?

    a. Patent.
    b. Inventory.
    c. Accounts Receivable.
    d. Cash.

_____ 6. Kim Corporation sold inventory which had a historical cost of $1,500 for $4,600 to a customer on account. This transaction is an example of which of the following:

    a. An investing activity.
    b. A financing activity.
    c. An operating activity.
    d. None of the above.

_____ 7. "Claims on the resources that result from benefits previously received by the company, which require that a specified amount be paid on a specified date." This statement describes which of the following?

    a. Shareholders' Equity.
    b. Contributed Capital.
    c. Liabilities.
    d. Retained Earnings.

_____ 8. Lonski Company reports total assets and total liabilities of $900,000 and $400,000, respectively, at the conclusion of its first year of business. The company earned $190,000 during the first year and distributed $100,000 in dividends. What was the firm's contributed capital?

    a. $500,000.
    b. $410,000.
    c. $310,000.
    d. $180,000.

_____ 9. Which of the following financial statements provides information about economic resources and claims on those resources?

    a. Income Statement.
    b. Balance Sheet
    c. Statement of Cash Flows.
    d. All of the above.

_____ 10. Ania Company reports total assets and total shareholders' equity of $750,000 and $440,000, respectively, at the end of its first year of business. The company reported earnings of $120,000 and distributed dividends of $40,000 during its first year. Also, during the year, the company issued additional shares of stock for $150,000. What are the firm's liabilities at year end and the firm's contributed capital at the beginning of the year, respectively?

    a. $150,000; $270,000.
    b. $160,000; $360,000.
    c. $310,000; $210,000.
    d. $310,000; $130,000.

_____ 11. During the year Doni Co. issued additional common stock. This transaction is an example of which of the following?

    a. An investing activity.
    b. A financing activity.
    c. An operating activity.
    d. None of the above.

_____ 12. During the year, Mariner Co., sold one of its warehouses for $250,000 cash. This transaction is an example of which of the following?

    a. An investing activity.
    b. A financing activity.
    c. An operating activity.
    d. None of the above.

_____ 13. Ikriche Corporation's retained earnings increased by $160,000 during the year. Also, during the year, dividends totaling $45,000 were declared and paid to shareholders. What was Ikriche Corporation's net income for the year?

    a. $ 45,000.
    b. $115,000.
    c. $160,000.
    d. $205,000.

_____ 14. Which of the following transactions does not result in an inflow of cash?

    a.   Sold surplus equipment.
    b.   Common stock was issued.
    c.   Dividends were distributed to shareholders.
    d.   Long-term debt was issued.

_____ 15. Which of the following does not describe an expense?

    a.   Paid dividends to shareholders.
    b.   Cost of merchandise sold.
    c.   Salaries earned by employees but not yet paid.
    d.   Depreciation for the period on the firm's building.

_____ 16. Which of the following transactions of the Idalia Company does not result in an inflow of cash?

    a.   Additional common stock was issued.
    b.   Additional equipment was acquired.
    c.   A long-term note was issued.
    d.   A tract of land was sold.

_____ 17. Which of the following assets is not a current asset?

    a.   Cash.
    b.   Land.
    c.   Merchandise Inventory.
    d.   Accounts Receivable.

_____ 18. Which of the following financial statements provides information about inflows and outflows of cash?

    a.   Income Statement.
    b.   Balance Sheet.
    c.   Statement of Cash Flows.
    d.   All of the above.

_____ 19. Which of the following equations is incorrect?

    a.   Shareholders' Equity = Contributed Capital + Retained Earnings.
    b.   Revenues - Expenses = Net Income.
    c.   Assets = Liabilities + Shareholders' Equity.
    d.   All of the above equations are correct.

_____ 20. Which one of the following liabilities is not a current liability?

    a.   Mortgage Payable.
    b.   Accounts Payable.
    c.   Salaries Payable.
    d.   Taxes Payable.

_____ 21. Which of the following would not appear on an Income Statement?

    a.   Rent Expense.
    b.   Salaries Payable.
    c.   Sales Revenue.
    d.   Cost of Goods Sold.

_____ 22. Revenues are a measure of the inflows of assets (or reductions in liabilities) from selling goods and providing services to customers. Which of the following is not a revenue transaction?

    a.   Sold merchandise for cash to a customer.
    b.   Sold merchandise on account to a customer.
    c.   Delivered weekly magazines to a subscriber, who had paid previously for a one-year's subscription.
    d.   Went to the local bank and borrowed money to be used in the business.

Exercises

1. The comparative balance sheets for the Bale Company for Year 1 and Year 2 are presented below:

	Year 1	Year 2
Cash	$ 36,000	$ 48,000
Noncurrent Assets	132,000	183,000
Total Assets	$168,000	$231,000
Noncurrent Liabilities	$ 99,000	$ 75,000
Contributed Capital	$ 49,500	$ 90,000
Retained Earnings	19,500	66,000
Total Shareholders' Equity	$ 69,000	$156,000
Total Equity	$168,000	$231,000

The company reported earnings and a cash inflow from operations of $60,000 in Year 2.

Identify five transactions during Year 2 that either provided or used cash. What was the amount of cash inflow or cash outflow in each transaction? Specify whether the transaction was an operating, financing, or investing activity.

2. The Isabel Corporation began operations in July, Year 1. Total shareholders' equity at that time was $32,000. On December 31, Year 1, the corporation reports assets of $136,000 and liabilities of $67,200.

    a. Determine the amount of shareholders' equity at December 31, Year 1. Has shareholders' equity increased or decreased?

b. Give several possible explanations for the change in shareholders' equity.

c. What items make up shareholders' equity?

3. Using the information given, determine the missing amount in each of the independent cases below:

	a	b	c
Inflows of Cash			
Operations	$_____	$ 15,000	$ 32,500
New Financing	$190,000	$ 42,500	$ 40,000
Sales of Noncurrent Assets	$ 35,000	$ 30,000	$ 20,000
Outflows of Cash			
Dividends	$ 15,000	$ _____	$ 10,000
Reduction in Financing	$ 95,000	$ 50,000	$ 30,000
Acquisition of Noncurrent Assets	$ 60,000	$ 35,000	$ 45,000
Increase (Decrease) in Cash	$ 85,000	$(10,000)	$_____

4. Using the information given, determine the missing amounts in each of the independent cases below:

	a	b	c
Current Assets	$ 31,500	$_____	$ 45,000
Noncurrent Assets	$ 36,000	$ 60,000	$ 66,000
Current Liabilities	$ 21,000	$ 15,000	$_____
Noncurrent Liabilities	$ 18,000	$ 30,000	$ 10,500
Contributed Capital	$_____	$ 33,000	$ 33,000
Retained Earnings	$ 12,000	$_____	$ 66,000
Shareholders' Equity	$_____	$ 54,000	$_____

5. Cash inflows and cash outflows can fit into one of three categories: (1) operating activities, (2) investing activities, and (3) financing activities. For each of the following transactions, indicate the appropriate category by placing the identifying number in the space provided.

_____ a. Purchased machinery.

_____ b. Sold additional stock to shareholders.

_____ c. Paid mortgage note at maturity date.

_____ d. Paid dividends to shareholders.

_____ e. Borrowed money on a five-year note.

_____ f. Sold a building.

_____ g. Sold merchandise to a customer on account.

_____ h. Collected cash on accounts receivable.

_____ i. Purchased merchandise from supplier on account.

_____ j. Paid accounts payable

_____ k. Paid weekly salaries to employees.

6. Using the information given, determine the missing amounts from the income statement and retained earnings statement in each of the independent cases below:

	a	b	c
Revenues	$ 68,000	$108,000	$_____
Expenses	$ 42,000	$_____	$ 80,000
Net Income	$_____	$_____	$ 20,000
Retained Earnings 1/1	$ 14,000	$ 18,000	$_____
Net Income	$_____	$ 21,600	$_____
Dividends	$ 16,000	$_____	$ 10,000
Retained Earnings 12/31	$_____	$ 27,600	$ 16,000

7. Using the information given, determine the missing amounts in each of the independent cases below:

	a	b	c
Assets	$_____	$288,000	$198,000
Liabilities	$ 36,000	$ 90,000	$132,000
Contributed Capital	$ 45,000	$_____	$ 48,000
Retained Earnings 1/1	$_____	$ 0	$ 6,000
Net Income	$ 10,800	$ 45,000	$ 33,000
Dividends	$ 6,000	$ 21,600	$_____
Retained Earnings 12/31	$ 24,000	$_____	$_____

Answers to Questions and Exercises

True/False

1.	F	6.	T	11.	T	16.	F	21.	T
2.	F	7.	F	12.	T	17.	T	22.	T
3.	F	8.	F	13.	F	18.	F	23.	T
4.	T	9.	T	14.	T	19.	T	24.	F
5.	F	10.	T	15.	F	20.	T	25.	T

Matching

1.	h	7.	l	13.	y	19.	f	25.	i
2.	m	8.	cc	14.	j	20.	z	26.	e
3.	t	9.	a	15.	u	21.	o	27.	n
4.	aa	10.	v	16.	d	22.	k	28.	p
5.	w	11.	s	17.	q	23.	x	29.	bb
6.	b	12.	r	18.	c	24.	g		

Multiple Choice

1.	b	7.	c	13.	d	19.	d
2.	d	8.	b	14.	c	20.	a
3.	c	9.	b	15.	a	21.	b
4.	d	10.	c	16.	b	22.	d
5.	a	11.	b	17.	b		
6.	c	12.	a	18.	c		

Exercises

1.

    1. ($ 51,000) Purchased a non-current asset, use of cash, investing activity.
    2. ($ 24,000) Paid liabilities, use of cash, financing activity.
    3. $ 40,500 Issued stock, source of cash, financing activity.
    4. $ 60,000 Cash inflows from operating activity.
    5. ($ 13,500) Paid distribution to owners, use of cash, financing activity.
       $ 12,000 Increase in cash during Year 2.

2.   a. Assets at 12/31, Year 1 $136,000
         Liabilities at 12/31, Year 1   67,200
         Shareholders' equity at 12/31, Year 1 $ 68,800

         Shareholders' equity has increased by $36,800 ($68,800 - $32,000) during the 6-month period, July 1 to December 31.

    b. The $36,800 increase may be attributable to the company earning net income and paying no dividends or earning net income and paying dividends; or the shareholders may have made additional purchases of the company's stock; or the increase could be attributed to a combination of the above-mentioned changes.

    c. Contributed capital represents the assets provided by the shareholders in exchange for an ownership interest in the firm. Retained earnings represents the earnings, or profits, realized by the firm since its formation in excess of dividends distributed to shareholders.

3.

	a	b	c
Inflows of Cash			
Operations	$ 30,000	$ 15,000	$ 32,500
New Financing	$190,000	$ 42,500	$ 40,000
Sales of Noncurrent Assets	$ 35,000	$ 30,000	$ 20,000
Outflows of Cash			
Dividends	$ 15,000	$ 12,500	$ 10,000
Reduction in Financing	$ 95,000	$ 50,000	$ 30,000
Acquisition of Noncurrent Assets	$ 60,000	$ 35,000	$ 45,000
Increase (Decrease) in Cash	$ 85,000	$(10,000)	$ 7,500

4.

	a	b	c
Current Assets	$ 31,500	$ 39,000	$ 45,000
Noncurrent Assets	$ 36,000	$ 60,000	$ 66,000
Current Liabilities	$ 21,000	$ 15,000	$ 1,500
Noncurrent Liabilities	$ 18,000	$ 30,000	$ 10,500
Contributed Capital	$ 16,500	$ 33,000	$ 33,000
Retained Earnings	$ 12,000	$ 21,000	$ 66,000
Shareholders' Equity	$ 28,500	$ 54,000	$ 99,000

5.

a.	2	g.	1
b.	3	h.	1
c.	3	i.	1
d.	3	j.	1
e.	3	k.	1
f.	2		

6.

	a	b	c
Revenues	$ 68,000	$108,000	$100,000
Expenses	$ 42,000	$ 86,400	$ 80,000
Net Income	$ 26,000	$ 21,600	$ 20,000
Retained Earnings 1/1	$ 14,000	$ 18,000	$ 6,000
Net Income	$ 26,000	$ 21,600	$ 20,000
Dividends	$ 16,000	$ 12,000	$ 10,000
Retained Earnings 12/31	$ 24,000	$ 27,600	$ 16,000

7.

	a	b	c
Assets	$105,000	$288,000	$198,000
Liabilities	$ 36,000	$ 90,000	$132,000
Contributed Capital	$ 45,000	$174,600	$ 48,000
Retained Earnings 1/1	$ 19,200	$ 0	$ 6,000
Net Income	$ 10,800	$ 45,000	$ 33,000
Dividends	$ 6,000	$ 21,600	$ 21,000
Retained Earnings 12/31	$ 24,000	$ 23,400	$ 18,000

Chapter 2

Balance Sheet: Presenting the Investments and Financing of a Firm

Chapter Highlights

1. The balance sheet is one of the three principal financial statements. It derives its name from the fact that it shows the following balance, or equality:

   Assets = Liabilities + Shareholders' Equity

   The firm's resources (the assets) must equal the firm's claims on the resources (the liabilities and shareholders' equity). The balance sheet presents a listing of the specific forms (for example cash, inventory, equipment) in which a firm holds resources and a listing of the people or entities that provided the financing and therefore have a claim on the resources.

2. An asset is a resource that has the potential for providing a firm with future economic benefits. The resources recognized as assets are those (a) for which the firm has acquired rights to their use in the future through a past transaction or exchange, and (b) for which the firm can measure or quantify the future benefits with a reasonable degree of precision. Assets are future benefits; not all future benefits are assets.

3. Accounting must assign a monetary amount to each asset on the balance sheet. Methods for determining this amount include: (a) acquisition or historical cost, (b) current replacement cost, (c) current net realizable value, and (d) present value of future net cash flows.

4. The acquisition, or historical, cost is the amount of cash payment (or cash equivalent value) made in acquiring an asset.

5. Current replacement cost (an entry value) represents the amount required currently to acquire the rights to receive future benefits from the asset.

6. Net realizable value (an exit value) is the net amount of cash (selling price less selling costs) that the firm would receive currently if it sold the asset.

7. The future benefits from an asset come from the asset's ability to generate future cash receipts or reduce future cash expenditures. A final way to express the valuation of an asset is in terms of the asset's present value, representing today's value of the stream of future cash flows. Because cash can earn interest over time, the present value is worth less than the sum of the cash amounts to be received or saved over time.   If future cash flows are to measure an asset's value, then accountants will discount the future net cash flows to find their present value as of the date of the balance sheet. Using discounted cash flows in the valuation of individual assets requires solving difficulties of: (a)

the uncertainty of the amounts of future cash flows, (b) how to allocate the cash receipts from the sale of merchandise to all of the assets involved in its production and distribution, and (c) how to select the appropriate rate to use in discounting the future cash flows to the present.

8. Financial statements prepared by publicly held firms are based primarily on one of two valuation methods, one for monetary assets and one for nonmonetary assets. Monetary assets, such as cash and accounts receivable, are shown at their current cash or cash-equivalent value. Nonmonetary assets, such as merchandise inventory, land, buildings, and equipment, are stated at acquisition cost, and in some cases are adjusted downward to reflect the services of the assets that have been consumed. The use of acquisition cost is supported by three important accounting concepts or conventions: (a) the going concern concept, (b) reliability, and (c) the conservatism convention.

9. The going concern concept assumes the firm is to remain in operations long enough for all of its current plans to be carried out.

10. Reliability refers to the ability of a measure, such as acquisition cost, to faithfully represent what it purports to measure. Reliability also encompasses the ability to verify, or audit, the measured amount.

11. Conservatism has evolved as a convention to justify acquisition cost valuations. Acquisition cost generally provides more conservative valuations of assets (and measures of earnings) relative to other methods. Many accountants feel that the possibility of misleading financial statements users will be minimized when assets are stated at lower rather than higher amounts.

12. The classification of assets within the balance sheet varies widely from firm to firm, but the principal asset categories are usually: (a) current assets, (b) investments, (c) property, plant, and equipment, and (d) intangible assets. Current assets include cash and other assets that are expected to be realized in cash or sold or consumed during the normal operating cycle. Investments include primarily long-term investments in securities of other firms. Property, plant, and equipment includes the tangible, long-lived assets used in a firm's operations and generally not acquired for resale. The balance sheet shows these items (except land) at acquisition cost reduced by the accumulated depreciation since the firm acquired the assets. Intangibles are long-lived assets that lack physical substance such as patents, trademarks, and franchises.

13. A liability is an obligation that arises when a firm receives benefits or services and in exchange promises to pay the provider of those goods or services a reasonably definite amount at a reasonably definite future time. All liabilities are obligations; not all obligations, however, are accounting liabilities.

14. Most liabilities are monetary in nature, requiring payments of specific amounts of cash. Those monetary liabilities due within one year or less are stated at the amount of cash expected to be paid to discharge the liability. Those liabilities with due dates extending more than one year into the future are stated at the present values of the future cash outflows. Liabilities that are discharged by delivering goods or rendering services are nonmonetary items and are stated at the amount of cash received or the estimated cost of providing the service.

15. Contingent liabilities, such as a loan guarantee or an unsettled lawsuit, require some future event to occur before accounting can establish the existence and amount of a liability. Obligations created by mutually unexecuted contracts, such as leases or employment contracts, are not recognized as liabilities.

16. Liabilities in the balance sheet are typically classified in one of the following categories: (a) current liabilities, (b) long-term debt, and (c) other long-term liabilities. Current liabilities are obligations expected to be paid or discharged during the normal operating cycle (they are usually paid using current assets). Long-term debt are those obligations having due dates more than one year from the balance sheet date. Obligations not properly considered as current liabilities or long-term debt are classified as other long-term liabilities.

17. The owners' (shareholders') equity, or interest, in a firm is a residual interest, since the owners have a claim only against those assets not required to meet the claims of creditors. Since owners' equity is a residual interest, its valuation on the balance sheet reflects the valuation of assets and liabilities.

18. The owners' (shareholders') equity section for a corporation is divided into two sections, contributed capital and retained earnings. Contributed capital represents amounts shareholders have provided for an interest in the firm (that is, common stock). Retained earnings are earnings subsequently realized by the firm in excess of dividends declared.

19. Contributed capital is usually further disaggregated into the par or stated value of the shares and amounts contributed in excess of par value or stated value. The par or stated value of a share of stock is a somewhat arbitrary amount assigned to comply with corporation laws of each state. The par or stated value rarely equals the market price of the shares at the time the firm issues them.

20. Firms organized as sole proprietorships or partnerships do not make a distinction between contributed capital and retained earnings in their balance sheet. The balance sheet reports a capital account for each owner containing their share of capital contributions plus their share of earnings in excess of distributions.

21. The balance sheet provides a constant equality between total assets and total equities (liabilities plus owners' equity). Any single transaction has a dual effect in maintaining this equality by either a/an:

    a. Increase in both an asset and a liability or shareholders' equity;

    b. Decrease in both an asset and a liability or shareholders' equity;

    c. Increase in one asset and a decrease in another asset; or

    d. Increase in one liability or shareholders' equity and a decrease in another liability or shareholders' equity.

22. Journal entries are used to record the dual effects of a transaction as to both accounts and amounts. Accountants refer to the first line of the journal entry as the debit line and the second line of the journal entry as the credit line. The standard journal entry format is

---

Date Account Debited ....   Amount Debited

       Account Credited........   Amount Credited

       Explanation of transaction

       or event being recorded.

Accountants follow the following rules for increases and decreases in asset, liability, and shareholders' equity accounts:

    a.   Debits increase an asset account or decrease a liability or shareholders' equity account.

    b.   Credits decrease an asset account or increase a liability or shareholders' equity account.

23. The preparation of a balance sheet requires that you recognize and understand the meaning of a large list of account titles that are commonly used. Careful attention should be given to this discussion in the text.

24. Analysts often use a common-size balance sheet to study the nature and mix of assets and their financing. In a common-size balance sheet, the analyst expresses each balance sheet item as a percentage of total assets or total liabilities plus shareholders' equity.

25. The balance sheet reflects the effects of a firm's investing and financing decisions. The user of the balance sheet should consider if the firm has the right mix of financing for its assets. Two principles guide decisions about financing:

    a.   Firms generally use short-term financing for assets that a firm expects to turn into cash soon, and long-term financing (debt or shareholders' equity) for assets that a firm expects to turn into cash over a longer period.

    b.   The mix of long-term financing depends on the nature of long-term assets and the amount of operating risk in the business.
        - Firms with tangible long-term assets and predictable cash flows tend to use a high proportion of long-term debt.

        - Firms with tangible long-term assets but less predictable cash flows tend to use a more balanced mix of long-term debt and shareholders' equity financing.

        - Firms with high proportion of intangibles tend to use low proportions of long-term debt.

26. The balance sheet does not always provide useful data because, as a result of following GAAP,

    a.   Not all resources of a firm appear on the balance sheet as assets,

    b.   Not all obligations of a firm appear on the balance sheet as liabilities,

    c.   Assets on the balance sheet do not typically reflect current market valuations, and

    d.   Liabilities on the balance sheet do not necessarily reflect current market valuations.

The user of the balance sheet should recognize these weaknesses when attempting to assess the financial condition of a firm.

27. The format and terminology of the balance sheet in many foreign countries differ from that used in the United States. Other countries accounting practice includes reporting some accounts seldom appearing on balance sheets in the U.S. and recognizing revaluation of assets not allowed in the U.S.

Questions and Exercises

True/False. For each of the following statements, place a T or F in the space provided to indicate whether the statement is true or false.

_____ 1. Research has not provided guidance as to the asset valuation basis most relevant to financial statements users.

_____ 2. Conservatism in accounting refers to the ability of several independent observers to come to the same conclusion about the valuation of an asset.

_____ 3. Some resources of a firm provide future economic benefits but are not capable of being reasonably measured or quantified and, therefore, are not classified as assets on the balance sheet.

_____ 4. The historical cost of an asset always represents its future economic value to the firm.

_____ 5. A lease transaction is an example of an unexecuted contract, which often is not recognized as a liability at the time of the agreement between the lessor and the lessee.

_____ 6. A balance sheet prepared for a sole proprietorship or partnership contains a contributed capital account and a retained earnings account for each owner.

_____ 7. A liability represents any obligation taken on by a firm.

_____ 8. Liabilities that will be discharged by the rendering of goods or services are considered nonmonetary liabilities.

_____ 9. Since owners' equity is a residual interest in the firm's assets, its valuation is dependent upon the valuations assigned to the assets and liabilities within the balance sheet.

_____ 10. Accumulated depreciation does not represent a fund set aside to replace fixed assets after they have been fully depreciated.

_____ 11. Retained earnings represent the cumulative amount of cash available for dividends.

_____ 12. Liability accounts are increased by debits and decreased by credits.

_____ 13. Accounting recognizes specifically identifiable intangible assets acquired in market exchanges from other entities as assets.

_____ 14. An example of an account included in the "other long-term liability" section is deferred income taxes.

_____ 15. The more specialized a firm's assets the more difficulty there is in determining either their replacement cost or net realizable value, because a well-organized secondhand market for these items may not exist.

_____ 16. The present value of future cash flows approach to assigning values to balance sheet items is likely to be employed with current liabilities such as accounts payable and taxes payable.

_____ 17. A parcel of land acquired for use should be classified as property, plant, and equipment.

_____ 18. For an obligation to be treated as a liability, it is necessary that it can be estimated with a reasonable degree of accuracy.

_____ 19. Current liabilities are usually paid from assets classified as current.

_____ 20. Treasury shares are usually shown as a deduction from the total of shareholders' equity accounts on the balance sheet.

_____ 21. If a firm accounts for the assets in a conservative manner, it is less likely that net income will be overstated.

_____ 22. All transactions have a dual effect upon the balance sheet equation, since both an asset and an equity account are affected in equal amounts in every transaction.

_____ 23. The format of the balance sheet in the United States is the same as the format of the balance sheet in the United Kingdom.

_____ 24. Some liabilities due within one year are not classified as current liabilities.

_____ 25. In a common-size balance sheet each balance sheet item is expressed as a percentage of either total assets or total liabilities plus stockholders' equity.

_____ 26. Par or stated value rarely equals the market price of the shares at the time of issuance.

_____ 27. All assets found on a balance sheet are recorded at their historical cost.

_____ 28. The balance sheet derives its name from the fact that it shows the following balance, or equality:

Assets + Liabilities = Owners' Equity.

_____ 29. In measuring net realizable value, we generally assume that the asset is not being sold at a distress price.

_____ 30. The valuation basis selected by a firm depends upon the purpose of the financial report being prepared.

_____ 31. Whenever a firm develops a good reputation over many years of operations, it is acceptable to assign a value to this resource and classify it as goodwill on the balance sheet.

_____ 32. Assets are only resources used by the firm for which legal title is held.

_____ 33. Land is a good example of a nonmonetary asset.

_____ 34. A company is considered to be a going concern only if it is expected to last forever.

_____ 35. The operating cycle for most companies is one year or less.

_____ 36. Depreciable assets such as buildings and machinery appear on the balance sheet at acquisition cost adjusted downward to reflect services consumed by the firm since acquisition.

_____ 37. Replacement cost and net realizable value are opposite approaches to determining the current value of an asset: replacement cost refers to an asset's exit value, and net realizable value refers to an asset's entry value.

_____ 38. Net realizable value is defined as the net amount of cash that could be realized from the sale of an asset.

_____ 39. The only accounts found in the investments section of the balance sheet are for the investments in the securities of other firms.

_____ 40. Intangibles are long-term assets that lack physical substance.

_____ 41. The present value of $20,000 to be received in one year at 10 percent is an amount greater than $20,000.

_____ 42. Interest receivable on ten-year bonds would represent the total interest to be received over the ten-year period.

_____ 43. The present value of future cash flows should be less than the total of the future cash flows.

_____ 44. Cash and accounts receivable are examples of monetary assets.

_____ 45. Unexecuted contracts, sometimes called executory contracts, generally do not result in recording an asset but always result in recording a liability.

_____ 46. Convertible bonds payable allow the holder to convert or "trade in" the bonds for shares of common stock.

_____ 47. Common stock is the same as preferred stock except the latter is issued only by companies with preferred credit ratings.

_____ 48. The mix of long-term financing depends on the nature of long-term assets and the amount of operating risk in the business.

_____ 49. The par value of stock is the same as its market value.

_____ 50. As long as a partnership has always been profitable, there will be a credit balance in the retained earnings account.

Matching

1. From the list of terms below, select the term most closely associated with each of the descriptive phrases or statements that follows and place the letter for that term in the space provided.

a. Accounts Payable

b. Accounts Receivable

c. Accumulated Depreciation

d. Acquisition Cost

e. Advances from Customers

f. Advance to Suppliers

g. Bonds Payable

h. Cash

i. Common-Size Balance Sheet

j. Common Stock

k. Contingent Obligations

l. Deferred Income Taxes

m. Executory Contracts

n. Finished Goods Inventory

o. Goodwill

p. Income Taxes Payable

q. Interest Payable

r. Interest Receivable

s. Leasehold

t. Marketable Securities

u. Merchandise Inventory

v. Monetary Assets

w. Nonmonetary Assets

x. Notes Receivables

y. Organization Costs

z. Patents

aa. Preferred Stock

bb. Premium on Preferred Stock

cc. Prepaid Insurance

dd. Raw Materials Inventory

ee. Retained Earnings

ff. Treasury Shares

_____ 1. Involves a contractual exchange of promises to perform in the future but neither party has yet performed.

_____ 2. Includes cash and claims to specified amounts of cash to be received in the future, such as accounts receivable.

_____ 3. These assets will generate unknown, rather than specified, amounts of cash in the future and include merchandise inventory, land, buildings, and equipment.

_____ 4. Includes all expenditures made or obligations incurred to prepare an asset for its intended use by a firm.

_____ 5. Requires some future event to occur before accounting can establish the existence and amount of a liability. An example is an unsettled lawsuit.

_____ 6. Each balance sheet item is expressed as a percentage of total assets or total liabilities plus shareholders' equity.

_____ 7. The amount subtracted from the cost of a fixed asset to get net book value.

_____ 8. Amounts received for the par value of a firm's voting stock.

_____ 9. Goods on hand that have been purchased for resale.

_____ 10. The right to use property owned by someone else.

_____ 11. The estimated and unpaid liability for current income taxes.

_____ 12. Amounts paid for various fees incurred in organizing a corporation.

_____ 13. Amounts due from customers, for which the claim is in the form of a written promise to pay.

_____ 14. The shares originally issued and outstanding that have been reacquired from the owners.

_____ 15. The financial obligation of the company associated with a loan that accrues with the passage of time.

_____ 16. A residual claim of owners having certain preferences relative to other owners' claims.

_____ 17. A type of liquid asset, an example of which is a demand deposit.

_____ 18. A right granted to exclude others from manufacturing, using, or selling a certain process or device.

_____ 19. The balance in this account is the amount owed to the company by its customers.

_____ 20. Payments made in advance for goods or services a firm will receive at a later date.

_____ 21. The amount of income taxes postponed for payments to future years.

_____ 22.   The amount of proceeds from the sales of Preferred Stock in excess of the par value.

_____ 23.   Cumulative amount of net income earned by a business since its inception in excess of dividends declared.

_____ 24.   Amounts owed for goods or services acquired under an informal credit agreement.

_____ 25.   Stock and bonds that can readily be converted into cash.

_____ 26.   Unused materials for manufacturing products.

_____ 27.   Recorded only when another business enterprise is acquired.

_____ 28.   Amounts borrowed by a business for a relatively long period of time under a formal written contract or indenture.

_____ 29.   Insurance premiums paid for future coverage.

_____ 30.   Obligation incurred when a firm receives payment in advance for goods or services it will furnish to customers in the future.

_____ 31.   Completed, but unsold, manufactured products.

_____ 32.   Has accrued through the passing of time but the firm has not yet collected.

2.   For the list of accounts below, select the balance sheet category in which that account should be classified.

a. Current Assets   f. Long-Term Debt

b. Investments   g. Other Long-Term Liabilities

c. Property, Plant, and Equipment   h. Capital Stock

d. Intangible Assets   i. Contributed Capital in Excess of Par Value

e. Current Liabilities   j. Retained Earnings

_____ 1.   Accounts Payable

_____ 2.   Accounts Receivable

_____ 3.   Accumulated Depreciation

_____ 4.   Additional Paid-in Capital

_____ 5.   Advances from Customers

_____ 6.   Advances to Suppliers

_____ 7.   Bonds Payable

_____ 8.   Buildings

_____ 9. Cash

_____ 10. Common Stock

_____ 11. Convertible Bonds Payable

_____ 12. Deferred Income Taxes

_____ 13. Equipment

_____ 14. Finished Goods Inventory

_____ 15. Furniture and Fixtures

_____ 16. Goodwill

_____ 17. Income Taxes Payable

_____ 18. Interest Receivable

_____ 19. Investment in Stock

_____ 20. Land

_____ 21. Leasehold

_____ 22. Marketable Securities

_____ 23. Merchandise Inventory

_____ 24. Mortgage Payable

_____ 25. Notes Payable (due in 3 years)

_____ 26. Notes Receivable (due in 6 months)

_____ 27. Patents

_____ 28. Preferred Stock

_____ 29. Prepaid Insurance

_____ 30. Prepaid Rent

_____ 31. Raw Materials Inventory

_____ 32. Rent Received in Advance

_____ 33. Retained Earnings

_____ 34. Supplies Inventory

_____ 35. Treasury Shares

_____ 36. Work-in-Process Inventory

3. From the list of terms below, select the term that is most closely associated with each of the descriptive phrases or statements that follows and place the letter for that term in the space provided.

a. Conservatism
b. Contributed capital
c. Current net realizable value
d. Current replacement cost
e. Going concern
f. Operating cycle
g. Par or stated value
h. Present value
i. Reliability

_____ 1. An entry value, the amount currently required to acquire the rights to receive future benefits from an asset.

_____ 2. An exit value, the amount obtainable if the firm currently disposed of an asset.

_____ 3. A firm will remain in operation long enough to carry out all of its current plans.

_____ 4. Today's value of a stream of future cash flows.

_____ 5. The reporting of assets at lower rather than higher amounts.

_____ 6. A stock's somewhat arbitrary face amount assigned to comply with corporation laws.

_____ 7. Refers to the ability of a measure, such as acquisition cost, to faithfully represent what it purports to measure.

_____ 8. Refers to the period of time during which a given firm converts cash into salable goods and services, sells those goods and services to customers, and receives cash from customers in payment for their purchases.

_____ 9. Refers to the amount that shareholders invested for an interest in the firm.

4. From the list of European accounts or balance sheet classifications listed below, select the term that is commonly used in the U.S. and place the letter for that term in the space provided.

a. Accounts Payable
b. Accounts Receivable
c. Additional Paid-in Capital
d. Bonds Payable
e. Common Stock
f. Inventories
g. Investment in Securities
h. Other Liabilities
i. Property, Plant, and Equipment
j. Retained Earnings

30

_____ 1.   Provisions

_____ 2.   Capital Reserve or Share Premium Account

_____ 3.   Debt or Borrowings

_____ 4.   Financial Assets

_____ 5.   Revenue Reserves

_____ 6.   Subscribed Capital or Called-up Share Capital

_____ 7.   Tangible Assets

_____ 8.   Trade Payables

_____ 9.   Trade Receivables or Debtors

_____ 10. Stocks

Multiple Choice. Choose the best answer for each of the following questions and enter the identifying letter in the space provided.

_____ 1.   The following are account titles for liabilities except for:

a.   Advances to suppliers.
b.   Advances from tenants.
c.   Rent received in advance.
d.   Advances from customers.

_____ 2.   From the list of accounts below, determine the amount that would be properly classified as property, plant, and equipment.

Land Used in Business	$100,000
Machinery Leased from Others (no liability has been recorded)	60,000
Accumulated Depreciation	(80,000)
Inventories	124,000
Land Held for Future Plant Site	40,000
Building	200,000
Investment in Stock of Construction Company	50,000

a. $220,000.
b. $360,000.
c. $260,000.
d. $280,000.

_____ 3.   The balance in all asset accounts combined is $300,000 on
           December 1. During December the following transactions took place.
           Purchase of $30,000 of inventory for cash.
           Purchase of $45,000 of machinery on account.
           Retirement of $60,000 in bonds with cash.

           What is the combined December 31 balance in the asset accounts?

           a. $240,000.
           b. $345,000.
           c. $315,000.
           d. $285,000.

_____ 4.   The balance sheet reflects the application of various valuation
           methods. Which of the methods listed below may be used on a balance
           sheet that follows generally accepted accounting principles?

           a.   Acquisition cost.
           b.   Current cash-equivalent value.
           c.   Present value of future cash flows.
           d.   All of the above.

_____ 5.   What account below would not be found on the balance sheet of a
           corporation?

           a.   Ferrero, Capital.
           b.   Retained Earnings.
           c.   Investment in Ladner Co. Stock.
           d.   Premium on Common Stock.

_____ 6.   Which of the journal entries below is incorrectly recorded?

           a.   Jan. 1: Cash $18,000
                            Investment in X Co.
                            Stock $18,000
                         Sale of an investment for
                         cash.

           b.   Jan. 2: Prepaid Insurance $ 500
                            Cash $ 500
                         Paid in Advance for a 1-year
                         insurance policy.

           c.   Jan. 3: Accounts Receivable $ 600
                            Merchandise Inventory $ 600
                         Returned defective merchandise
                         for credit. The merchandise
                         has not yet been paid for.

           d.   Jan. 4: Machinery $25,000
                            Notes Payable $25,000
                         Gave a 1-year note to
                         acquire machinery.

_____ 7.   All of the assets listed below are nonmonetary assets except one. Which one is not a nonmonetary asset?

   a.   Patent.
   b.   Land.
   c.   Inventory.
   d.   Accounts receivable.

_____ 8.   The concept of present value:

   a.   Can be simply defined as the value today of a stream of future cash flows.
   b.   Implies that the value of receiving cash today will be less than the value of receiving it in the future.
   c.   Is employed extensively in the valuation of assets under current generally accepted accounting principles.
   d.   Determines the minimum amount that a buyer would be willing to pay for an asset.

_____ 9.   Different balance sheet items employ different valuation methods. Which valuation application below is not generally accepted?

   a.   A major line of inventory has increased in value substantially above its cost and has been restated to its current replacement cost.
   b.   Machinery is stated at its historical cost less the estimated amount of benefits consumed to date.
   c.   Cash is received for goods to be delivered next month. The liability is stated at the amount of cash received and not the cost of goods to be delivered.
   d.   Common stock is stated at the amount at which it was originally sold.

_____ 10.   The following entry was made on March 12 for Tanya Co.

Mar. 12 Machinery $ 55,000
            Accounts Payable $ 55,000

This entry was made for which of the following transactions?

   a.   Payment for purchase of machinery.
   b.   Sale of machinery.
   c.   Depreciation of machinery.
   d.   Purchase of machinery.

_____ 11.   All of the following would normally be classified as a current liability account except for:

   a.   Accounts Payable.
   b.   Interest Payable.
   c.   Rent Received in Advance.
   d.   All of the above would be classified as a current liability.

_____ 12. The Pugh Corporation failed to record the purchase of inventory on account at the end of 2007. In which of the following ways is the balance sheet misstated?

    a.   Assets and liabilities are both understated.
    b.   Assets are understated and liabilities are overstated.
    c.   Assets and shareholders' equity are both understated.
    d.   Assets, liabilities, and shareholders' equity are all correctly stated.

_____ 13. Which equation below does not represent an acceptable presentation of the balance sheet equation?

    a.   Assets - Liabilities = Owners' Equity.
    b.   Assets = Liabilities + Capital Stock + Capital Contributed in Excess of Par Value + Retained Earnings.
    c.   Assets = Equities.
    d.   All of the above represent acceptable presentations of the balance sheet equation.

_____ 14. Which of the liabilities below would be accounted for at the present value of future cash payments?

    a.   Accounts Payable.
    b.   Bonds Payable.
    c.   Income Taxes Payable.
    d.   Advances from Customers.

_____ 15. Vadim Corp. has assets and liabilities of $45,000 and $36,000, respectively. If Vadim issues an additional $4,500 of stock for cash, what will be the balance in shareholders' equity following this transaction?

    a. $45,000.
    b. $76,500.
    c. $13,500.
    d. $49,500.

_____ 16. From the following list of selected account balances, determine the total for the shareholders' equity section of the balance sheet for Roma Co.:

Investment in Stock of Ania Co.	$10,000
Retained Earnings	20,000
Cash (in special bank account for payment of dividends)	12,000
Note Payable to Suppliers	8,000
Common Stock	40,000
8% Preferred Stock	30,000

    a. $ 82,000.
    b. $ 90,000.
    c. $ 98,000.
    d. $102,000.

Exercises

1. Indicate the effect of each transaction below on the balance sheet equation. After each transaction is properly recorded, compute new subtotals for the Assets, Liabilities, and Owners' Equity, being sure to maintain the equality of the equation. Use the following format:

Transaction Number	Assets	=	Liabilities + Owners' Equity
Example	$+600,000		$+600,000
Subtotal	$ 600,000		$ 600,000

Example: Issued 4,000 shares of $100 par value common stock for $600,000 cash.

   a. Received $12,000 for a magazine subscription to be delivered to customers over the next year.

   b. Paid $7,000 in advance for one year of insurance.

   c. Purchased for $500,000 cash a building to be used for office space.

   d. Paid $15,000 to an advertising agency for a promotional campaign which will start in one month.

   e. Bought $115,000 of merchandise inventory on account.

   f. Paid $65,000 to the supplier for inventory purchase in (e) and gave a note for the remaining $50,000.

   g. Loaned $30,000 to an officer and accepted his 90-day note.

   h. Bought $42,000 of merchandise for cash.

   i. Borrowed $75,000 from the bank.

   j. Ten shares of $100 par value common stock are issued in settlement of an account payable of $26,000.

   k. The company agrees to buy four trucks six months from now for $178,000.

2. Below is a list of balance sheet account titles that may be needed in recording the transactions that follow. For each transaction, select those accounts that would be used in recording the transaction and place the letters accompanying the account title in the appropriate columns for debit and credit.

a. Accounts Payable	h. Notes Payable
b. Additional Paid-in-Capital	i. Notes Receivable
c. Capital Stock	j. Organization Costs
d. Cash	k. Prepaid Insurance
e. Machinery and Equipment	l. Rent Received in Advance
f. Marketable Securities	m. Retained Earnings
g. Merchandise Inventory	n. Supplies Inventory

Transaction	Account Debited	Account Credited
Example: Acquired supplies for cash.	n	d
1. Owners invested $30,000 cash in the company in exchange for 4,000 shares of stock having a par value of $5.	_____	_____
2. Advanced money to an officer and received a 90-day note as recognition of the debt.	_____	_____
3. Machinery and equipment were bought on open account.	_____	_____
4. Purchased stock of another company as a temporary use of cash.	_____	_____
5. Sold stock purchased in previous transaction (no. 4 above).	_____	_____
6. Paid the lawyers in company stock for the legal work performed in organizing the company.	_____	_____
7. Purchased merchandise on open account.	_____	_____
8. Purchased for cash a 1-year insurance policy for $900.	_____	_____
9. Received a 1-year advance from tenants for rental property.	_____	_____
10. Bought inventory for cash.	_____	_____

11. A 120-day note was given to
    the bank for a loan.   _____   _____

12. Paid off the creditors for
    inventory purchases.   _____   _____

3.   Vonderheid's balance sheet for December 31, 2006 is presented below:

Vonderheid Company
Balance Sheet
December 31, 2006

Current Assets			Current Liabilities		
Cash	$30,000		Accounts Payable	$20,000	
Interest Receivable	1,000		Notes Payable	16,000	
Notes Receivable	8,000		Interest Payable	800	
Inventory	50,000		Total		$ 36,800
Total		$ 89,000			
Property, Plant & Equipment			Long Term Liabilities		
Land	$15,000		Bonds Payable		$ 20,000
Building	$70,000		Total Liabilities		$ 56,800
Total		$ 85,000			
			Shareholders' Equity		
			Common Stock	$80,000	
			Pd in Cap in Excess	20,000	
			Retained Earnings	17,200	
			Total Shareholders' Equity		$117,200
			Total Liabilities		
Total Assets		$174,000	and Shareholders Equity		$174,000

The following transactions (a-g) occurred during January 2007. For each
transaction, make the appropriate entry to record the transaction.

   a.   The note receivable of $8,000 and the related accrued interest of
        $1,000 were collected on January 2.

   b.   The note payable for $16,000 and the related accrued interest of $800
        were paid on January 2.

c. The January 1 balance in Accounts Payable was paid on January 15.

d. On January 20, the company issued $80,000 of bonds at face value and used the proceeds to pay for an addition to the building.

e. On January 21, merchandise inventory costing $30,000 was acquired with payment of $16,000 in cash and the remainder due in 30 days on open account.

f. On January 25, the plot of land costing $15,000 was sold for $15,000.

g. On January 28, the company issued an additional 400 shares of common stock for $125 per share. The par value of the stock is $100.

4. Indicate whether or not each of the following items should be recognized as an asset on a company's 12/31/2007 Balance Sheet. Indicate the correct answer by placing a "Yes" or "No" in the space provided.

_____ 1. Amounts paid for legal and incorporation fees.

_____ 2. The value to be derived by the firm from having a key location for selling its product.

     3. Costs incurred to develop a new patent.

     4. Interest to be received for the previous six months, on a long-term note receivable.

     5. Cash received from subscribers for publications to be shipped in 2008.

     6. The benefit to the firm of its employees receiving advanced college degrees.

     7. The goodwill paid for when acquiring another business enterprise.

     8. A union agreement that promises a higher quality of performance in the upcoming year.

     9. A piece of machinery worth $1,000, purchased originally for use, but subsequently retired from use and awaiting sale.

    10. Shares of the company's own stock purchased back from the original shareholders.

5. Indicate whether or not each of the following items should be recognized as a liability on a company's 12/31/2007 Balance Sheet. Indicate the correct answer by placing a "Yes" or "No" in the space provided.

     1. The expectation of replacing worn out equipment in 2008.

     2. An agreement to purchase inventory in 2008.

     3. An agreement to publish and deliver magazines in 2008 for cash already received.

     4. The obligation to pay dividends from income earned during 2008.

     5. The obligation to pay interest in 2008 on bonds that were issued on 12/31/2007.

     6. The obligation to repay a loan made in the current year and due in 2009.

     7. Unpaid income taxes from 2007.

     8. The obligation to pay workers for services already rendered.

     9. The burden of having a senile president.

    10. The obligations of the president to pay for his son's traffic fines.

6. From the list of account balances below, prepare in good form a Balance Sheet for Reyna's Department Store at December 31, 2007.

Cash	$ 3,000	
Marketable Securities	13,500	
Accounts Receivable	28,500	
Building	37,500	
Notes Payable (due in one year)		$ 16,500
Patent	6,000	
Building - Accumulated Depreciation		9,000
Property Taxes Payable		6,000
Accounts Payable		21,750
Retained Earnings		58,350
Common Stock		37,500
Bonds Payable		60,000
Inventory	22,500	
Land	75,000	
Investment in IBM Stock	21,000	
Investments in Florida Power Bonds	9,000	
Prepaid Insurance	750	
Withheld Income Tax		1,650
Capital Contributed in Excess of Par Value		17,250
Goodwill	11,250	
	$228,000	$228,000

Answers to Questions and Exercises

True/False

1. T	11. F	21. T	31. F	41. F
2. F	12. F	22. F	32. F	42. F
3. T	13. T	23. F	33. T	43. T
4. F	14. T	24. T	34. F	44. T
5. T	15. T	25. T	35. T	45. F
6. F	16. F	26. T	36. T	46. T
7. F	17. T	27. F	37. F	47. F
8. T	18. T	28. F	38. T	48. T
9. T	19. T	29. T	39. F	49. F
10. T	20. T	30. T	40. T	50. F

Matching

1.

1. m	8. j	15. q	22. bb	29. cc
2. v	9. u	16 aa	23. ee	30. e
3. w	10. s	17. h	24. a	31. n
4. d	11. p	18. z	25. t	32. r
5. k	12. y	19. b	26. dd	
6. i	13. x	20. f	27. o	
7. c	14. ff	21. l	28. g	

2.	1. e	10. h	19. b	28. h
	2. a	11. f	20 c	29. a
	3. Reduction of c	12 g	21. c or d	30. a
	4. i	13. c	22. a	31. a
	5. e	14. a	23. a	32. e
	6. a	15 c	24. f	33. j
	7. f	16. d	25. f	34. a
	8. c	17. e	26. a	35. reduction of (h,i,j)
	9. a	18. a	27. d	36. a

3.	1. d	3. e	5. a	7. i	9. b
	2. c	4. h	6. g	8. f	

4.	1. h	3. d	5. j	7. i	9. b
	2. c	4. g	6. e	8. a	10. f

Multiple Choice

1. a	5. a	9. a	13. d
2. a	6. c	10. d	14. b
3. d	7. d	11. d	15. c
4. d	8. a	12. a	16. b

Exercises

1.

Transaction Number	Assets	=	Liabilities	+	Owners' Equity
Example	$600,000				$600,000
Subtotal	$600,000	=			$600,000
a.	+ 12,000		+ 12,000		
Subtotal	$612,000	=	$ 12,000		$600,000
b.	+ 7,000				
	- 7,000				
Subtotal	$612,000	=	$ 12,000	+	$600,000
c.	+500,000				
	-500,000				
Subtotal	$612,000	=	$ 12,000	+	$600,000
d.	+ 15,000				
	- 15,000				
Subtotal	$612,000	=	$ 12,000	+	$600,000
e.	+115,000		+115,000		
Subtotal	$727,000	=	$127,000	+	$600,000
f.	- 65,000		-115,000		
			+ 50,000		
Subtotal	$662,000	=	$ 62,000	+	$600,000
g.	+ 30,000				
	- 30,000				
Subtotal	$662,000	=	$ 62,000	+	$600,000
h.	+ 42,000				
	- 42,000				
Subtotal	$662,000	=	$ 62,000	+	$600,000
i.	+ 75,000		+ 75,000		
Subtotal	$737,000	=	$137,000	+	$600,000
j.			- 26,000		+ 26,000
Subtotal	$737,000	=	$111,000	+	$626,000
k. (no effect)					
Total	$737,000	=	$111,000	+	$626,000

2.

		Account Debited	Account Credited
1.		d	c, b
2.		i	d
3.		e	a
4.		f	d
5.		d	f
6.		j	c (possibly b as well)
7.		g	a
8.		k	d
9.		d	l
10.		g	d
11.		d	h
12.		a	d

3.

a. Jan 2   Cash   9,000
                 Notes Receivable   8,000
                 Interest Receivable   1,000
              To record collection of note
              and interest

b. Jan 2   Notes payable   16,000
              Interest Payable   800
                 Cash   16,800
              Paid note and interest

c. Jan 15   Accounts Payable   20,000
                 Cash   20,000
              Paid accounts payable

d. Jan 20   Cash   80,000
                 Bonds Payable   80,000
              Issued bonds payable

    Jan 20   Building   80,000
                 Cash   80,000
              Paid for building addition

e. Jan 21   Inventory   30,000
                 Cash   16,000
                 Accounts payable   14,000
              Purchased inventory

f. Jan 25   Cash   15,000
                 Land   15,000
              Sold land

g. Jan 28   Cash   50,000
                 Common Stock   40,000
                 Paid in Capital in Excess of Par   10,000
              Issued 400 shares of common stock

4.

1.	Yes	4.	Yes	7.	Yes	10.	No
2.	No	5.	Yes	8.	No		
3.	No	6.	No	9.	Yes		

5.

1.	No	4.	No	7.	Yes	10.	No
2.	No	5.	No	8.	Yes		
3.	Yes	6.	Yes	9.	No		

6.

Reyna's Department Store
Balance Sheet
December 31, 2007

Assets

Current Assets
Cash	$ 3,000	
Marketable Securities	13,500	
Accounts Receivable	28,500	
Inventory	22,500	
Prepaid Insurance	750	$ 68,250

Investments
Investment in Stock	$ 21,000	
Investment in Bonds	9,000	30,000

Property, Plant & Equipment
Land		$ 75,000	
Building	$ 37,500		
Accumulated Depreciation	(9,000)	28,500	103,500

Intangibles
Patent	$ 6,000	
Goodwill	11,250	17,250
Total Assets		$219,000

Liabilities

Current Liabilities
Accounts Payable	$ 21,750	
Notes Payable	16,500	
Prop. Taxes Payable	6,000	
Withheld Income Tax	1,650	$ 45,900

Long-Term Debt
Bonds Payable	60,000
Total Liabilities	$105,900

Shareholders' Equity

Common Stock	$ 37,500	
Capital Contributed in Excess of Par Value	17,250	
Retained Earnings	58,350	
Total Shareholders' Equity		$113,100
Total Liabilities and Shareholders' Equity		$219,000

Chapter 3

Income Statement: Reporting the Results of Operating Activities

Chapter Highlights

1. The income statement provides a measure of the operating performance of a firm for a particular period of time. Net income is produced when revenues exceed expenses. A loss results when expenses exceed revenues.

2. Revenues measure the net assets (assets less liabilities) that flow into a firm when goods are sold or services are rendered.

3. Expenses measure the net assets that a firm consumes in the process of generating revenues.

4. Most companies use the calendar year as the time span for preparing financial statements for distribution to stockholders and potential investors.

5. Other companies use a natural business year or fiscal period for their accounting period. A natural business year ends when the firm has concluded most of its operating activities for the period.

6. Interim reports are reports of performance for periods shorter than a year. These reports do not eliminate the need to prepare annual reports but are prepared as indicators of progress during the year.

7. The cash basis and the accrual basis are two approaches for measuring operating performance.

8. A company applying the cash basis recognizes revenues when cash is received from customers and recognizes expenses when cash is expended for merchandise, salaries, insurance, taxes, and similar items. The cash basis of accounting is subject to three important criticisms. First, the cost of the efforts required in generating revenues are not adequately matched with those revenues. Second, the cash basis postpones unnecessarily the time when revenue is recognized. Third, the cash basis provides an opportunity for firms to distort the measurement of operating performance by timing their cash expenditures.

9. Some companies use a modified cash basis, which is the same as a cash basis except that long-lived assets (buildings, equipment, etc.) are treated as assets (not expenses) when purchased. A portion of the asset's acquisition cost is recognized as an expense over several accounting periods as the asset's services are consumed.

10. The accrual basis of accounting typically recognizes revenues when goods are sold or services are rendered. It reports costs as expenses in the period when the revenues that they help produce are recognized. Thus accrual accounting attempts to match expenses with associated revenues.

11. Costs that cannot be closely identified with specific revenues are treated as expenses of the period in which the benefits of the asset are consumed.

12. Accrual accounting focuses on the inflows of net assets from operations, and the use of net assets in operations regardless of whether those inflows and outflows currently produce or use cash.

13. The accrual basis provides a superior measure of operating performance compared to the cash basis because (a) revenues more accurately reflect the results of sales activity and (b) expenses are associated more closely with reported revenues.

14. Under the accrual basis, revenue is recognized when the following two criteria have been met: (a) a firm has performed all, or a substantial portion, of the services it expects to provide and (b) the firm has received either cash, a receivable, or some other asset whose cash-equivalent value can be measured with reasonable precision. For most companies, revenues are recognized at the point of sale.

15. The amount of revenue recognized is measured by the cash or cash-equivalent value of other assets received from customers. The gross revenue for some companies needs to be adjusted for amounts estimated to be uncollectible, discounts for early payment, and sales returns and allowances.

16. Expenses measure the assets consumed in generating revenue. Assets are unexpired costs. Expenses are expired costs. The amount of an expense equals the cost of the asset consumed.

17. Asset expirations associated directly with revenues are expenses in the period when a firm recognizes revenues. This treatment is called the matching principle.

18. Asset expirations not clearly associated with revenues become expenses of the period when a firm consumes the benefits of the asset in operations. These expenses are called period expenses. Most selling and administrative costs receive this treatment.

19. The cost of merchandise sold is generally the easiest to associate directly with revenue. For a merchandising firm, such as a department store, the acquisition cost of inventory is an asset until it is sold, at which time it becomes an expense. A manufacturing firm incurs costs (product costs) of direct materials, direct labor, and manufacturing overhead in producing its product. Manufacturing overhead is a mixture of indirect costs, which provides the capacity to produce the product. Manufacturing overhead often includes items such as plant utilities, property taxes and insurance on the factory, and depreciation on the factory plant and equipment. In both the merchandising firm and the manufacturing firm, product costs are expensed when revenues are generated from the sale of the product.

20. Net Income, or earnings, for a period measures the excess of revenues (net asset inflows) over expenses (net asset outflows) from selling goods and providing services.

21. Dividends measure the net assets distributed to shareholders. Dividends are not expenses and do not appear in the income statement.

22. The Retained Earnings account on the balance sheet measures the cumulative excess of earnings over dividends since the firm began operations.

23. Revenues increase owners' equity. Conversely, expenses decrease owners' equity. Although they are not expenses, dividends also decrease owners' equity.

24. At the end of the accounting period, entries are recorded that adjust or correct account balances in order to match all revenues and expenses for the proper reporting of net income and financial position. Examples of such adjustments include adjusting for insurance that has expired, adjusting for salaries that have been earned but not paid, or recording interest payable or interest receivable.

25. Depreciation accounting is a cost-allocation procedure whereby the cost of a long-lived asset is allocated to the periods in which benefits are received and used. The charge made to the current operations for the portion of the cost of such assets consumed during the current period is called depreciation. An account called Accumulated Depreciation is used to record the write-down in the cost of the asset for services used during the period. The Accumulated Depreciation account appears on the balance sheet as a subtraction from the acquisition cost of the asset. Accountants refer to accounts such as Accumulated Depreciation as contra accounts because they appear as subtractions from the amounts in other related accounts.

26. The income statement provides information for assessing the operating profitability of a firm. Common-size income statements express each expense and net income as a percentage of revenues and permit an analysis of changes or differences in the relations between revenues, expenses, and net income.

27. Financial statement users can employ common-size income statements in time series analysis and cross section analysis.

28. Time series analysis compares common-size income statements for two or more periods. Such comparisons may reveal trends that would help the statement reader interpret and analyze the firm's operations.

29. Cross section analysis involves using common-size income statements to compare two or more firms. Such analysis provides information about the different strategies that firms follow.

QUESTIONS AND EXERCISES

True/False. For each of the following statements, place a T or F in the space provided to indicate whether the statement is true or false.

_____ 1. Dividends represent distributions of earnings and decrease owners' equity.

_____ 2. The Depreciation Expense account reflects the cumulative depreciation on the asset since acquisition.

_____ 3. Product costs represent only the costs of raw material for a manufacturing firm.

_____ 4. Assets = Liabilities + Contributed Capital + Revenues - Expenses - Dividends.

_____ 5. Assets = Liabilities + Contributed Capital + Retained Earnings.

_____ 6. The major difference between the cash basis and the accrual basis is in expense recognition, because revenues are the same for both methods.

_____ 7. Product costs are recorded as expenses of the period in which the services are consumed, since these costs rarely create assets with future benefits.

_____ 8. The balance in the Accumulated Depreciation account represents the cumulative depreciation on the asset since acquisition.

_____ 9. For accounting purposes the cash-basis income statement provides the most meaningful measure of operating performance during a particular period, because cash flow is the most objective measure of a company's performance.

_____ 10. Revenues - Expenses - Dividends = Net Income.

_____ 11. Revenues reflect an increase in owners' equity.

_____ 12. The income statement provides a measure of the operating performance of the firm for a particular period of time.

_____ 13. Expenses measure the net assets (assets less liabilities) that flow into a firm when goods are sold or services are rendered.

_____ 14. The Parker Company recorded the purchase of a 1-year insurance policy on July 1, Year 1, as an asset, Prepaid Insurance. On December 31, Year 1, the company should increase insurance expense and decrease Prepaid Insurance for the amount of the expired insurance.

_____ 15. Assets may be referred to as unexpired costs, while expenses may be referred to as expired costs.

_____ 16. Net income is produced when revenues exceed expenses.

_____ 17. Expenses measure the net assets used in the process of generating revenue.

_____ 18. A natural business year for a company is always the one that coincides with the calendar year.

_____ 19. Expenses cause a decrease in owners' equity.

_____ 20. Under the accrual basis of accounting, revenue is recognized in the period when the cash is received as opposed to when the sale is made.

_____ 21. Common-size income statements express revenues and expenses as a percentage of net income.

_____ 22. Time series analysis involves using common-size income statements to compare two or more firms.

Matching.
From the list of terms below, select that term that is most closely associated with each of the descriptive phrases or statements that follows and place the letter for that term in the space provided.

a. Accrual Basis   h. Expenses

b. Accumulated Depreciation   i. Matching Convention

c. Cash Basis   j. Natural Business Year or Fiscal Period

d. Common-size Income Statement   k. Owners' Equity

e. Contra Accounts   l. Period Expenses

f. Depreciation   m. Product Costs

g. Dividends   n. Revenues

_____ 1. Deduction or valuation accounts that accumulate amounts that are subtracted from another account.

_____ 2. A manufacturing firm's cost of producing its product.

_____ 3. The charge made to the current operations for the portion of cost of long-lived assets consumed during the current period.

_____ 4. The balance in this account reflects the cumulative depreciation of an asset since acquisition.

_____ 5. A measure of the inflow of net assets from selling goods and providing services.

_____ 6. This account represents distributions of earnings to shareholders of the firm.

_____ 7. Recognizes revenues and expenses as cash flows (inflow and outflow) takes place.

_____ 8. A measure of the outflow of net assets that are used or consumed, in the process of generating revenues.

_____ 9. The year ends when most earnings activities of a firm have been substantially completed.

_____ 10. The basis that recognizes revenues upon the completion of a critical event in the earnings process.

_____ 11. Asset expirations associated directly with revenues are expenses in the period when a firm recognizes revenues.

_____ 12. Asset expirations not clearly associated with revenues become expenses of the period when a firm consumes services in operations.

_____ 13. Contributed Capital plus Retained Earnings.

_____ 14. Expenses and net income are expressed as a percentage of revenues which permits an analysis of changes or differences in the relations between revenues, expenses, and net income.

Multiple Choice. Choose the best answer for each of the following questions and enter the identifying letter in the space provided.

_____ 1. Miro Company has just completed its first year of operations in Year 1. The company distributed dividends of $50,000. If the ending balance of Retained Earnings on 12/31, Year 1, is $70,000 and the company had revenues of $400,000 from Year 1 sales, the company's Year 1 expenses totaled

    a. $350,000.
    b. $330,000.
    c. $280,000.
    d. None of the above.

_____ 2. At the beginning of the year, Valentina reported a $4,320 balance in its Prepaid Insurance account. At year end, the company reported Insurance Expense of $5,400 in its income statement and a balance of $2,280 in the Prepaid Insurance account. What was the cost of the additional insurance that was purchased during the year?

    a. $5,400.
    b. $7,440.
    c. $3,360.
    d. $7,680.

_____ 3. Igor Company reported a balance in Accounts Receivable of $113,400 on 1/1, Year 2. During Year 2, Igor collected $357,000 from its customers who had purchased on account. On 12/31, Year 2, Igor reported a balance in Accounts Receivable of $59,500. How much was Igor's credit sales for Year 2?

    a. $303,100.
    b. $362,600.
    c. $410,900.
    d. $416,500.

_____ 4. All of the following are examples of period expenses except

    a. Administrative costs.
    b. Inventory costs.
    c. Accounting costs.
    d. Selling costs.

_____ 5. Firms may prepare reports of performance

    a. Using the calendar year as the accounting period.
    b. Using a natural business year as the accounting period.
    c. For interim periods.
    d. Answers (a), (b), and (c) above are correct under appropriate circumstances.

_____ 6. The account Accumulated Depreciation reflects

    a. Depreciation for the current accounting period only.
    b. Cumulative depreciation on the asset since acquisition.
    c. The amount of depreciation that can be taken in future periods.
    d. None of the above.

_____ 7. In preparing its Year 1 adjustments, Dotsenko neglected to adjust prepaid insurance for the amount of insurance expired during Year 1. As a result of this error

    a. Year 1 net income is understated, the balance in retained earnings is understated, and assets are understated.
    b. Year 1 net income is overstated, the balance in retained earnings is overstated, and assets are correctly stated.
    c. Year 1 net income is overstated, the balance in retained earnings is overstated, and assets are overstated.
    d. None of the above.

_____ 8. Sergey Company completed its second year of operations in Year 2. On 1/1, Year 2, the balance in Retained Earnings was $63,000. During the year, the company declared and paid a dividend of $48,750 to share-holders. The company reported net earnings of $78,750 in its Year 2 income statement. What was the 12/31, Year 2 balance in Retained Earnings?

    a. $141,750.
    b. $127,500.
    c. $111,750.
    d. $ 93,000.

_____ 9. In preparing its Year 1 adjustments, the Cavallini Company neglected to adjust rental fees received in advance for the amount of rental fees earned during Year 1. As a result of this error:

    a. Year 1 net income is understated, the balance in retained earnings is understated, and liabilities are overstated.
    b. Year 1 net income is overstated, the balance in retained earnings is overstated, and liabilities are correctly stated.
    c. Year 1 net income is understated, the balance in retained earnings is understated, and liabilities are understated.
    d. None of the above.

_____ 10. At the beginning of the year, Dominguez reported Accounts Receivable of $27,300. During the year, the company had credit sales totaling $201,600. At year end, the Accounts Receivable balance was $32,900. How much cash was collected on the accounts during the year?

    a. $207,200.
    b. $201,600.
    c. $196,000.
    d. $190,400.

_____ 11. Rodenko, Inc., publishes a monthly sports magazine. On July 1, Year 1, the company sold 1,000 2-year subscriptions for $100 each. On December 31, Year 1, the amount reported as a liability on the balance sheet and the amount reported as revenue on the income statement are, respectively

    a. $ -0- ; $100,000.
    b. $25,000; $ 75,000.
    c. $50,000, $ 50,000.
    d. $75,000; $ 25,000.

_____ 12. Which of the following accounts in not an expense?

    a. Depreciation.
    b. Sales Salaries.
    c. Dividends Declared.
    d. Delivery Expense.

_____ 13. J. R. Moss, an attorney, collects a retainer fee from all of his new clients. At the beginning of the year, the Unearned Retainer Fee account had a balance of $48,000. Moss collected additional retainer fees totaling $188,000 from his clients during the year. His year end balance sheet reports a $32,000 balance in the Unearned Retainer Fee account. How much of the retainer fees were earned by Moss during the year?

    a. $216,000.
    b. $220,000.
    c. $172,000.
    d. $204,000.

_____ 14. Garcia Company purchased a 1-year insurance policy on April 1, Year 1, for $6,000. After year-end adjustments, the amount of prepaid insurance and the amount of insurance expense at December 31, Year 1, are, respectively

    a. $ 1,500;$4,500.
    b. $ 4,500;$1,500.
    c. $ 2,000;$4,000.
    d. $ 4,000;$2,000.

_____ 15. Which of the following transactions did not result in revenue being reported?

    a. Sold merchandise for cash.
    b. Sold merchandise on account.
    c. Collected an account receivable.
    d. All of the above transactions would result in revenue being reported.

Exercises

1. Assume that the accrual basis of accounting is used and revenue is recognized at the time goods are sold or services rendered. Indicate in the space provided the dollar amount of revenue recognized in the month of January. (Each case is independent of the others.)

    _____ a. In January, a company sold its product for a sales price totaling $450,000, of which $270,000 was collected in January, $100,000 collected in February, and the remainder in March.

    _____ b. A theatrical company sells $600,000 of season tickets to its plays, which will be given the second Saturday in each month for 10 months beginning in January. Also, the company sells $80,000 of tickets for January's play.

    _____ c. The Laker Gators, a pro football team, receives $6,000,000 as its portion of the gate receipts for the playoffs held in the previous December.

    _____ d. Bonilla, Co., an owner of office buildings, collected $1,800,000 in January for office rental fees for the 12 month period, January through December.

_____ e. On January 1, a company loans $300,000 to a customer. The customer agrees to repay the $300,000 plus 12 percent interest (total of $336,000) on December 31.

2. Lonski, Inc. began operations on January 1, Year 4. The owners invested $48,000 and the company borrowed $36,000 from a bank. The bank loan is due on January 1, Year 6, with interest at 10 percent per year.

On January 1, the company paid $15,000 for a one-year lease of a building. Also, on January 1 the company purchased a one-year insurance policy for $1,800. The company purchased $80,000 of inventory on account on January 2. On January 10 a payment of $60,000 was made to the supplier. At the end of January, inventory costing $10,000 was still on hand.

During January, cash sales totaled $80,000 and sales to customers on account totaled $66,000. During January, $45,000 was collected from customers who bought on credit.

Other costs paid in cash during January were as follows: salaries, $8,000; utilities, $2,400; supplies, $1,500.

Salaries earned by employees but not paid at January 31 totaled $1,200.

a. Determine Lonski's accrual basis income for January.

b. Determine Lonski's cash basis income for January.

3. Assume that the accrual basis of accounting is used and that revenue is recognized at the time goods are sold or services are rendered. Indicate the amount of expense recognized during the month of September in each of the following situations.

_____ a.   During September, a wholesale company purchased $1,200,000 of its product for resale. A portion, $250,000, was the cost of goods ordered by their customers in August to be delivered in September. Customers placed orders and received goods with a cost to the wholesale company of $450,000 in September. In September, customers ordered goods with a cost of $225,000 to be delivered in October. The remaining portion of September's purchases was maintained for future orders.

_____ b.   A manufacturing firm has two insurance policies covering their property against casualty events. Each policy covers a 6-month period. On August 15, the premium for the first policy, $4,500, is paid to cover the period August 15 through February 15. On September 1, the second policy's premium, $2,880, is paid to cover the period September 1 through February 28.

_____ c.   A pro football team incurred in September a cost of $354,000 for an advertising campaign that will produce full-page ads in local papers, as follows: two in September, three in October, two in November, and one in December.

_____ d.   A swimming pool company purchased concrete supplies totaling
           $166,000 in August. At the end of August there were still
           unused supplies totaling $140,000, and at the end of
           September there were unused supplies totaling $24,000. The
           remaining $24,000 was used in October.

_____ e.   An accounting firm leases its office space. The annual lease
           payment of $270,000 was paid on July 1.

_____ f.   Sales commissions for a cosmetics company are based on a
           percentage of each sales dollar generated by the sales staff.
           The commission is paid at the end of each 3-month period. In
           September $105,000 was paid for July, August, and September
           sales. Sales related to commissions for the 3-month period
           were as follows: July, $262,500; August, $367,500;
           September, $420,000.

4.   Determine the missing amounts in each of the following independent cases:

	a	b	c	d
Assets		$205,000	$145,000	$380,000
Liabilities	$ 185,000		$ 80,000	$125,000
Contributed Capital	$ 92,000	$ 85,000	$	$150,000
Beginning Retained Earnings	$	$ 40,000	$ 37,500	$ 50,000
Revenues	$ 300,000	$195,000	$	$325,000
Expenses	$ 202,500	$175,000	$107,500	$
Dividends	$ 40,000	$	$ 6,250	$ 35,000
Ending Retained Earnings	$ 80,000	$ 27,500	$ 47,500	$

Answers to Questions and Exercises

True/False

1.	T	6.	F	11.	T	16.	T	21.	F
2.	F	7.	F	12.	T	17.	T	22.	F
3.	F	8.	T	13.	F	18.	F		
4.	F	9.	F	14.	T	19.	T		
5.	T	10.	F	15.	T	20.	F		

Matching

1.	e	5.	n	9.	j	13.	k
2.	m	6.	g	10.	a	14.	d
3.	f	7.	c	11.	i		
4.	b	8.	h	12.	l		

Multiple Choice

1.	c	5.	d	9.	a	13.	d
2.	c	6.	b	10.	c	14.	a
3.	a	7.	c	11.	d	15.	c
4.	b	8.	d	12.	c		

Exercises

1. a. $450,000.
   b. $140,000.
   c.   -0-
   d. $150,000.
   e. $ 3,000.

2. a. Accrual basis income:

Sales Revenue		$146,000
Less Expenses:		
Cost of Goods Sold	$70,000	
Salaries	9,200	
Utilities	2,400	
Supplies	1,500	
Rent	1,250	
Insurance	150	
Interest	300	
Total Expenses		84,800
Net Income		$ 61,200

2. b. Cash basis income:

Sales Revenue		$125,000
Less Expenses:		
Cost of Goods Sold	$60,000	
Salaries	8,000	
Utilities	2,400	
Supplies	1,500	
Rent	15,000	
Insurance	1,800	
Total Expenses		88,700
Net Income		$ 36,300

3. a. $700,000.
   b. $ 1,230.
   c. $ 88,500.
   d. $116,000.
   e. $ 22,500.
   f. $ 42,000.

4.

	a	b	c	d
Assets	$357,000	$205,000	$145,000	$380,000
Liabilities	$185,000	$ 92,500	$ 80,000	$125,000
Contributed Capital	$ 92,000	$ 85,000	$ 17,500	$150,000
Beginning Retained Earnings	$ 22,500	$ 40,000	$ 37,500	$ 50,000
Revenues	$300,000	$195,000	$123,750	$325,000
Expenses	$202,500	$175,000	$107,500	$235,000
Dividends	$ 40,000	$ 32,500	$ 6,250	$ 35,000
Ending Retained Earnings	$ 80,000	$ 27,500	$ 47,500	$105,000

Chapter 4

Statement of Cash Flows:
Reporting the Effects of Operating, Investing,
and Financing Activities on Cash Flows

Chapter Highlights

1.   The statement of cash flows, the third major statement discussed in this text, reports the impact of a firm's operating, investing, and financing activities on cash flows during an accounting period. The statement explains the reasons for the change in cash between balance sheet dates and classifies the reasons for the change as operating, investing or financing activity.

2.   The operating section of the statement of cash flows shows the adjustments required to convert net income, measured on an accrual basis, to the amount of net cash flows generated from operations during the period. The revenues and expenses reported on the income statement will differ from the cash receipts and disbursements because (a) the recognition of revenues will not necessarily coincide with the receipts of cash from customers and (b) the recognition of expenses will not necessarily coincide with the disbursements of cash to suppliers, employees, and other creditors.

3.   In presenting cash flows from operations, a firm may use either the indirect method or the direct method. Most firms report cash flow from operations using the indirect method. The indirect method begins with net income for a period and then shows adjustments to net income to convert revenues to cash received from customers and to convert expenses to cash disbursed to various suppliers of goods and services. Under the direct method, cash flows from operations are calculated by subtracting all expenses that use cash from all cash receipts from customers. Cash flow from operations is identical under the two methods.

4.   Investing activities include cash received from sales of investments and property, plant, and equipment and the cash paid for acquisition of investments and property, plant, and equipment.

5.   Cash received from issuing debt or capital stock and cash paid for dividends and reacquisitions of debt or capital stock are reported as financing activities in the statement of cash flows.

6.   Free cash flow is the excess of cash flow from operations over cash flow for investing. Firms can use free cash flow to repay borrowing, pay a dividend, repurchase common stock, and add to cash on the balance sheet.

7.   Ambiguities exist for classifying some cash transactions into either operations, investing or financing activities. For example cash flows from interest and dividend revenues are correctly classified as operating activities, but the cash flows related to the purchase and sale of investments in securities are classified as an investing activity.

Another example is interest expense which is classified as an operating activity but the issue or redemption of debt is classified as a financing activity. A dividend paid to shareholders is considered to be a financing activity.

8. Some financing and investment transactions do not directly affect cash but must be disclosed either in a separate note or in a supplementary schedule. An example of such a transaction is the acquisition of a parcel of land by issuing a mortgage.

9. The effects of various transactions on cash might be seen by reexamining the accounting equation. The accounting equation states that

$$\text{Assets} = \text{Liabilities} + \text{Shareholders' Equity}$$
$$C + N\$A = L + SE$$

If the start-of-the-period and the end-of-the-period balance sheets maintain the accounting equation, the following equation must also be valid:

$$DC + DN\$A = DL + DSE$$

Rearranging terms, we obtain the <u>cash change equation</u>:

$$DC = DL + DSE - DN\$A$$

where:

> D = The change in an item, whether positive or negative, from the beginning to the end of the period.
> C = Cash
> $N\$A$ = Non-cash Assets
> L = Liabilities
> SE = Shareholders' Equity

The cash change equation states that changes in cash (left-hand side) equal the changes in liabilities plus the changes in shareholders' equity less the changes in non-cash assets (right-hand side).

10. Stated another way, the causes of the change in cash can be identified by studying the changes in non-cash accounts and classifying those changes as operating, investing, and financing activities.

11. A columnar work sheet is used in preparation of the statement of cash flows. The following steps are followed in preparing the statement of cash flows:

a. Compute the change in each balance sheet account between the beginning and end of the year. Enter the changes in the non-cash balance sheet accounts in the first column of the upper panel of the work sheet. (Increases in non-cash assets appear with negative signs. Decreases in non-cash assets appear with positive signs. Increases in liability and shareholders' equity accounts appear with positive signs. Decreases in liability and shareholders' equity accounts appear with negative signs). Enter the net change in cash on the last line of the top panel of the work sheet.

Also, enter the amounts of revenues and expenses for the period in the first column of the lower panel of the work sheet. The information in this lower panel is used to compute cash flow from operations under the direct method.

b. Classify the change in each balance sheet account as an operating, investing or financing activity and enter it in the appropriate column of the work sheet using the same sign as in the first column.

Also, enter the change in each balance sheet account that relates to an operating activity on the revenue or expense line in the lower panel to which it relates. For example, changes in accounts receivable relate to sales revenue. Changes in inventory and accounts payable relate to cost of goods sold.

c. Sum the entries in the Operations, Investing, and Financing columns and net the three sums to ensure that they equal the net change in cash. Also sum the amounts in each of the columns in the lower panel and check to ensure that net income plus changes in operating balance sheet accounts equals cash received from customers minus cash disbursed to suppliers of various goods and services, which in turn equals cash flow from operations.

d. The work sheet provides the information needed to prepare the statement of cash flows using either the direct method or the indirect method of computing cash flows from operations.

12. Statement No. 7 of the International Accounting Standards Board recommends the preparation of a statement of cash flows that reports cash flows from operating, investing and financing activities. Standard-setting bodies in most countries have adopted this standard.

13. The statement of cash flows provides information that helps the reader in:

a. assessing the impact of operations on liquidity, and

b. assessing the relations between cash flows from operating, investing, and financing activities.

14. Users find interpreting a statement of cash flows requires an understanding of the economic characteristics of the firm's industry. The interpretation is enhanced by examining the statement of cash flows over several years.

Questions and Exercises

True/False. For each of the following statements, place a T or F in the space provided to indicate whether the statement is true or false.

_____ 1. It is correct to assume that, if a firm has a loss for a period of time, the firm has also decreased its liquidity.

_____ 2. If the only noncurrent item to change was shareholders' equity, and it decreased, then cash must have increased.

_____ 3.   The most important source of cash for successful firms is the return on funds invested in profitable securities.

_____ 4.   Like the balance sheet and income statement, the statement of cash flows is generated as a regular output of the firm's record-keeping system.

_____ 5.   An increase in accounts payable is added to net income in determining the cash flow from operations.

_____ 6.   A decrease in inventory is added to net income in calculating the cash flow from operations.

_____ 7.   A reason that revenues and expenses differ from cash receipts and disbursements is that the accrual basis of accounting is used in determining net income.

_____ 8.   The statement of cash flows is related to both the balance sheet and the income statement, but also discloses information that is unavailable or only partially available by analysis of the balance sheet and income statements alone.

_____ 9.   Accumulated depreciation increased by $10,000 during the year. As long as no depreciable assets have been retired during the year, this $10,000 increase can be attributed to depreciation expense.

_____ 10. If a creditor allows a firm to owe money on account, this is effectively a use of cash to the firm.

_____ 11. When all other things remain the same, an increase in non-cash assets causes cash to decrease.

_____ 12. In determining cash from operations, depreciation expense is added to the net income since it represents a fund of cash set aside during the year for the replacement of long-lived assets.

_____ 13. Financing and investing activities that do not directly affect cash do not need to be disclosed.

_____ 14. Whenever there are sales on account, the amount of sales revenue will always exceed the amount of cash receipts.

_____ 15. The statement of cash flows, although providing useful information to readers, is not considered a major financial statement.

_____ 16. One of the most important factors not reported on the balance sheet and income statement is how the operations of the period affected the liquidity of the firm.

_____ 17. Dividends are an example of a cash disbursement that did not affect operations.

_____ 18. Since the exchange of a parcel of land for a new machine does not involve cash, it should not be disclosed when reporting cash flows.

_____ 19. The fact that the balance in cash increased over time does not necessarily mean that the cash generated from operations was positive.

_____ 20. Depreciation is added back to net income in a statement of cash flows because it is a source of cash.

_____ 21. One difference between the income statement and the statement of cash flows is that the former is based upon the accrual basis of accounting and the latter is prepared on a cash basis.

_____ 22. If the balance in accounts receivable increases over the year, this means that the sales revenue exceeds the cash received from customers who bought on credit.

_____ 23. Cash receipts from operations are the only source of cash for a company.

_____ 24. The declaration of dividends has no effect on cash.

_____ 25. The cash change equation is:

$$DC = DL + DSE + DN\$A$$

_____ 26. Cash flow from financing includes cash paid for retirement of debt but does not include cash paid for dividends.

_____ 27. Cash flow from operations includes cash received from sales of services.

_____ 28. Cash flow from operations is always positive unless a company is in bankruptcy.

_____ 29. Cash flow from investing activities include cash received from sales of investments and cash paid for acquisition of property, plant, and equipment.

_____ 30. The cash flow from investing section of the statement of cash flows is the same whether a firm follows the direct or indirect method of computing cash flow from operations.

_____ 31. A cash flow for interest expense is shown in the statement of cash flows as a financing activity.

_____ 32. A cash flow for the purchase of marketable securities is shown in the statement of cash flows as an investing activity.

_____ 33. Cash equivalents represent short-term, highly liquid investments in which a firm has temporarily placed excess cash.

_____ 34. "Cashflows" refers only to flows of cash.

_____ 35. "Free cash flow" refers to an excess of cash flow from operations over cash flow for investing.

Matching

1. For each transaction below, indicate the effects on cash and non-cash accounts and place the letters for your answer in the space provided. The first one is shown as an example:

    a. (a) = Increase (decrease) in cash
    b. (b) = Increase (decrease) in liabilities
    c. (c) = Increase (decrease) in shareholders' equity
    d. (d) = Increase (decrease) in non-cash assets

a, (d) 1. Sale of temporary investments, with no gain or loss.

_____ 2. Sale of used equipment at its book value.

_____ 3. Pay accounts payable.

_____ 4. Issuance of capital stock for cash.

_____ 5. Borrowing on a 60-day note payable.

_____ 6. Issuance of 10-year bonds.

_____ 7. Payment of dividends previously declared.

_____ 8. Purchase of equipment for cash.

_____ 9. Collect accounts receivable.

_____ 10. Paid cash to retire preferred stock.

_____ 11. Purchased merchandise inventory on account.

_____ 12. Collection of 1-year note receivable from customer.

_____ 13. Purchased a parcel of land in exchange for a mortgage payable.

_____ 14. Accrual of income taxes to be paid in following year.

_____ 15. Declaration of dividends to be paid in 30 days.

_____ 16. Expiration of insurance policy during year after purchase.

_____ 17. Recording of depreciation expense.

_____ 18. Receipt of cash for delivery of merchandise next month.

_____ 19. Acceptance of a 30-day note for an overdue account receivable.

_____ 20. Early retirement of bonds due in four years.

_____ 21. Prepayment for a 1-year insurance policy.

_____ 22. Recognition of accrued interest expense, which is payable in 30 days, on long-term notes.

2.   Using the designated letters, classify each of the following cash flows of the current period as either

  a.   operating activity.
  b.   investing activity.
  c.   financing activity.

_____ 1.   Receipt of $111,000 from customers for sales made this period.

_____ 2.   Disbursement of $95,000 to merchandise suppliers.

_____ 3.   Disbursement of $19,000 for insurance for the next 18 months.

_____ 4.   Disbursement for dividends declared in the current year.

_____ 5.   Disbursement for acquisition of marketable securities.

_____ 6.   Receipt of $350,000 from issuing bonds payable.

_____ 7.   Receipt of $18,000 from customers for sales made last period.

_____ 8.   Disbursement of $101,000 for a patent.

_____ 9.   Disbursement of $6,700 to employees for services performed last period.

_____ 10. Disbursement of $50,000 to acquire equipment.

3.   For each transaction below, indicate the effects on a statement of cash flows (indirect method) using the following choices:

Cash flows from operations
a.   Net income will be increased or adjusted upward.
b.   Net income will be decreased or adjusted downward.

Cash flows from investing
c.   Cash received.
d.   Cash paid.

Cash flows from financing
e.   Cash received.
f.   Cash paid.

_____ 1.   Purchase of a building for cash.

_____ 2.   Paid cash dividends.

_____ 3.   Sale of a long-term investment (no gain or loss).

_____ 4.   Depreciation on equipment.

_____ 5.   Sale of equipment at book value.

_____ 6.   Issuance of preferred stock.

_____ 7.   Accounts Receivable increased during the period.

_____ 8. Issuance of long-term debt.

_____ 9. Prepaid Insurance decreased during the period.

_____ 10. Accounts Payable increased during the period.

_____ 11. Inventory decreased during the period.

_____ 12. Salaries Payable decreased during the period.

Multiple Choice. Choose the best answer for each of the following questions and enter the identifying letter in the space provided.

_____ 1. The Adam Company had a net loss of $480,000 in 2007. These additional facts are also given:

Dividends paid	$120,000
Depreciation expense	$ 90,000
Increase in accounts payable	$ 45,000
Issuance of stock	$300,000
Retirement of debt	$150,000

What was the amount of cash flow from operations?

a. ($345,000).
b. $615,000.
c. ($225,000).
d. $195,000.

_____ 2. Referring to the question above, what was the net change in cash for 2007?

a. ($315,000).
b. $ 30,000.
c. $645,000.
d. ($495,000).

_____ 3. During 2007, the Varner Company had a net income of $100,000. In addition, selected balance sheet accounts showed the following changes:

Accounts Receivable	$ 6,000 increase
Accounts Payable	2,000 increase
Building	8,000 decrease
Accumulated Depreciation	3,000 increase
Bonds Payable	16,000 increase

What was the amount of cash flow from operations?

a. $100,000.
b. $ 99,000.
c. $119,000.
d. $103,000.

_____ 4.   The major components of the statement of cash flows include the following:

   a.   Cash flow from operations, cash flow from investing, and cash flow from financing.
   b.   Cash flow from operations, other sources of cash, and other uses of cash.
   c.   Sources of cash from investments, application of cash for financing activities, and other cash transactions.
   d.   Cash received from customers, cash paid to customers, and other sources of cash.

_____ 5.   Which transaction below is presented as a cash flow from financing?

   a.   Cash paid for investments acquisition.
   b.   Cash received from sale of property, plant, and equipment.
   c.   Cash received from customers.
   d.   Cash paid for dividends.

_____ 6.   Which of the following would be an addition to net income in determining cash flow from operations?

   a.   Increased accounts receivable.
   b.   Increased merchandise inventory.
   c.   Increased accounts payable.
   d.   Decreased notes payable to suppliers.

_____ 7.   Which transaction listed below is shown on a statement of cash flows but does not affect cash?

   a.   Sale of bonds for cash.
   b.   Exchange of land for stock.
   c.   Collection of customer accounts.
   d.   Dividends paid to owners.

_____ 8.   During 2007 the Whaley Company had net income of $450,000. In addition, selected additional facts are also given.

Depreciation expense	$ 63,000
Issuance of debt	$360,000
Loss on sale of equipment	$ 69,000
Purchase of building	$330,000
Increase in inventory	$ 36,000

   What was the amount of cash flow from operations?

   a. $546,000.
   b. $513,000.
   c. $477,000.
   d. $414,000.

_____ 9.   Depreciation expense

a.   Provides cash from operations.
b.   Should be added to net income in determining cash provided by operations.
c.   Should be deducted from net income in determining cash provided by operations.
d.   Is an example of a cash expense.

_____ 10.   The method of presenting cash from operations by listing all revenues providing cash followed by all expenses using cash is the:

a.   Direct method.
b.   Operations method.
c.   Indirect method.
d.   Funds method.

_____ 11.   The most popular method of presenting cash from operations in the statement of cash flows is the:

a.   Direct method.
b.   Operations method.
c.   Indirect method.
d.   Funds method.

_____ 12.   During 2007 the Luna Company had net income of $78,000. In addition, selected additional facts are also given:

Decrease in accounts receivable	$ 2,500
Gain on sale of building	3,500
Increase in accounts payable	3,000
Issuance of common stock	22,500
Retirement of debt	11,500

What was the amount of cash flow from operations?

a. $83,500.
b. $80,500.
c. $80,000.
d. $81,000.

_____ 13.   Cash received from the issue of debt is shown as

a.   Cash flow from operations.
b.   Cash flow from investing.
c.   Cash flow from financing.
d.   A non-cash transaction.

_____ 14.   Cash received from the sale of an investment is shown as

a.   Cash flow from operations.
b.   Cash flow from investing.
c.   Cash flow from financing.
d.   A non-cash transaction.

_____ 15. Cash paid for dividends is shown as

a. Cash flow from operations.
b. Cash flow from investing.
c. Cash flow from financing.
d. A non-cash transaction.

_____ 16. Cash received from the sale of services is shown as

a. Cash flow from operations.
b. Cash flow from investing.
c. Cash flow from financing.
d. A non-cash transaction.

_____ 17. Cash paid for operating expenses is shown as

a. Cash flow from operations.
b. Cash flow from investing.
c. Cash flow from financing.
d. A non-cash transaction.

_____ 18. Bonds Payable had the following balances at the beginning and end of 2007:

January 1	$300,000
December 31	$420,000

In addition $180,000 of bonds were retired in 2007. How much was issued during the year?

a. $300,000.
b. $ 60,000.
c. $480,000.
d. $540,000.

_____ 19. The Harper Company had the following selected amounts taken from its balance sheet.

	Building	Accumulated Depreciation
01/01/07	$900,000	$210,000
12/31/07	$775,000	$250,000

During 2007, a building having a cost of $190,000 was purchased. Was any building sold during the year, and if so, what was its original cost?

a. No building was sold in 2007.
b. Yes, but its cost cannot be determined.
c. Yes, and its original cost was $125,000.
d. Yes, and its original cost was $315,000.

_____ 20.   The balance in the Accumulated Depreciation account was $65,000 on
             1/1/07 and $60,000 on 12/31/07. During 2007, an asset costing
             $50,000 (accumulated depreciation of $40,000) was sold for $10,000.
             What was the depreciation expense for 2007?

             a. $ 5,000.
             b. $45,000.
             c. $55,000.
             d. $35,000.

_____ 21.   Which statement below is true concerning depreciation expense?

             a.   Depreciation expense increases the expense for a period but
                   does not use cash.
             b.   Depreciation expense is added back to net income in
                   determining cash flow from operations because it had
                   originally been subtracted in computing net income but was not
                   a use of cash.
             c.   Depreciation expense is not a source of funds.
             d.   All of the above are true.

_____ 22.   Which statement below expresses the objective of the statement of
             cash flows?

             a.   To report the amount of cash flow from a firm's operating
                   activities.
             b.   To report the principal inflows and outflows of cash from
                   investing activities.
             c.   To report the principal inflows and outflows of cash from
                   financing activities.
             d.   All of the above.

_____ 23.   Which of the following would be a deduction from net income in
             determining cash flow from operations?

             a.   Depreciation expense.
             b.   Increased accounts receivable.
             c.   Decreased accounts receivable.
             d.   Increased accounts payable.

_____ 24.   During the year 2007 the following changes took place:

Current Liabilities	$75,000 increase
Noncurrent Liabilities	45,000 decrease
Owners' Equity	51,000 decrease
Noncurrent Assets	42,000 increase
Current Assets (other than cash)	18,000 increase

             What has been the change in cash for 2007?

             a.   ($57,000).
             b. $30,000.
             c. $39,000.
             d.   ($81,000).

_____ 25.   Cash paid for land is shown as:

       a.   Cash flow from operations.
       b.   Cash flow from investing.
       c.   Cash flow from financing.
       d.   A non-cash transaction.

_____ 26.   It is common practice in most countries to prepare:

       a.   A statement of cash flows.
       b.   A statement of financing activities.
       c.   A statement of investing activities.
       d.   A statement of sources and uses of funds.

_____ 27.   Free cash flow can be used for which of the following:

       a.   For operating activities.
       b.   For investing activities.
       c.   For financing activities.
       d.   All of the above.

_____ 28.   Which of the following is considered to be a cash equivalent?

       a.   Accounts receivable to be collected within 15 days.
       b.   A line of credit from the company's bank.
       c.   A short-term, highly liquid investment.
       d.   None of the above

Exercises

1. Assume that, during the current year, Victor Corporation engages in the transactions listed in the left column of the table shown below. Analyze the transactions to show their effect on cash (C), liabilities (L), shareholders' equity (SE) and non-cash asset (N$A) accounts. Use the table below. The first transaction is shown as an example.

	Changes in Cash		Effect on Cash — Changes in Non-cash Accounts				
Transactions	DC	=	DL	+	DSE	-	DN$A
a. Acquires merchandise costing $70 on account.		=	$ 70	+		-	(+$ 70)
b. Sells merchandise costing $60 to customers on account for $124.		=		+		-	
c. Collects $90 of accounts receivable.		=		+		-	
d. Pays salaries of $20.		=		+		-	
e. Issues long-term debt for $100.		=		+		-	
f. Pays other expenses of $10.		=		+		-	
g. Records depreciation for the year of $8.		=		+		-	
h. Acquires equipment costing $130 for cash.		=		+		-	
i. Declares and pays dividends of $8.		=		+		-	
j. Pays accounts payable, $50, to suppliers of merchandise.		=		+		-	
k. Accrues and pays $4 interest on bonds payable.		=		+		-	
Net change in cash and non-cash accounts		=		+		-	

2. You are given below a list of several key transactions, along with other relevant information for Gloria Company in 2007. You are to prepare the Statement of Cash Flows for 2007.

a. Net income for 2007 was $110,000.

b. Depreciation expense for the year was $30,000, and patent amortization was $3,750.

c. Dividends of $27,000 were paid in December.

d. 1,000 shares of preferred stock were issued for total cash consideration of $100,000.

e. A parcel of land was acquired for $30,000.

f. A $5,000 loan was made to one of the company's officers to be repaid in 2009.

g. A long-term investment, having originally cost $1,650, was sold for $1,650.

h. A used piece of equipment was sold for $12,750. It had an original cost of $30,000 and accumulated depreciation of $17,250.

i. The beginning cash balance was $10,000.

j. There were the following changes in other non-cash accounts:

Accounts Receivable	$40,500 Increase
Inventory	$36,000 Decrease
Accounts Payable	$25,000 Decrease

3. Financial Statement data for Bonnie Company are presented below for the years ended December 31, 2007 and December 31, 2008.

Bonnie Company
Comparative Balance Sheets

	Year Ended December 31			
Assets	2008		2007	
Current Assets				
Cash	$ 96,000		$ 84,000	
Accounts Receivable	120,000		87,000	
Inventories	200,000	$416,000	132,000	$303,000
Fixed Assets				
Land	$ 76,000		$ -0-	
Equipment (cost)	240,000		289,000	
Less Accumulated Depreciation	(156,000)	160,000	(128,000)	161,000
Intangibles				
Goodwill		40,000		44,000
Total Assets		$616,000		$508,000

Liabilities				
Current Liabilities				
Accounts Payable	$116,000		$ 96,000	
Notes Payable	140,000		-0-	
Interest Payable	4,000	$260,000	4,000	$100,000
Long-Term Liabilities				
Notes Payable, due in 2009		-0-		140,000
Total Liabilities		$260,000		$240,000
Shareholders' Equity				
Capital Stock	$140,000		$100,000	
Retained Earnings	216,000	$356,000	168,000	$268,000
Total Liabilities and Shareholders' Equity		$616,000		$508,000

Bonnie Company
Income Statement
For the Year Ended December 31, 2008

Sales $200,000

Deduct Expenses:
  Depreciation $ 28,000
  Amortization of Goodwill   4,000
  Income Tax   48,000
  Interest Expense   4,000
  Other Expenses   44,000   128,000

Net Income $ 72,000

Bonnie Company
Retained Earnings Statement
For the Year Ended December 31, 2008

    Retained Earnings 1/1/08 $168,000
    Plus Net Income   72,000
                                           240,000
    Less Dividends   24,000
    Retained Earnings 12/31/08 $216,000

Additional Information: There were no purchases of equipment during 2008.
Equipment was sold in 2008 for $49,000.

Prepare a statement of cash flows for 2008 (use the indirect method).

4. A Statement of Cash Flows for the Elvin Corporation is presented below:

Elvin Corporation
Statement of Cash Flows
For the Year Ended December 31, 2008

Operations
  Net income $24,000
  Depreciation Expense   2,800
  Changes in Working Capital Accounts   (10,000)
    Cash Flow from Operations $16,800

Investing
  Acquisition of Equipment   (8,800)

Financing
  Issue of Common Stock   6,000
  Net Increase in Cash   14,000
  Cash, January 1, 2008   2,800
  Cash, December 31, 2008 $16,800

After preparing this condensed statement of cash flows for 2008, you discover that Elvin sold a building on the last day of the year but failed to record it in the accounts or to deposit the check received from the sale. The building originally cost $100,000 and had accumulated depreciation of $90,000 at the time of sale. Recast the statement of cash flows above assuming that Elvin Corporation sold the building for cash in the following amounts (ignore income taxes):

a. $15,000.

b. $ 7,000.

5. Presented below are the comparative balance sheets for Bennett Company for 12/31/08 and 12/31/07.

	12/31/08		12/31/07	
Cash		$ 36,000		$ 20,000
Accounts Receivable		82,000		60,000
Inventory		34,000		52,000
Prepaid Insurance		2,400		7,200
Land		110,000		44,000
Equipment	$270,000		$240,000	
Acc. Dep-Equip	70,000	200,000	60,000	180,000
Goodwill		32,000		38,000
Total Assets		$496,400		$401,200
Accounts Payable		$ 28,000		$ 20,000
Salaries Payable		6,000		11,000
Notes Payable		10,000		0
Bonds Payable		200,000		230,000
Common Stock		240,000		108,000
Retained Earnings		12,400		32,200
Total Liabilities &				
Shareholder Equity		$496,400		$401,200

Bennett's income statement for the year ending 12/31/08 reported a net loss of $13,800:

Sales		$190,600
Cost of Goods Sold	$170,800	
Insurance Expense	5,600	
Depreciation Expense	10,000	
Interest Expense	12,000	
Goodwill Amortization	6,000	204,400
Net Income (Loss)		($13,800)

Other information:
   The company declared and paid a $6,000 dividend to shareholders in 2008.

   Prepare a statement of cash flows (use the indirect method).

Answers to Questions and Exercises

True/False

1.	F	8.	T	15.	F	22.	T	29.	T
2.	F	9.	T	16.	T	23.	F	30.	T
3.	F	10.	F	17.	T	24.	T	31.	F
4.	F	11.	T	18.	F	25.	F	32.	T
5.	T	12.	F	19.	T	26.	F	33.	T
6.	T	13.	F	20.	F	27.	T	34.	F
7.	T	14.	F	21.	T	28.	F	35.	T

Matching

1.
1. a, (d)	6. a,b	11. d,b	16. (c), (d)	21. d, (a)
2. a, (d)	7. (b), (a)	12. a, (d)	17. (c), (d)	22. (c),b
3. (b), (a)	8. d, (a)	13. d,b	18. a,b	
4. a,c	9. a, (d)	14. (c),b	19. d, (d)	
5. a,b	10. (c), (a)	15. (c),b	20. (b), (a)	

2.
1. a	3. a	5. b	7. a	9. a
2. a	4. c	6. c	8. b	10. b

3.
1. d	3. c	5. c	7. b	9. a	11. a
2. f	4. a	6. e	8. e	10. a	12. b

Multiple Choice

1.	a	6.	c	11.	c	16.	a	21.	d	26.	a
2.	a	7.	b	12.	c	17.	a	22.	d	27.	c
3.	b	8.	a	13.	c	18.	a	23.	b	28.	c
4.	a	9.	b	14.	b	19.	d	24.	d		
5.	d	10.	a	15.	c	20.	d	25.	b		

Exercises

1.

Victor Corporation
Analysis of the Effects of Transactions during the year
on Cash and Non-cash Accounts

Transactions	Changes in Cash DC	=	Changes in Non-cash Accounts DL	+	DSE	-	DN$A
a. Acquires merchandise costing $70 on account, increasing a non-cash asset and a liability.		=	$ 70	+		-	(+$ 70)
b. Sells merchandise costing $60 to customers on account for $124, increasing a non-cash, accounts receivable, by $124, decreasing the noncash asset, inventory by $60, and increasing shareholders☐ equity by $64.		=		+	$ 64	-	(+$124) (-$ 60)
c. Collects $90 of accounts receivable, increasing cash and decreasing the non-cash asset, accounts receivable.	$ 90	=		+		-	(-$ 90)
d. Pays salaries of $20, decreasing cash and shareholders☐ equity.	(-$ 20)	=		+	(-$ 20)	-	
e. Issues long-term debt for $100, increasing cash and a liability.	$100	=	$100	+		-	
f. Pays other expenses of $10, decreasing cash and shareholders☐ equity.	(-$10)	=		+	(-$ 10)	-	
g. Records depreciation for the year of $8, decreasing shareholders☐ equity and non-cash assets.		=		+	(-$ 8)	-	(-$ 8)

h. Acquires equipment costing $130, for cash, decreasing cash and increasing non-cash assets.

h.	(-$130)	=		+		-	(+$130)
i.	(-$ 8)	=		+	(-$ 8)	-	
j.	(-$ 50)	=	(-$ 50)	+		-	
k.	(-$ 4)	=		+	(-$ 4)	-	
Net change in cash and non-cash accounts	-$ 32	=	$120	+	$ 14	-	$166

i. Declares and pays dividends of $8, decreasing cash and shareholders' equity.

j. Pays accounts payable, $50, to suppliers of merchandise , decreasing cash and a liability.

k. Accrues and pays $4 interest on bonds payable decreasing cash and shareholders' equity.

2.

Gloria Company
Statement of Cash Flows
For the Year Ended December 31, 2007

Operations:
Net Income $110,000

Additions:
Depreciation Expense Not Using Cash	30,000
Patent Amortization Not Using Cash	3,750
Decreased Merchandise Inventory	36,000

Subtractions:
Increased Accounts Receivable	(40,500)	
Decreased Accounts Payable	(25,000)	
Cash Flow From Operations		$114,250

Investing:
Acquisition of Land	$(30,000)	
Loan to Officer	(5,000)	
Sale of Long-Term Investment	1,650	
Sale of Equipment	12,750	
Cash Flow from Investments		(20,600)

Financing:
Dividends Paid	$(27,000)	
Issue Preferred Stock	$100,000	
Cash Flow from Financing		73,000
Net Change in Cash		$166,650
Cash, January 1, 2007		10,000
Cash, December 31, 2007		$176,650

3.
Bonnie Company
Statement of Cash Flows
For the Year Ended December 31, 2008

Operations:
Net Income		$72,000	
Additions			
Depreciation	$28,000		
Amortization	4,000		
Accounts Payable Increase	20,000		
Deductions			
Accounts Receivable Increase	(33,000)		
Inventories Increase	(68,000)	(49,000)	
Cash Flow From Operations			$23,000

Investing:
Sale of Equipment		$49,000	
Acquisition of Land		(76,000)	
Cash Flow From Investments			(27,000)

Financing:
Sale of Stock		$40,000	
Paid Dividends		(24,000)	
Cash Flow From Financing			$16,000
Net Change in Cash			$12,000
Cash, January 1, 2008			84,000
Cash, December 31, 2008			$96,000

4.
Elvin Corporation
Statement of Cash Flows
For Year Ended December 31, 2008

Operations	(a)	(b)
Net Income [includes $5,000 Gain in (a) and $3,000 Loss in (b)]	$29,000	$ 21,000
Depreciation	2,800	2,800
(Gain) Loss on Sale of Building	(5,000)	3,000
Changes in Working Capital Accounts	(10,000)	(10,000)
Cash Flow from Operations	$16,800	$ 16,800
Investing		
Acquisition of Equipment	(8,800)	(8,800)
Sale of Building	15,000	7,000
Cash Flow from Investing	$ 6,200	$(1,800)
Financing		
Issue of Common Stock	$ 6,000	$ 6,000
Net Change in Cash	29,000	21,000
Cash, January 1, 2008	2,800	2,800
Cash, December 31, 2008	$31,800	$ 23,800

Bennett Company
Statement of Cash Flows
For Year Ended December 31, 2008

Operations:
Net Loss $(13,800)
Additions:
    Inventory decrease $18,000
    Prepaid Insurance decrease   4,800
    Accounts Payable increase   8,000
    Depreciation Expense   10,000
    Goodwill Amortization   6,000
Deductions:
    Accounts Receivable increase   (22,000)
    Salaries Payable decrease   (5,000)
Cash Flow from Operations $ 6,000

Investing:
    Purchased Land $(66,000)
    Purchased Equipment   (30,000)
Cash Flow from Investments   (96,000)

Financing:
    Issued Common Stock $132,000
    Note Payable Issued   10,000
    Retired Bonds Payable   (30,000)
    Paid Dividends   (6,000)
Cash Flow from Financing $ 106,000
Net Change in Cash $ 16,000
Cash, January 1, 2008 $ 20,000
Cash, December 31, 2008 $ 36,000

Chapter 5

Introduction to Financial Statement Analysis

Chapter Highlights

1. When comparing investment alternatives, the investor's decision is based on the return anticipated from each investment and the risk associated with that return. Most financial statement analysis, therefore, is directed at some aspect of a firm's profitability or its risk, or both.

2. Ratios are useful tools in financial statement analysis because they conveniently summarize data in a form that is more easily understood, interpreted, and compared. Ratios should be used carefully. Once calculated, the ratio must be compared with some criterion or standard. Several possible criteria might be used: (a) the planned ratio for the period being analyzed; (b) the value of the ratio during the preceding period for the same firm; (c) the value of the ratio for a similar firm in the same industry; or (d) the average ratio for other firms in the same industry.

3. Three measures of profitability are (a) rate of return on assets; (b) rate of return on common shareholders' equity; and (c) earnings per share of common stock.

4. The rate of return on assets (ROA) is a measure of a firm's performance in using assets to generate earnings independent of the financing of those assets. The rate of return on assets relates the results of operating performance to the investments of a firm without regard to how the firm financed the acquisition of those investments. The rate of return is computed as follows:

$$\frac{\text{Net Income + Interest Expense Net of Income Tax Savings}}{\text{Average Total Assets}}.$$

5. The rate of return has particular relevance to lenders or a firm's creditors because, when extending credit or providing debt capital to a firm, creditors want to be sure that the firm can generate a rate of return on that capital exceeding its cost.

6. The rate of return on assets is dependent upon a firm's profit margin ratio and total asset turnover ratio. The relationship between the three ratios can be expressed as follows:

Rate of Return on Assets = Profit Margin Ratio $\times$ Total Assets Turnover Ratio.

OR

$$\frac{\text{Net Income +}}{\text{Interest Expense}} = \frac{\text{Net Income +}}{\text{Interest Expense}} \times \frac{}{}$$

$$\frac{\text{Net of Income}}{\text{Tax Savings}} = \frac{\text{Net of Income}}{\text{Tax Savings}} \times \frac{\text{Sales}}{\text{Average Total Assets}}$$

Therefore, an improvement in the rate of return on assets can be accomplished by increasing the profit margin ratio, the total assets turnover ratio, or both.

7. The profit margin ratio, the percentage of net income plus interest expense net of tax savings to sales, is a measure of a firm's ability to control the level of expenses relative to sales. By controlling costs, a firm will be able to increase the profits from a given amount of sales and improve its profit margin ratio.

8. To identify the reasons for a change in the profit margin ratio, changes in a firm's expenses must be examined. Any important expense can be watched by management by comparing the expense with sales in an effort to note the trend of the expense and to take prompt action to control the expense if it appears to be getting out of line.

9. The total assets turnover ratio, the ratio of sales to average total assets during the period, provides a measure of the sales generated from a particular level of investment in assets. Changes in the total assets turnover ratio can be analyzed by computing an accounts receivable turnover, an inventory turnover, and a fixed asset turnover.

10. The accounts receivable turnover, which is computed by dividing net sales on account by average accounts receivable, indicates how quickly the firm collects cash. The average number of days that accounts receivable are outstanding can be computed by dividing 365 days by the accounts receivable turnover. The average number of days can be compared with the firm's credit sale terms to determine if any corrective action is needed in the firm's credit and collection activity.

11. The inventory turnover indicates how fast firms sell their inventory items. It is computed by dividing cost of goods sold by average inventory. The average number of days that merchandise is held can be computed by dividing 365 days by the inventory turnover.

12. The fixed asset turnover (or the fixed asset productivity ratio) is computed by dividing sales by average fixed assets (property, plant, equipment) during the year. It measures the relation between the investment in fixed assets and sales. The reciprocal of the fixed assets turnover ratio measures dollars of fixed assets required to generate one dollar of sales.

13. Changes in the fixed asset turnover ratio should be interpreted cautiously. A decreasing rate of fixed asset turnover may indicate that a firm is expanding and preparing for future growth while an increasing rate of fixed asset turnover may indicate that a firm is anticipating a decline in sales and is cutting back its capital expenditures.

14. The rate of return on assets measures the profitability of a firm before any payments to the suppliers of capital. A portion of the return on assets must be allocated to the various providers of capital. The share allocated to creditors equals any contractual interest net of tax savings. The share allocated to preferred shareholders equals the stated dividend amounts on the preferred stock. The common shareholders have a residual claim on all earnings after creditors and preferred shareholders have received amounts contractually owed them.

15. The rate of return on common shareholders' equity (ROCE) measures a firm's performance in using and financing assets to generate earnings and is of primary interest to common shareholders. The ratio is computed as follows:

$$\frac{\text{Net Income} - \text{Dividends on Preferred Stock}}{\text{Average Common Shareholders' Equity}}$$

This measure of profitability assesses a firm's performance in using assets to generate earnings and explicitly considers the financing of those assets. The rate of return on common shareholders' equity will exceed the rate of return on assets if the rate of return on assets exceeds the after-tax cost of debt and any dividends required for preferred shareholders.

16. Financing with debt and preferred stock to increase the return to the residual common shareholders' equity is referred to as financial leverage. The common shareholders benefit from leverage when capital contributed by creditors and preferred shareholders earns a greater rate of return than the payments made to creditors and preferred shareholders.

17. In financial leverage, the common shareholders take extra risk (because the firm incurred debt obligations with fixed payments dates) for a potentially higher return. As more debt is added to the capital structure, the risk of default or insolvency increases and lenders will require a higher return to compensate for this additional risk. A point will be reached where leverage can no longer increase the potential rate of return to common shareholders' equity because the after tax cost of debt will exceed the rate of return earned on assets.

18. The rate of return on common shareholders' equity can be disaggregated as follows:

Rate of Return on Common Shareholders' Equity		Profit Margin Ratio (after Interest Expense & Preferred Dividends)	x	Total Assets Turnover Ratio	x	Capital Structure Leverage Ratio
	=					

OR

Net Income - Dividends on Preferred Stock / Average Common Shareholders' Equity	=	Net Income - Dividends on Preferred Stock / Sales	x	Sales / Average Total Assets	x	Average Total Assets / Average Common Shareholders' Equity

19. The profit margin percentage indicates the portion of the sales dollar left over for the common shareholders after covering all operating costs and subtracting all claims of creditors and preferred shareholders. The total assets turnover indicates the sales generated from each dollar of assets. The capital structure leverage ratio indicates the relative proportion of capital provided by common shareholders contrasted with that provided by creditors and preferred shareholders.

20. The larger the capital structure leverage ratio, the smaller the portion of capital provided by common shareholders and the larger the proportion provided by creditors and preferred shareholders. Therefore, the larger the capital structure leverage ratio, the greater the extent of financial leverage.

21. Earnings per share of common stock is computed as follows:

$$\frac{\text{Net Income - Preferred Stock Dividends Declared}}{\text{Weighted Average Number of Common Shares Outstanding}}$$

Earnings per share amounts are often compared with the market price of the stock. This is called a price-earnings ratio (or P/E ratio) and is computed as follows:

$$\frac{\text{Market Price per Share}}{\text{Earnings per Share}}$$

22. A dual presentation of basic earnings per share and diluted earnings per share is required when a firm has outstanding securities that, if exchanged for shares of common stock, would decrease basic earnings per share by 3 percent or more. Basic earnings per share is the net income attributable to common stock divided by the average number of common shares outstanding. Diluted earnings per share is the amount of earnings per share reflecting the maximum dilution that would occur if all options, warrants, and convertible securities outstanding at the end of the accounting period were exchanged for common stock.

23. When assessing risk, the focus is generally on the firm's relative liquidity. Cash and near-cash assets provide a firm with the resources needed to adapt to the various types of risk. Four measures for assessing short-term liquidity risk are (a) current ratio; (b) quick ratio; (c) operating cash flow to current liabilities ratio; and (d) working capital turnover ratio.

24. The current ratio, which is calculated by dividing current assets by current liabilities, is of particular significance to short-term creditors because it indicates the ability of the firm to meet its short-term obligations.

25. The current ratio can be manipulated. When the current ratio exceeds 1 to 1, an increase of equal amount in both current assets and current liabilities will decrease the current ratio. An equal decrease in both current assets and current liabilities will increase the current ratio.

26. A company's management can take deliberate steps to produce a financial statement that presents a better current ratio at the balance sheet date than the normal current ratio. These actions taken by management to increase the current ratio are referred to as "window dressing."

27. The quick ratio, or acid test ratio, is computed by including in the numerator of the fraction only those current assets that could be converted into cash quickly (cash, marketable securities, and receivables). The denominator includes all current liabilities.

28. The current ratio and quick ratio are criticized because they are calculated using amounts at a specific point in time. The cash flow from operations to current liabilities ratio, which is calculated by dividing cash flow from operations by average current liabilities, overcomes this deficiency because it measures short-term liquidity for a period of time. A ratio of 40 percent or more is common for a healthy firm.

29. The operating cycle of a firm is a sequence of activities in which (a) inventory is purchased on account from suppliers; (b) inventory is sold on account to customers; (c) customers pay amounts due; and (d) suppliers are paid amounts due. The longer the cycle, the longer the time that funds are tied up in receivables and inventories and the less liquid is the firm.

30. The operating cycle of a firm can be evaluated by computing several ratios. The inventory turnover ratio indicates the length of the period between the purchase and sale of inventory during each operating cycle. The accounts receivable turnover ratio indicates the length of the period between the sale of inventory and the collection of cash from customers during each operating cycle. The accounts payable turnover ratio indicates the length of the period between the purchase of inventory on account and the payment of cash to suppliers during each operating cycle. The accounts payable turnover ratio is computed by dividing purchases on account by average accounts payable.

31. Measures of long-term liquidity risk are used in assessing the firm's ability to meet interest and principal payments on long-term debt and similar obligations as they come due. A good indicator of long-term liquidity risk is a firm's ability to generate profits over a period of years. If a firm is profitable, it will either generate sufficient cash from operations or be able to obtain needed capital from creditors and owners. In addition to measures of profitability, three other measures of long-term liquidity risk are debt ratios, the cash flow from operations to total liabilities ratio, and the interest coverage ratio.

32. The long-term debt ratio (which is calculated by dividing total long-term debt by the sum of total long-term debt and total shareholders' equity) and the debt-equity ratio (which is calculated by dividing total liabilities by total equities) are used to measure a firm's long-term liquidity risk. These ratios must be evaluated in relation to the stability of the firm's earnings and cash flows from operations. In general, the more stable the earnings and cash flows, the higher the debt ratio that is considered acceptable or safe.

33. The debt ratios do not consider the availability of liquid assets to cover various levels of debt. A ratio that overcomes this deficiency is the cash flow from operations to total liabilities ratio. The ratio is calculated as follows:

$$\frac{\text{Cash Flow from Operations}}{\text{Average Total Liabilities}}$$

A financially healthy company normally has a cash flow from operations to total liabilities ratio of 20 percent or more.

34. Another measure of long-term liquidity risk, the number of times that earnings cover interest charges, is calculated by dividing income before interest and income taxes by interest expense. The interest coverage ratio is used to indicate the relative protection that operating profitability provides bondholders and permits them to assess the probability of a firm's failing to meet required interest payments. Analysts typically view an interest coverage ratio below 3.0 as risky. If bond indentures require periodic repayments of principal on long-term liabilities, the denominator of the ratio might include such repayments. The ratio would then be called the fixed charges coverage ratio.

35. Accountants use the term "pro forma financial statements" to refer to financial statements prepared under a particular set of assumptions. The usefulness of the pro forma financial statements depends on the reasonableness of those assumptions.

36. The preparation of pro forma financial statements typically begins with the income statement, followed by the balance sheet and then the statement of cash flows. The level of operating activity usually dictates the amount of assets required, which in turn affects the level of financing needed. Amounts for the statement of cash flows come directly from the income statement and comparative balance sheets.

37. Managers, security analysts, and others analyze financial statements (both historical and pro forma) to form judgments about the market value of a firm. One approach to approximating market value projects the amount of cash flows a firm will generate from operating, investing, and financing activities over some number of years in the future and discounts this net amount at an appropriate discount rate to find the present value of these future cash flows.

38. Other approaches to approximating a firm's market value rely on market multiples of certain financial statement items for similar firms in the market. One common valuation approach relates market prices to multiples of earnings. Another valuation approach relates market values to the book values of common shareholders' equity of similar firms.

Questions and Exercises

True/False. For each of the following statements, place a T or F in the space provided to indicate whether the statement is true or false.

_____ 1. If the inventory of a company turns over five times each year, the average number of days that merchandise is held during the year is 73 days.

_____ 2. The long-term debt ratio is calculated by dividing total liabilities by total equities.

_____ 3. If the common stock of the Burrell Company is selling for $50 per share and the earnings per share for the current year is $2, then the price-earnings ratio is 100 to 1.

_____ 4. If the average number of days that an accounts receivable is outstanding is about 46 days, the accounts receivable turnover for the year is about six times.

_____ 5. The rate of return on assets measures the profitability of a firm before any payments to the suppliers of capital.

_____ 6. Ratios are more meaningful if they are compared to a budgeted standard or an industry standard.

_____ 7. Improving the rate of return on assets can be accomplished by increasing the profit margin ratio, the rate of asset turnover ratio, or both.

_____ 8. To determine the amount of earnings assignable to the common shareholders, any dividends on preferred stock declared during the period must be deducted from net income.

_____ 9. In some situations, it may be preferable to compute the number of times that earnings cover interest charges by using cash flows rather than earnings in the numerator.

_____ 10. Basic earnings per share is the amount of earnings per share reflecting the maximum dilution that would occur if all options, warrants, and convertible securities outstanding at the end of the accounting period were exchanged for common stock.

_____ 11. The operating cash flow from operations to average current liabilities is a measure of profitability.

_____ 12. The current ratio is susceptible to "window dressing" by completing certain transactions just before the end of the period.

_____ 13. A person concerned with the long-term liquidity risk of a firm is primarily interested in whether the firm will have sufficient cash available to pay current debt.

_____ 14. The quick ratio is a measure of the relationship between sales and the investment in plant assets.

_____ 15. The cash flow from operations to total liabilities ratio is one measure of long-term liquidity risk.

_____ 16. The accounts payable turnover is computed by dividing cost of goods sold by average accounts payable.

_____ 17. The inventory turnover ratio indicates the length of the period between the sale of inventory and the collection of cash from customers.

_____ 18. A dual presentation of basic and diluted earnings per share is required when a firm has outstanding securities that, if exchanged for more shares of common stock, would decrease basic earnings per share by 3 percent or more.

_____ 19. Financial leverage increases the rate of return on common shareholders' equity when the rate of return on assets is less than the after-tax cost of debt.

_____ 20. Rate of return on assets is computed using income before deducting any payment or distributions to the providers of capital.

_____ 21. In computing the rate of return on assets, the denominator should reflect average total assets during the year.

_____ 22. The rate of return on assets can be disaggregated into two other ratios as follows:

$$\text{Rate of Return on Assets} = \text{Profit Margin Ratio} \times \text{Current Ratio}.$$

_____ 23. The preparation of pro forma financial statements usually begins with the preparation of a statement of cash flows.

_____ 24. The interest coverage ratio is used to indicate the relative protection of bondholders and to assess the probability of a firm's failing to meet required interest payments.

_____ 25. The capital structure leverage ratio indicates the relative proportion of capital provided by common shareholders contrasted with that provided by creditors and preferred shareholders.

_____ 26. A point will be reached where financial leverage can no longer increase the potential rate of return to common shareholders' equity.

_____ 27. The shorter the time that funds are tied up in receivables and inventories, the shorter is the operating cycle.

_____ 28. The accounts payable turnover ratio indicates the length of the period between the purchase of inventory on account and the payment of cash to suppliers.

_____ 29. In computing the quick ratio, inventories are usually omitted from the listing of assets that can be converted into cash quickly.

_____ 30. In computing the rate of return on common shareholders' equity, dividends on preferred stock must be added to net income.

_____ 31. Time-series analysis involves comparing a given firm's ratios with those of other firms for a specific period.

_____ 32. In computing the rate of return on assets, dividends paid to shareholders must be added to net income in determining the ratio's numerator.

_____ 33. The reciprocal of the fixed asset turnover ratio measures dollars of fixed assets required to generate one dollar of sales.

_____ 34. Another name for the fixed asset turnover ratio is the fixed asset productivity ratio.

_____ 35. Insolvency refers to a legal condition in which liabilities usually exceed assets.

Matching.
From the list of terms below, select that term which is most closely associated with each of the descriptive phrases or statements that follows and place the letter for that term in the space provided.

a. Accounts Payable Turnover Ratio

b. Accounts Receivable Turnover Ratio

c. Bankruptcy

d. Cash Flow from Operations to Current Liabilities Ratio

e. Cash Flow from Operations to Total Liabilities Ratio

f. Cross-Section Analysis

g. Current Ratio

h. Debt-Equity Ratio

i. Earnings Per Share

j. Financial Leverage

k. Fixed Asset Turnover Ratio

l. Fixed Charges Coverage Ratio

m. Insolvency

n. Interest Coverage Ratio

o. Inventory Turnover Ratio

p. Liquidity

q. Long-Term Debt Ratio

r. Operating Cycle

s. Price Earnings Ratio

t. Pro forma Financial Statements

u. Profit Margin Ratio (before interest effects)

v. Quick Ratio

w. Rate of Return on Assets

x. Rate of Return on Common Shareholders' Equity

y. Reciprocal of Fixed Asset Turnover Ratio

z. Time-Series Analysis

aa. Total Assets Turnover Ratio

_____ 1. This ratio indicates the length of the period between the purchase of inventory on account and the payment of cash to suppliers.

_____ 2. This analysis involves comparing the changes in a firm's ratios over a multiple-year period.

_____ 3. This ratio considers the availability of liquid assets to cover various levels of debt. For a financially healthy firm, the ratio should be 20 percent or more.

_____ 4. Refers to the "nearness of cash" of a firm's assets.

_____ 5. This ratio provides a measure of the sales generated for each dollar invested in fixed assets.

_____ 6. This ratio assesses the firm's operating performance independently of financing decisions.

_____ 7. This ratio measures how many times during each period accounts receivable are turned over (or converted to cash).

_____ 8. This analysis involves comparing a given firm's ratios with those of other firms for a particular period.

_____ 9. This ratio indicates the proportion of total capital supplied by creditors.

_____ 10. This ratio is used to indicate the relative protection of bondholders and to assess the probability of a firm's failing to meet required interest payments.

_____ 11. This ratio is a measure of a firm's ability to control the level of costs, or expenses, relative to sales.

_____ 12. This ratio provides a measure of the sales generated for each dollar invested in assets.

_____ 13. This ratio indicates the proportion of a firm's long-term capital that is provided by creditors.

_____ 14. Financial statements prepared using a particular set of assumptions.

_____ 15. This ratio is supposed to indicate the ability of the firm to meet its current obligations.

_____ 16. This ratio generally includes cash, marketable securities, and accounts receivable in its numerator.

_____ 17. This ratio is computed by dividing cash flow from operations by average current liabilities.

_____ 18. Refers to a firm's financing with debt and preferred stock to increase the return to the common shareholders' equity.

_____ 19. This ratio is computed by dividing net income attributable to common stock by the average number of common shares outstanding during the period.

_____ 20. This ratio indicates the number of times that the average inventory has been sold during the period.

_____ 21. This ratio measures the firm's performance in generating earnings that are assignable to the common shareholders' equity.

_____ 22. If bond indentures require periodic repayments of principal on long-term liabilities, the denominator of the interest coverage ratio might include such repayments.

_____ 23. The sequence of activities in which inventory is purchased on account from suppliers, inventory is sold on account to customers, customers pay the amounts due and suppliers are paid the amounts due to them.

_____ 24. Earnings per share amount is compared with the market price of the stock.

_____ 25. This ratio measures dollars of fixed assets required to generate one dollar of sales.

_____ 26. Refers to a condition in which the firm has insufficient cash to pay its current debts.

_____ 27. Refers to a legal condition in which liabilities usually exceed assets.

Multiple Choice. Choose the best answer for each of the following questions and enter the identifying letter in the space provided.

_____ 1. Which of the following is not a component of the rate of return on common shareholders' equity?

    a. Capital Structure Leverage Ratio.
    b. Profit Margin Ratio.
    c. Total Assets Turnover Ratio.
    d. All three of the above ratios are components of the rate of return on common shareholders' equity.

_____ 2. Which of the following would not be used to evaluate a firm's operating cycle?

    a. Accounts Payable Turnover Ratio.
    b. Inventory Turnover Ratio.
    c. Current Ratio.
    d. Accounts Receivable Turnover Ratio.

_____ 3. The Sebring Company sells on credit with terms of "net 30 days." If the company's credit policy and collection activity is working efficiently, how many times should the company's accounts receivable turn over in a year?

    a. Approximately 6 times.
    b. Approximately 8 times.
    c. Approximately 10 times.
    d. Approximately 12 times.

_____ 4. Which of the following ratios would not be used in assessing a firm's long-term liquidity risk?
    a. Debt-Equity Ratio.
    b. Long-Term Debt Ratio.
    c. Interest Coverage Ratio.
    d. Current Ratio.

_____ 5. Which of the following is not a measure of profitability?

    a. Rate of Return on Assets.
    b. Accounts Payable Turnover Ratio.
    c. Rate of Return on Common Shareholders' Equity.
    d. Earnings Per Common Share.

_____ 6. Assume that J. Williams, Inc. has a current ratio of 2:1. Which of the following transactions would result in an increase in the company's current ratio?

    a.   Declaring cash dividend payable next period.
    b.   Paying long-term debt.
    c.   Paying accounts payable.
    d.   Borrowing money on a 6-month note.

_____ 7. If a company's rate of return on assets is 20 percent and the profit margin percentage is 5 percent, the company's total assets turnover must be which of the following?

    a.   1.
    b.   4.
    c.   5.
    d.   20.

_____ 8. The Rate of Return on Assets can be disaggregated into two other ratios. Which of the following is one of the two ratios?

    a.   Fixed Asset Turnover Ratio.
    b.   Debt-Equity Ratio.
    c.   Profit Margin Ratio.
    d.   Inventory Turnover Ratio.

_____ 9. A company wants to increase its rate of return on assets from 8 percent to 14 percent. It is believed that the firm's total assets turnover of .667 cannot be easily increased at the present time. What must the profit margin percentage be to achieve the desired 14 percent rate of return on assets?

    a.   7 percent.
    b.   14 percent.
    c.   21 percent.
    d.   28 percent.

_____ 10. Comparisons of a given firm's ratios with those of other firms for a particular period is referred to as

    a.   Times-Series Analysis.
    b.   Defensive Interval Analysis.
    c.   Cross-Section Analysis.
    d.   None of the above.

_____ 11. In computing the rate of return on assets, interest expense net of income tax savings is added to net income. Assume that the RBC Company has interest expense of $20 million and net income of $50 million. Assume that the income tax rate is 40 percent. In computing the rate of return on assets, the numerator would be:

    a. $38 million.
    b. $42 million.
    c. $58 million.
    d. $62 million.

_____ 12. The phenomenon of common shareholders trading extra risk for a potentially higher return is called:

a. Financial Leverage.
b. Operating Leverage.
c. Liquidity.
d. Interest Coverage Ratio.

_____ 13. Assume that the current ratio of the Nokomis Company is 2.5 to 1. What effect would an equal dollar increase in current assets and current liabilities have on the current ratio?

a. Increase the current ratio.
b. Decrease the current ratio.
c. No effect on the current ratio.
d. Answer cannot be determined from information given.

_____ 14. Which of the following ratios would probably not be used to analyze the total assets turnover ratio?

a. Fixed Asset Turnover.
b. Accounts Receivable Turnover.
c. Inventory Turnover.
d. Long-Term Debt Ratio.

_____ 15. Which of the following ratios uses "Sales" in its numerator?

a. Total Assets Turnover Ratio.
b. Profit Margin Ratio.
c. Fixed Asset Turnover Ratio.
d. Both a and c use "Sales" in their numerators.

_____ 16. Financial leverage can increase the return to common shareholders as long as

a. The rate of return earned on assets equals the rate paid for the capital used to acquire those assets.
b. The rate of return earned on assets is less than the rate paid for the capital used to acquire those assets.
c. The rate of return earned on assets exceeds the rate paid for the capital used to acquire those assets.
d. The firm has a "good" earnings year.

_____ 17. Which of the following is not used to assess short-term liquidity risk?

a. Accounts Receivable Turnover.
b. Operating Cash Flow to Current Liabilities Ratio.
c. Current Ratio.
d. Quick Ratio.

_____ 18. In computing the quick ratio, which of the following items is customarily excluded from the numerator?

    a. Cash.
    b. Inventory.
    c. Marketable Securities.
    d. Accounts Receivable.

_____ 19. Assume that the debt-equity ratio of the Davidson Company is .5 to 1. If the company issued a long-term note in the purchase of some land, what effect would this transaction have on the debt-equity ratio?

    a. Decrease debt-equity ratio.
    b. Increase debt-equity ratio.
    c. No effect on the debt-equity ratio.
    d. Answer cannot be determined from information given.

_____ 20. This ratio is a useful measure for assessing a firm's performance in using assets to generate earnings.

    a. Profit Margin Ratio.
    b. Financial Leverage.
    c. Rate of Return on Assets.
    d. Working Capital.

Exercises

1. Joel Company's balance sheet indicates that the company has $20 million of 8 percent debt and total shareholders' equity of $10 million.

Monika Company's balance sheet indicates that the company has no debt and total shareholders' equity of $30 million.

Assume that both companies are identical in all respects except for the difference outlined above. Both companies report income before interest and taxes of $6,000,000 and the tax rate is 30 percent. Both companies have average total assets of $30 million and sales of $45 million.

a. Compute the Rate of Return on Assets for both companies.

b. Compute the Rate of Return on Common Shareholders' Equity.

c. Explain any difference in the computed ratios for the two companies.

d. For both companies, disaggregate the rate of return on common shareholders' equity into its component parts:

Rate of Return On Common Shareholders' Equity	=	Profit Margin Ratio (after Interest Expense and Preferred Dividends)	x	Total Assets Turnover Ratio	x	Capital Structure Leverage Ratio

e. Explain what the capital structure leverage ratio reveals about the two companies.

2. The Comparative Balance Sheets for Year 1 and Year 2 and the Year 2 Income Statement for Royal Bros., Inc. are as follows:

Royal Bros, Inc.
Balance Sheet

Assets	12/31 Year 2	12/31 Year 1
Cash	$ 180,000	$ 54,000
Accounts Receivable	360,000	540,000
Inventory	1,080,000	720,000
Property, Plant, and Equipment	2,520,000	2,646,000
Total Assets	$4,140,000	$3,960,000

Liabilities and Shareholders' Equity	12/31 Year 2	12/31 Year 1
Accounts Payable	$ 680,400	$ 900,000
5% Mortgage Payable	1,440,000	1,494,000
Common Stock (250,000 shares outstanding)	1,080,000	1,080,000
Retained Earnings	939,600	486,000
Total Equities	$4,140,000	$3,960,000

Royal Bros., Inc.
Income Statement
For Year Ended December 31, Year 2

Sales on Account		$3,240,000
Less Expenses:		
Cost of Sales	$1,800,000	
Salary Expense	594,000	
Depreciation Expense	126,000	
Interest Expense	72,000	
Total Expenses		$2,592,000
Income before Taxes		$ 648,000
Income Tax Expense (35% rate)		226,800
Net Income		$ 421,200

Compute the following ratios for Royal Bros., Inc. for Year 2.

a. Current Ratio.

b. Quick Ratio (inventory cannot be quickly converted to cash).

c.   Debt-Equity Ratio.

d.   Rate of Return on Assets.

e.   Rate of Return on Common Shareholders' Equity.

f.   Earnings per Share of Common Stock.

g.   Profit Margin Ratio (before interest expense and related income tax effects).

h.   Total Assets Turnover Ratio.

i.   Interest Coverage Ratio.

j.   Inventory Turnover Ratio.

k.   Average Number of Days Inventory on Hand.

l.   Accounts Receivable Turnover Ratio.

m.   Average Collection Period for Accounts Receivable.

n.   Long-Term Debt Ratio.

o.   Fixed Asset Turnover Ratio.

p.   Capital Structure Leverage Ratio.

q.   Accounts Payable Turnover Ratio.

r.   Profit Margin Ratio (after interest expense and preferred dividends).

3.   This exercise is a continuation of Exercise 2, Royal Bros, Inc.

   a.   Disaggregate the rate of return on assets into its two components:

Rate of Return on Assets	=	Profit Margin Ratio (before interest expense and related income tax effects)	x	Total Assets Turnover Ratio
_____	=	_____	x	_____

b. Disaggregate the rate of return on common shareholders' equity into its three components:

Rate of Return on Common Shareholder Equity	=	Profit Margin Ratio (after interest expense and preferred dividends)	x	Total Assets Turnover Ratio	x	Capital Structure Leverage Ratio

_____ = _____ x _____ x _____

c. Why is Royal Bros.' rate of return on common shareholders' equity (part b above) greater than its rate of return on assets (part a above)?

4. This exercise is a continuation of Exercise 2, Royal Bros., Inc. Given below is information about cost of goods sold, beginning and ending inventories, and average accounts payable for Years 3, 4 and 5:

	Year 3	Year 4	Year 5
Cost of Goods Sold	$1,895,400	$2,079,000	$2,250,000
Beginning Inventory	1,080,000	540,000	1,116,000
Ending Inventory	540,000	1,116,000	525,600
Average Accounts Payable	226,800	482,400	324,000

All of Royal Bros.' purchases are made on credit terms of "net 45 days".

a. Compute the accounts payable turnover for each year.

b. Evaluate Royal Bros.' management of its accounts payable over the 3-year period.

5. This exercise is a continuation of Exercise 2, Royal Bros, Inc. Given below is information about sales, cost of goods sold, and average inventory for Years 3, 4, and 5:

	Year 3	Year 4	Year 5
Sales (all on credit)	$3,510,000	$3,960,000	$4,500,000
Cost of Goods Sold	1,895,400	2,079,000	2,250,000
Average Inventory	810,000	828,000	820,800

a. Compute the inventory turnover for each year.

b. Compute the average number of days that inventory is on hand each year.

c. What percentage is cost of goods sold to sales for each year?

d. Evaluate Royal Bros.' management of its inventories over the 3 years.

6. This exercise is a continuation of Exercise 2, Royal Bros., Inc. Given below is information about sales and average accounts receivable for Years 3, 4, and 5. Royal Bros.' credit terms are net 30 days.

	Year 3	Year 4	Year 5
Sales (all on credit)	$3,510,000	$3,960,000	$4,500,000
Average Accts. Rec.	540,000	720,000	900,000

a. Compute the accounts receivable turnover for each year.

b. Compute the average collection period for accounts receivable for each year.

c. Evaluate Royal Bros.' management of its accounts receivable over the 3-year period.

7. This exercise is a continuation of Exercise 2, Royal Bros., Inc. For the year ending 12/31 Year 2, the company reported current assets (Cash, Account Receivable and Inventory) totaling $1,620,000; current liabilities (Accounts Payable) of $680,400; and a current ratio of 2.38:1 ($1,620,000/$680,400).

a. Assume that, at the end of Year 2, the company failed to record a credit purchase of inventory in the amount of $225,000. What would have been the company's current ratio at 12/31 Year 2 if the credit purchase of inventory had been correctly recorded at 12/31 Year 2?

b. Assume that, at the end of Year 2, the company recorded a $270,000 credit sale that should have been recorded as a Year 3 sale. Also assume that the 12/31 Year 2 inventory of $1,080,000 correctly includes the cost of the inventory item sold for $270,000 in Year 3. What would have been the company's current ratio at 12/31 Year 2 if the credit sale had been correctly recorded as a Year 3 sale?

c. What is meant by "window dressing"?

8. Maresca, Inc. reported net income of $630,000 for the current year. The company had 100,000 shares of $10 par value Common stock and 20,000 shares of $50 par value Convertible Preferred stock outstanding during the year. The dividend rate on the Preferred stock is $3 per share. Each share of the Convertible Preferred stock can be converted into four shares of Common stock. None of the Convertible Preferred stock was converted during the year.

a. Compute the company's basic earnings per share.

b. Compute the company's diluted earnings per share.

c. Will the company be required to report a dual presentation of earnings per share? Why?

Answers to Questions and Exercises

True/False

1.	T	8.	T	15.	T	22.	F	29.	T
2.	F	9.	T	16.	F	23.	F	30.	F
3.	F	10.	F	17.	F	24.	T	31.	F
4.	F	11.	F	18.	T	25.	T	32.	F
5.	T	12.	T	19.	F	26.	T	33.	T
6.	T	13.	F	20.	T	27.	T	34.	T
7.	T	14.	F	21.	T	28.	T	35.	F

Matching

1.	a	7.	b	13.	q	19.	i	25.	y
2.	z	8.	f	14.	t	20.	o	26.	m
3.	e	9.	h	15.	g	21.	x	27.	c
4.	p	10.	n	16.	v	22.	l		
5.	k	11.	u	17.	d	23.	r		
6.	w	12.	aa	18.	j	24.	s		

Multiple Choice

1.	d	6.	c	11.	d	16.	c
2.	c	7.	b	12.	a	17.	a
3.	d	8.	c	13.	b	18.	b
4.	d	9.	c	14.	d	19.	b
5.	b	10.	c	15.	d	20.	c

Exercises

1. a.

Computation of Net Income for:	Joel Company	Monika Company
Income before Interest and Taxes	$6,000,000	$6,000,000
Interest Expense	1,600,000	-0-
Income before Taxes	$4,400,000	$6,000,000
Tax Expense	1,320,000	1,800,000
Net Income	$3,080,000	$4,200,000

$$\text{Rate of Return on Assets} = \frac{\text{Net Income + Interest Expense (Net of Tax Savings)}}{\text{Average Total Assets}}$$

Joel Company: $\dfrac{\$3,080,000 + \$1,120,000}{\$30,000,000} = .14$

Monika Company: $\dfrac{\$4,200,000}{\$30,000,000} = .14$

b. Rate of Return on Common Shareholders' Equity

$$= \frac{\text{Net Income - Preferred stock dividends}}{\text{Average shareholders' equity}}$$

Joel Company: $\dfrac{\$3,080,000}{\$10,000,000} = .308$

Monika Company: $\dfrac{\$4,200,000}{\$30,000,000} = .14$

c. The rate of return on assets is 14 percent for both companies. Joel is using financial leverage to increase the return to its common shareholders. Monika has financed its assets through common share-holders' equity and is not using any financial leverage. Joel's return to common shareholders' equity is 30.8 percent, which is greater than the company's rate of return on assets of 14 percent.

Leverage increased the rate of return to shareholders because the capital provided by long-term creditors earned 14 percent but required an after tax interest payment of only 5.6 percent: (.08) x (1-.30 tax rate). The additional 8.4 percent (.14 - .056) return on assets financed by creditors increased the return to common shareholders:

Excess return of 8.4 percent on assets financed by creditors:

(.084) x ($20,000,000) $1,680,000

Return of 14 percent on assets financed by common
shareholders:
(.14 x $10,000,000) $1,400,000

Total return to common shareholders $3,080,000

Rate of return on common shareholders' equity
($3,080,000/$10,000,000)   30.8%

d.

Net Income- Dividends on Preferred Stock Average Common Shareholders' Equity	=	Net Income - Dividends on Preferred Stock Sales	x	Sales Average Total Assets	x	Average Total Assets Average Common Shareholders' Equity

Joel Company: $\frac{\$ 3,080,000}{\$10,000,000}$ = $\frac{\$ 3,080,000}{\$45,000,000}$ x $\frac{\$45,000,000}{\$30,000,000}$ x $\frac{\$30,000,000}{\$10,000,000}$

.308 = .0684 x 1.5 x 3.0

Monika Company: $\frac{\$ 4,200,000}{\$30,000,000}$ = $\frac{\$ 4,200,000}{\$45,000,000}$ x $\frac{\$45,000,000}{\$30,000,000}$ x $\frac{\$30,000,000}{\$30,000,000}$

.14 = .0933 x 1.5 x 1

e. The capital structure leverage ratio indicates the proportion of total assets, or total capital, provided by common shareholders contrasted with the capital provided by creditors and preferred shareholders. Monika's capital structure leverage ratio of 1.0 indicates that 100% of the company's total assets (or total capital) was provided by common shareholders and, therefore, the company is not using financial leverage. Joel's capital structure leverage ratio of 3.0 indicates that one-third of the company's assets (or total capital) was provided by common shareholders while creditors have provided two-thirds of the company's assets (or total capital). Comparing Joel and Monika's capital structure leverage ratios, one can see that (a) the larger the capital structure leverage ratio, the smaller is the proportion of capital provided by common shareholders and (b) the larger the capital structure leverage ratio, the larger is financial leverage.

2. a. Current Ratio

$$= \frac{\text{Current Assets}}{\text{Current Liabilities}}$$

$$= \frac{\$1,620,000}{\$ \ \ \ 680,400} = 2.38{:}1$$

b. Quick Ratio

$$= \frac{\text{Cash + Receivables + Marketable Securities}}{\text{Current Liabilities}}$$

$$= \frac{\$180,000 + \$360,000}{\$680,400} = .794{:}1$$

c. Debt-Equity Ratio

$$= \frac{\text{Total Liabilities}}{\text{Total Liabilities + Shareholders' Equity}}$$

$$= \frac{\$2,120,400}{\$4,140,000} = .512$$

d. Rate of Return on Assets

$$= \frac{\text{Net Income + Interest Expense (Net of Income Tax Savings)}}{\text{Average Total Assets}}$$

$$= \frac{\$421,200 + \$46,800}{\frac{1}{2} \ (\$4,140,000 + \$3,960,000)} = .116$$

e. Rate of Return on Common Shareholders' Equity

$$= \frac{\text{Net Income - Dividends on Preferred Stock}}{\text{Average Common Shareholders' Equity During Period}}$$

$$= \frac{\$421,200}{\frac{1}{2} \ (\$2,019,600 + \$1,566,000)} = .235$$

f.   Earnings per Share of Common Stock

$$= \frac{\text{Net Income - Preferred Stock Dividends}}{\text{Weighted Average Number of Common Shares Outstanding During Period}}$$

$$= \frac{\$421,200}{250,000} = \$1.68$$

g.   Profit Margin Ratio
     (before interest expense and related income tax effects)

$$= \frac{\text{Net Income + Interest Expense Net of Tax Savings}}{\text{Sales}}$$

$$= \frac{\$421,200 + \$46,800}{\$3,240,000} = .144$$

h.   Total Assets Turnover Ratio

$$= \frac{\text{Sales}}{\text{Average Total Assets During Period}}$$

$$= \frac{\$3,240,000}{\frac{1}{2}\ (\$4,140,000 + \$3,960,000)} = .8$$

i.   Interest Coverage Ratio

$$= \frac{\text{Net Income before Interest and Income Taxes}}{\text{Interest Expense}}$$

$$= \frac{\$648,000 + \$72,000}{\$\ 72,000} = 10 \text{ times}$$

j.   Inventory Turnover Ratio

$$= \frac{\text{Cost of Goods Sold}}{\text{Average Inventory During Period}}$$

$$= \frac{\$1,800,000}{\frac{1}{2}\ (\$1,080,000 + \$720,000)} = 2$$

k.   Average Number of Days Inventory on Hand

$$= \frac{365}{\text{Inventory Turnover Ratio}}$$

$$= \frac{365}{2} = 182.5$$

l.   Accounts Receivable Turnover Ratio

$$= \frac{\text{Net Sales on Account}}{\text{Average Accounts Receivable During Period}}$$

$$= \frac{\$3,240,000}{\frac{1}{2}\ (\$360,000 + \$540,000)} = 7.2$$

m.   Average Collection Period for Accounts Receivable

$$= \frac{365}{\text{Accounts Receivable Turnover Ratio}}$$

$$= \frac{365}{7.2} = 50.7 \text{ days}$$

n.   Long-Term Debt Ratio

$$= \frac{\text{Total Long-Term Debt}}{\text{Total Long-Term Debt Plus Shareholders' Equity}}$$

$$= \frac{\$1,440,000}{\$1,440,000 + \$2,019,600} = .416$$

o.   Fixed Asset Turnover Ratio

$$= \frac{\text{Sales}}{\text{Average Fixed Assets During Period}}$$

$$= \frac{\$3,240,000}{\frac{1}{2} (\$2,520,000 + 2,646,000)} = 1.25$$

p.   Capital Structure Leverage Ratio

$$= \frac{\text{Average Total Assets During Period}}{\text{Average Common Shareholders' Equity During Period}}$$

$$= \frac{\frac{1}{2} (\$4,140,000 + \$3,960,000)}{\frac{1}{2} (\$2,019,600 + \$1,566,000)} = 2.26$$

q.   Accounts Payable Turnover Ratio

$$= \frac{\text{Purchases*}}{\text{Average Accounts Payable}}$$

$$= \frac{\$2,160,000}{\frac{1}{2} (\$680,400 + \$900,000)} = 2.73$$

   * Purchases = Cost of Goods Sold + Ending Inventory - Beginning Inventory

$$= \$1,800,000 + \$1,080,000 - \$720,000$$
$$= \$2,160,000$$

r.   Profit Margin Ratio (after interest expense and preferred dividends)

$$= \frac{\text{Net Income - Preferred Stock Dividends}}{\text{Sales}}$$

$$= \frac{\$ \ 421,200}{\$3,240,000} = .13$$

3. a. Rate of Return = Profit Margin Ratio x Total Assets
on Assets (before interest Turnover
expense and Ratio
related income
tax effects)

$$.116 = .144 \times .8$$

b. Rate of Return   Profit Margin   Total Assets   Capital
on Common Share- = Ratio (after x Turnover x Structure
holders' Equity   interest   Ratio   Leverage
expense and   Ratio
preferred
dividends)

$$.235 = .13 \times .8 \times 2.26$$

c. The rate of return on common shareholders' equity is greater than the rate of return on assets because the company is using financial leverage to increase the return to its common shareholders.

4. a. Account Payable Turnover $= \dfrac{\text{Purchases *}}{\text{Average Accounts Payable}}$

      * Purchases = Cost of Goods Sold
                + Ending Inventory
                - Beginning Inventory

Year 3: Accounts Payable Turnover $= \dfrac{\$1,355,400}{\$226,800} = 5.98$

Year 4: Accounts Payable Turnover $= \dfrac{\$2,655,000}{\$482,400} = 5.50$

Year 5: Accounts Payable Turnover $= \dfrac{\$1,659,600}{\$324,000} = 5.12$

b. Since all purchases are made on credit terms of "net 45 days," the accounts payable turnover should be about 8.11 (365 days/45 days). For the 3 years, Royal Bros. is taking longer to pay for the purchases than the credit terms offered. The average payment period (in days) is as follows:

Year 3: 61 days (365/5.98)
Year 4: 66 days (365/5.50)
Year 5: 71 days (365/5.12)

5. a. Inventory Turnover = $\dfrac{\text{Cost of Goods Sold}}{\text{Average Inventory During Period}}$

Year 3: Inventory Turnover = $\dfrac{\$1,895,400}{\$\ 810,000}$ = 2.34

Year 4: Inventory Turnover = $\dfrac{\$2,079,000}{\$\ 828,000}$ = 2.51

Year 5: Inventory Turnover = $\dfrac{\$2,250,000}{\$\ 820,800}$ = 2.74

b. Av. Number of Days Inventory on Hand = $\dfrac{365}{\text{Inventory Turnover}}$

Year 3: Av. Number of Days Invty. on Hand = $\dfrac{365}{2.34}$ = 156

Year 4: Av. Number of Days Invty. on Hand = $\dfrac{365}{2.51}$ = 145

Year 5: Av. Number of Days Invty. on Hand = $\dfrac{365}{2.74}$ = 133

c. Cost of Goods Sold Percentage = $\dfrac{\text{Cost of Goods Sold}}{\text{Sales}}$

Year 3: Cost of Goods Sold Percentage = $\dfrac{\$1,895,400}{\$3,510,000}$ = 54%

Year 4: Cost of Goods Sold Percentage = $\dfrac{\$2,079,000}{\$3,960,000}$ = 52.5%

Year 5: Cost of Goods Sold Percentage = $\dfrac{\$2,250,000}{\$4,500,000}$ = 50%

d. Royal Bros. has made steady progress in managing its inventories over the 3-year period. Inventory turnover has increased each year; the number of days that inventory is on hand has decreased each year; and the cost of goods sold percentage has decreased each year which means that the gross profit margin percentage has increased each year.

6. a. Accounts Receivable Turnover = $\dfrac{\text{Net Sales on Account}}{\text{Average Accounts Receivable}}$

Year 3: Accounts Receivable Turnover = $\dfrac{\$3,510,000}{\$\ 540,000}$ = 6.5

Year 4: Accounts Receivable Turnover = $\dfrac{\$3,960,000}{\$\ 720,000}$ = 5.5

Year 5: Accounts Receivable Turnover = $\dfrac{\$4,500,000}{\$\ 900,000}$ = 5

b. Av. Collection Period for Accts. Rec. = $\dfrac{365}{\text{Accts. Rec. Turnover}}$

    Year 3: Collection Period for Accts. Rec. = $\dfrac{365}{6.5}$ = 56 days

    Year 4: Collection Period for Accts. Rec. = $\dfrac{365}{5.5}$ = 66 days

    Year 5: Collection Period for Accts. Rec. = $\dfrac{365}{5}$ = 73 days

c. Royal Bros. has experienced steady erosion in its ability to collect its accounts receivable on a timely basis. Royal Bros. should be able to collect its accounts in 30 days since that is the credit policy. The buildup in accounts receivable is occurring because accounts are not being collected on a timely basis. As a result, the turnover of accounts receivable is decreasing each year.

7. a. Current Ratio = $\dfrac{\text{Current Assets}}{\text{Current Liabilities}}$

    = $\dfrac{\$1,620,000 + \$225,000}{\$\ \ 680,400 + \$225,000}$

    = $\dfrac{\$1,845,000}{\$\ \ 905,400}$

    = 2.04:1

b. Current Ratio = $\dfrac{\text{Current Assets}}{\text{Current Liabilities}}$

    = $\dfrac{\$1,620,000 - \$270,000}{\$680,400}$

    = $\dfrac{\$1,350,000}{\$\ \ 680,400}$

    = 1.98:1

c. "Window dressing" refers to actions taken by a company's management to increase the current ratio. As a result of "window dressing" the company's financial statements present a better current ratio at the balance sheet date than would have been reported otherwise.

The current ratio computed in Ex. 2(a) was 2.38:1.

(a) above illustrates that, by failing to record a purchase of inventory and accounts payable, the current ratio of 2.38:1 is higher than it would have been if the inventory had been included in current assets and the accounts payable had been included in current liabilities.

(b) above illustrates that, by recording a year 3 sale in year 2, the company's current ratio of 2.38:1 is higher than it would have been if the sale had been correctly reported in year 3.

8. a. Basic earnings per share:

$$\frac{\text{Net Income} - \text{Preferred Stock Dividends}}{\text{Weighted Average Number of Common Shares Outstanding During Period}}$$

$$\frac{\$630,000 - \$60,000}{100,000} = \$5.70$$

b. Diluted earnings per share:

$$\frac{\text{Net Income}}{\text{Weighted Average Number of Common Shares Outstanding During Period}}$$

$$\frac{\$630,000*}{100,000 + 80,000*} = \$3.50$$

*For purposes of computing diluted earnings per share, it is assumed that the Convertible Preferred Stock is converted into Common Stock, resulting in 80,000 additional shares of Common Stock, outstanding. Since it is assumed that the Convertible Preferred Stock was converted, there is no Preferred Stock dividend to subtract from net income.

c. The company will be required to report a dual presentation of earnings per share because issuance of Common Stock upon conversion of the Preferred Stock would decrease (dilute) basic earnings per share by more than 3%. When a firm has securities outstanding that, if exchanged for shares of Common Stock, would decrease basic earnings per share by 3 percent or more, GAAP require a dual presentation.

Receivables and Revenue Recognition

Chapter Highlights

1. Generally accepted accounting principles (GAAP) are the methods of accounting that firms use to measure the results of their business transactions, with a principal aim of measuring net income for a period and financial position at the end of a period.

2. Standard-setting bodies within each country currently set GAAP. In the United States, the Financial Accounting Standards Board (FASB) sets acceptable accounting principles. The International Accounting Standards Board (IASB) promotes the establishment of more uniform GAAP worldwide.

3. In some situations, alternative GAAP for reporting a particular transaction are permitted. In such cases, standard-setting bodies recognize that the economic effects of certain transactions may differ across firms and that a single method may not provide the best measure of earnings and financial position.

4. Standard-setting bodies generally provide broad guidelines rather than detailed rules for applying their pronouncements because (a) economic differences may exist between firms and (b) firms should have latitude to apply pronouncements to reflect these economic differences.

5. The flexibility and latitude of GAAP do have economic consequences to managers, investors, lenders, and others.

6. Controls do exist to constrain the opportunistic actions of management. In their audits, a firm's independent accountant makes judgements about the appropriateness of the accounting principles a firm selects and the reasonableness of the way the firm applies the accounting principles. Another control is the oversight provided by government regulators, such as the Securities and Exchange Commission (SEC) in the United States.

7. The term "quality of earnings" encompasses the following ideas:

    (a) the representative faithfulness of earnings as a measure of value added

    (b) the ability managers have to use discretion in measuring and reporting earnings in their particular industry

    (c) the extent to which the managers have exercised this discretion

    (d) the extent to which earnings include unusual or nonrecurring items.

8. It is believed that managers will usually make choices that enhance current earnings and present the firm in the best light. By their selection of accounting principles or standards when GAAP allow a choice, by their use of estimates in the application of accounting principles, and by their timing transactions to recognize nonrecurring items in earnings, managers can influence the firm's earning and its present value. To the extent managers make choices enhancing currently reported income, analysts will say the firm has a lower quality of earnings. All the management choices that affect the quality of earnings affect <u>when</u> the firm reports its income, not its <u>total amount</u>, over time.

9. Under the accrual basis of measuring income, revenue is recognized when (a) all, or a substantial portion, of the services expected to be provided have been performed and (b) cash, or another asset whose cash equivalent value can be objectively measured, has been received. Satisfying the first criterion means that a firm can estimate the total expected cash outflows related to an operating activity. If a firm cannot estimate the total expected cash outflows, it will not know the amount of expense to match against revenue, and therefore it will not know the amount of income. Satisfying the second criterion means that a firm can estimate the amount of expected cash flows from customers. If a firm cannot estimate expected cash inflows, it will not know the amount of revenues and therefore the amount of income.

10. A more informed judgement about whether (a) delivery has occurred or services have been performed, (b) the price is fixed or determinable and (c) collectibility is reasonably assured can be made if there is persuasive evidence that an arrangement exists. The arrangement may take the form of a contract, prior business dealings with a particular customer, or customary business practices by a firm and its industry.

11. Most firms satisfy the criteria for revenue recognition at the time of sale or delivery of goods and services. Recognizing revenues at the time of sale and properly matching expenses with revenues require firms to estimate the cost of uncollectible accounts, returns, and similar items and recognize them as income reductions at the time of sale.

12. When credit is extended there will be some customers whose accounts will never be collected. The principal accounting issue related to uncollectible accounts concerns <u>when</u> firms should recognize the loss from uncollectibles.

13. The direct write-off method recognizes losses from uncollectible accounts in the period when a firm decides that specific customers' accounts are uncollectible.

14. The direct write-off method has three shortcomings: (a) it does not usually recognize the loss from uncollectible accounts in the period in which the firm recognizes revenue; (b) it provides firms with an opportunity to manipulate earnings each period by deciding when particular customers' accounts are uncollectible; and (c) the amount of accounts receivable on the balance sheet under the direct write-off method does not reflect the amount a firm expects to collect in cash.

15. Generally accepted accounting principles do not allow the direct write-off method for financial reporting when losses from uncollectible accounts are significant in amount and are reasonably predictable. The direct write-off method is required for income tax reporting.

16. When the amount of uncollectibles can be estimated with reasonable precision, GAAP require that the allowance method be used. The allowance method involves (a) estimating the amount of uncollectibles that will occur in connection with the sales of each period and (b) making an adjusting entry that reduces the reported income on the income statement and reduces the Accounts Receivable on the balance sheet for the net amount of accounts expected to be uncollectible. The adjusting entry involves a debit to Bad Debts Expense to reduce income and a credit to Allowance for Uncollectible Accounts, a contra account to Accounts Receivable.

17. Views differ as to the type of account that "Bad Debts Expense" is-- expense or revenue contra. Arguments for treating it as a revenue contra may be persuasive, but treatment as an expense is more widely used in practice.

18. When a particular account is judged uncollectible, it is written off by debiting Allowance for Uncollectible Accounts and crediting Accounts Receivable. Writing off the specific account does not affect either net assets or income. The reduction in net assets and the affect on income took place in the year of sale when the firm estimated the amount of eventual uncollectibles and recorded Bad Debts Expense and credited the Allowance for Uncollectible Accounts.

19. The allowance method for uncollectible accounts (a) provides a better matching of revenues and expenses in the period of sale, (b) reduces management's opportunity to manipulate earnings through the timing of write-offs, and (c) results in reporting accounts receivable at the amount the firm expects to collect in cash in future periods. Because the allowance method requires firms to estimate the amount of future uncollectibles, a firm's management could manipulate earnings by over- stating or understating bad debts expense.

20. There are two basic approaches for calculating the amount of the adjustment for uncollectible accounts under the allowance method. The easiest method in most cases is to apply an appropriate percentage to total sales on account for the period. Another method, called aging the accounts, involves the analysis of customers' accounts classified by the length of time the accounts have been outstanding. The rationale is that the longer an account has been outstanding, the greater the probability that it will never be collected. By applying judgment to the aging analysis, an estimate is made of the approximate balance needed in the allowance for uncollectible accounts at year end.

21. When the percentage-of-sales method is used, the periodic provision for uncollectible accounts is merely added to the existing balance in the account, Allowance for Uncollectible Accounts. When the aging method is used, the balance in the account, Allowance for Uncollectible Accounts, is adjusted to reflect the desired ending balance.

22. The allowance method requires estimates of uncollectible accounts. When the amount of actual uncollectible accounts differs from the estimated amount, the previous misestimates should be corrected by adjusting the provision for bad debts during the current period. GAAP's reasoning is that the making of estimates is an integral part of measuring earnings under the accrual basis. Presuming that firms make conscientious estimates each year, adjustments for misestimates, although recurring, should be small.

23. Accountants use the allowance method when the firm knows that, at the time of sale, it will suffer some reduction in future cash flows but can only estimate the amount at the time of sale. The allowance method permits firms to reduce reported earnings in the period of sale to the amount of the expected net cash collections. The allowance method can be used when the customer has the right to return the product for a refund or when the customer has the right to repairs or replacement under warranty if the purchased product is defective.

24. Often, a seller of merchandise offers a reduction from the invoice price for prompt payment, called a sales discount or cash discount. The amount of sales discounts appears as an adjustment in measuring net sales revenue.

25. When a customer returns merchandise, the sale has in effect been canceled and an entry that reverses the recording of the sale is appropriate. The account, Sales Returns, is treated as a sales contra account on the income statement. GAAP do not allow a firm to recognize revenue from a sale when the customer has the right to return goods unless the firm can reasonably estimate the amount of the return and does so, using an allowance method.

26. A sales allowance is a reduction in price granted to a customer, usually after the goods have been purchased and found to be unsatisfactory or damaged. The effect of the allowance is to reduce sales revenue. It may be desirable to accumulate the amount of such an adjustment in a Sales Allowances account.

27. In some cases, a firm may find itself temporarily short of cash and unable to obtain financing from its usual sources. In such cases accounts receivable may be assigned, pledged, or factored.

28. Accounts are assigned to a bank or finance company in order to obtain a loan. The borrowing company usually maintains physical control of the receivables, collects customers' remittances, and forwards the proceeds to the lending institution to liquidate the loan.

29. Accounts may be pledged as collateral for a loan. If the borrower fails to repay the loan when due, the lending agency has the right to sell the accounts receivable in order to obtain payment.

30. Accounts receivable may be factored, which is in effect a sale of the receivables to a bank or finance company. In this case, the firm sells accounts receivable to the lending institution, which physically controls the receivables and collects payments from customers.

31. If a firm has pledged accounts receivable, a footnote to the financial statements should indicate this fact. The collection of pledged accounts receivable will not increase the liquid resources available to the firm to pay general trade creditors. Accounts receivables that the firm has factored or assigned do not appear on the balance sheet because the firm has sold them.

32. Contractors engaged in long-term construction projects may recognize revenue using the percentage-of-completion method or the completed-contract method.

33. Under the percentage-of-completion method, a portion of the total contract price is recognized as revenue each period. Corresponding proportions of the total estimated costs of the contract are recognized as expenses. The percentage-of-completion method measures the proportion of total work carried out during the accounting period either from engineers' estimates of the degree of completion or from the ratio of costs incurred to date to the total costs expected for the entire contract. The percentage-of-completion method follows the accrual basis of accounting because expenses are matched with related revenues.

34. Under the completed contract method, revenue is recognized when the project is completed and sold. The total costs of the project are expensed in the period when revenue is recognized.

35. In some cases, firms use the completed contract method because the contracts take a short time to complete. Firms also use the completed contract method when they have not found a specific buyer while construction progresses or when uncertainty obscures the total costs the contractor will incur in carrying out the project even when the firm has a contract with a specific price.

36. The percentage-of-completion method provides information on the profitability of a contractor as construction progresses while the completed contract method reports all income from contracts in the period of completion. GAAP require the use of the percentage-of-completion method whenever firms can make reasonable estimates of revenues and expenses.

37. Because the percentage-of-completion method requires estimates of revenues and expenses prior to completion, management is provided with the opportunity to manage earnings through its estimates of total expenses or its estimates of the degree of completion of the project. For this reason, most analysts view earnings reported under the percentage-of-completion method as having lower quality than earnings under the completed contract method.

38. When substantial uncertainty exists at the time of sale regarding the amount of cash or cash equivalent value of assets that a firm will ultimately receive from customers, it delays the recognition of revenues and expenses until it receives cash. Such sellers recognize revenue at the time of cash collection using either the installment method or the cost-recovery-first method. GAAP permit the seller to use the installment method and the cost-recovery-first method only when the seller cannot make reasonably certain estimates of cash collection.

39. The installment method recognizes revenue as cash is collected and recognizes as expenses each period the same portion of the cost of the good or service sold as the portion of total revenue recognized.

40. The cost-recovery-first method is appropriate when there is substantial uncertainty about cash collection. Under this method, costs of generating revenues are matched dollar for dollar with cash receipts until all such costs are recovered. When cumulative cash receipts exceed total costs, profit will be reported on the income statement.

41. To summarize, a firm can recognize revenue when it has delivered products or services to customers so long as the firm can estimate with reasonable statistical certainty the events remaining to complete the transaction. When significant uncertainty exists at the time of delivery about the events remaining to complete the transactions, firms must delay revenue recognition until the uncertainties resolve to the level of reasonable statistical certainty.

42. In evaluating a firm's past profitability and projecting its likely future profitability, the nature of income items must be considered. Does the income item result from the firm's primary operating activity or from an activity incidental or peripheral to the primary operating activities? Is the income item recurring or nonrecurring?

43. Revenues and expenses result from the recurring primary operating activities of a business. Gains and losses result from either peripheral activities or nonrecurring activities. Revenues and expenses are reported as gross amounts, whereas gains and losses are reported as net amounts.

Questions and Exercises

True/False. For each of the following statements, place a T or F in the space provided to indicate whether the statement is true or false.

_____ 1. The percentage-of-completion method of revenue recognition allows firms with long-term construction contracts to recognize a portion of the total contract price, based on the degree of completion of the work, during each accounting period of the life of the contract.

_____ 2. In assessing the quality of a firm's earnings, one factor to consider is the recurring or nonrecurring nature of various income items.

_____ 3. If a firm's management chooses estimates that lead to lower current income, analysts refer to the resulting reported earnings as lower quality.

_____ 4. Because the allowance method for reporting bad debts expense requires firms to estimate the amount of future uncollectibles, a firm's management could manipulate earnings by overstating or understating bad debts expense.

_____ 5. Most analysts view earnings reported under the percentage-of-completion method as having higher quality than earnings under the completed contract method.

_____ 6. Gains and losses are a gross concept and result from the recurring, primary operating activities of a business.

_____ 7. "Quality of earnings" refers to the ability managers have to use discretion in measuring and reporting earnings.

_____ 8. The cost-recovery-first method of income recognition matches costs of generating revenues dollar for dollar with cash receipts until all such costs are recovered.

_____ 9. Generally accepted accounting principles permit the installment method and the cost-recovery-first method only when substantial uncertainty exists about cash collection.

_____ 10. A contractor would not use the percentage-of-completion method to recognize revenues if there is substantial uncertainty regarding the total cost of the project.

_____ 11. The installment method of revenue recognition allows a firm to take a cash sale and recognize revenue from the sale equally over a 3-to-5 year period in the future.

_____ 12. The completed contract method of recognizing revenue is the same as the completed sale basis.

_____ 13. The computation of bad debt expense using the percentage-of-sales method involves multiplying the bad debt percentage times the credit sales for the period.

_____ 14. Under the allowance method for uncollectible accounts, writing off a specific account decreases net assets and decreases net income.

_____ 15. Under the allowance method, when a particular account is judged uncollectible, it is written off by debiting Bad Debts Expense and crediting Accounts Receivable.

_____ 16. The allowance method recognizes losses from uncollectible accounts in the period when a firm decides that specific customers' accounts are uncollectible.

_____ 17. When the aging method is used to estimate uncollectible accounts, the balance in the Allowance for Uncollectible Accounts is adjusted to bring the account balance to a desired ending balance.

_____ 18. The principal accounting issue related to uncollectible accounts concerns when firms should recognize the loss from uncollectibles.

_____ 19. For all firms the optimal amount of bad debts is zero.

_____ 20. The allowance method for uncollectible accounts results in reporting accounts receivable at the amount the firm expects to collect in cash in future periods.

_____ 21. The direct write-off method provides a better matching of revenues and expenses in the period of sale than the allowance method for uncollectible accounts.

_____ 22. A cash discount that is offered as an incentive for prompt payment is actually a form of interest expense to the buyer.

_____ 23. The appearance of the Allowance for Uncollectible Accounts on the balance sheet indicates the use of the direct write-off method.

_____ 24. The method of accounting for uncollectible accounts that recognizes a loss when a customer's account has clearly been demonstrated to be uncollectible is the direct write-off method.

_____ 25. Under the direct write-off method, the amount of accounts receivable on the balance sheet reflects the amount the firm expects to collect in cash.

_____ 26. One method of obtaining cash from accounts receivable is to pledge the accounts, which is equivalent to a sale.

_____ 27. When accounts receivable are factored, the lending institution physically controls the receivables and collects payments from customers.

_____ 28. Revenues and expenses are net concepts and result from either peripheral activities or nonrecurring activities.

Matching. From the following list of terms, select that term which is most closely associated with each of the descriptive phrases or statements that follows and place the letter for that term in the space provided.

a. Accounts Receivable

b. Aging of Accounts Receivable

c. Allowance for Uncollectible Accounts

d. Allowance Method

e. Assigning of Accounts Receivable

f. Bad Debts Expense

g. Direct Write-Off Method

h. Factor Accounts Receivable

i. Higher Quality of Earnings

j. Lower Quality of Earnings

k. Percentage of Sales

l. Pledging of Accounts Receivable

m. Quality of Earnings

n. Sales Returns & Allowances

_____ 1. A negative consequence of extending credit.

_____ 2. Treated as a contra to sales revenue.

_____ 3. Refers to the ability managers have to use discretion in measuring and reporting earnings.

_____ 4. A trade receivable.

_____ 5. A contra to Accounts Receivable.

_____ 6. A firm sells its accounts receivable to a bank or finance company to obtain cash.

_____ 7. The preferable method of accounting for uncollectible accounts.

_____ 8. If the borrower does not repay a note when due, the lending institution can sell the accounts receivable maintained as collateral for the loan.

_____ 9. How analysts refer to earnings when managers choose estimates that lead to lower current income.

_____ 10. A method in which uncollectible accounts are charged to expense when they are clearly demonstrated to be uncollectible.

_____ 11. When this method is used to estimate uncollectible accounts, the balance in the Allowance for Uncollectible Accounts is adjusted to reflect the desired ending balance.

_____ 12. In this situation, a company uses its accounts receivable to obtain a loan. The company usually maintains control of the receivables, collects from customers, and forwards the proceeds to the lending institution to liquidate the loan.

_____ 13. When this method is used to estimate uncollectible accounts, the provision for uncollectible accounts is added to the existing balance in the Allowance for Uncollectible Accounts.

_____ 14. How analysts refer to earnings when managers choose estimates that lead to higher current income.

Multiple Choice. Choose the best answer for each of the following questions and enter the identifying letter in the space provided.

The following information relates to Questions 1 - 3. Maguire Co. reported Accounts Receivable of $15,000 and an Allowance for Uncollectible Accounts of $1,500 on its 12/31, Year 1, Balance Sheet. During Year 2, credit sales totaled $450,000; collections on account totaled $420,000; and write-offs totaled $2,400. After aging its Accounts Receivable, Maguire estimated that 10 percent of its Accounts Receivable at 12/31, Year 2, will be uncollectible.

_____ 1. What is the balance in Accounts Receivable on 12/31, Year 2?

   a. $41,100.
   b. $41,700.
   c. $42,600.
   d. $43,500.

_____ 2. What amount would Maquire report as Bad Debts Expense in its Year 2 Income Statement?

   a. $ 4,260.
   b. $ 4,500.
   c. $ 5,400.
   d. $ 5,160.

_____ 3. Assume that Maguire estimates its bad debts to be 2 percent of credit sales. What balance would Maguire report in Allowance for Uncollectible Accounts on its 12/31, Year 2, balance sheet?

   a. $ 6,600.
   b. $ 8,100.
   c. $ 9,000.
   d. $10,500.

4. Espana Van Conversions had credit sales of $2,000,000 during Year 1. At 12/31, Year 1, the balance in Accounts Receivable was $81,000. The company estimates bad debts to equal 1 percent of credit sales. What effect will the company's 12/31 adjusting entry have on the company's income statement and balance sheet?

   a. Decrease income by $20,000; no effect on balance sheet.
   b. Decrease income by $20,000; decrease assets by $20,000.
   c. No effect on either income statement or balance sheet.
   d. None of the above.

5. Refer to the previous question. During Year 2, a customer's account for $3,600 was written off as uncollectible. What effect will the write-off have on the company's Year 2 income statement and balance sheet?

   a. No effect on income; decrease assets by $3,600.
   b. Decrease income by $3,600; decrease assets by $3,600.
   c. No effect on either income statement or balance sheet.
   d. None of the above.

6. Fridman Co. had $585,000 of sales during Year 1, $260,000 of which were on account. The balances in its Accounts Receivable and its Allowance for Uncollectible Accounts on December 31, Year 1, were $78,000 and $10,400, respectively. Past experience indicates that 5 percent of all credit sales will not be collected. What is the correct amount for Fridman to debit to Bad Debts Expense?

   a. $39,000.
   b. $13,000.
   c. $ 6,500.
   d. $26,000.

7. Refer to the question above, but assume that an aging of accounts indicated that $19,500 of the receivable balance would not be collected. What is the correct amount for Fridman to debit to Bad Debts Expense?

   a. $29,800.
   b. $13,000.
   c. $19,500.
   d. $ 9,100.

8. The proper handling in the financial statements of the account, Allowance for Uncollectible Accounts, is:

   a. A revenue contra account.
   b. A selling expense.
   c. A contra to Accounts Receivable.
   d. A current liability.

9. When a firm uses its accounts receivable as collateral for a loan, this transaction is known as a(an):

   a. Factoring of accounts receivable
   b. Assignment of accounts receivable.
   c. Pledging of accounts receivable.
   d. Sale of accounts receivable.

_____ 10. Which of the following events reduces total assets?

      a. A customer returns merchandise for credit.
      b. The write-off of uncollectible accounts under the allowance method.
      c. The collection of an account receivable.
      d. None of the above.

_____ 11. Of the numerous ways of turning receivables into cash, which one below is the same as an outright sale?

      a. Assignment of receivables.
      b. Factoring of receivables.
      c. Pledging of receivables.
      d. Collection of receivables.

_____ 12. Which of the accounts below would not be treated as a reduction in sales revenue on the income statement?

      a. Sales Discounts.
      b. Sales Allowances.
      c. Sales Returns.
      d. Bad Debts Expense.

The information which follows relates to Questions 13 - 16. Choose the answer to each question from the following four choices:

      a. Primary operating activity, which is recurring.

      b. Primary operating activity, which is nonrecurring.

      c. A recurring activity, which is peripheral to primary operations.

      d. A nonrecurring activity, which is peripheral to primary operations.

_____ 13. A manufacturing firm sold a parcel of land next to one of its warehouses.

_____ 14. A fast food restaurant chain sold a division that operated movie theaters.

_____ 15. A professional soccer team paid a signing bonus to one of its new players.

_____ 16. A Florida hotel chain's properties located on the "Emerald Coast" were destroyed when the area was devastated by an earthquake.

The information which follows relates to Questions 17-19.
Osprey Land Development Company sold a residential lot to Mr. Rosa for $420,000.
The cost assigned to the lot by Osprey was $168,000. The contract calls for five
annual payments of $84,000. Each payment was received, on time, at the end of
each of the 5 years.

_____ 17.   If Osprey recognizes income under the installment method, how much
            income would Osprey recognize in Year 1?

            a. $420,000.
            b. $252,000.
            c. $ 84,000.
            d. $ 50,400.

_____ 18.   If Osprey recognizes income under the cost-recovery-first method,
            how much income would Osprey recognize in Year 2?

            a.   -0-   .
            b. $ 50,400.
            c. $ 84,000.
            d. $100,800.

_____ 19.   If Osprey recognizes income under the cost-recovery-first method,
            how much income would Osprey recognize in Year 3?

            a.   -0-.
            b. $ 50,400.
            c. $ 84,000.
            d. $151,200.

The information which follows relates to Questions 20-22.
The Byrd Company signed a contract late in Year 1 to construct a bridge for the
Florida Department of Transportation. The contract price was $16,800,000. The
schedule below summarizes the costs during the 3-year construction period:

Year	Construction Costs Incurred
2	$4,000,000
3	$6,000,000
4	$2,000,000

Assume that Byrd follows the percentage-of-completion method.

_____ 20.   How much income would Byrd recognize in Year 2 on the bridge
            contract?

            a. $1,600,000.
            b. $4,000,000.
            c. $4,800,000.
            d. $5,600,000.

_____ 21. How much income would Byrd recognize in Year 3 on the bridge contract?

      a. $8,400,000.
      b. $4,800,000.
      c. $4,000,000.
      d. $2,400,000.

_____ 22. How much income would Byrd recognize in Year 4 on the bridge contract?

      a.   -0-
      b. $ 800,000.
      c. $2,800,000.
      d. $4,800,000.

The information which follows relates to Questions 23 and 24.
The Samuel Construction Company began construction of an office building early in Year 1. The project, which was completed during Year 3, incurred costs as follows:

Year	Costs Incurred
1	$5,200,000
2	$6,500,000
3	$3,900,000

The contract price for the construction of the building was $23,400,000.

Assume that Samuel follows the completed contract method.

_____ 23. How much revenue would Samuel recognize in Year 1 on the office building contract?

      a. $7,800,000.
      b. $5,200,000.
      c. $2,600,000.
      d.   -0-

_____ 24. How much income would Samuel recognize in Year 3 on the office building contract?

      a. $1,950,000.
      b. $3,900,000.
      c. $5,850,000.
      d. $7,800,000.

_____ 25. If a reasonable estimate of the amount of cash to be received can be made, and the firm has performed all, or a substantial portion, of the services it expects to provide, when should revenue be recognized?

      a.   At the time of sale.
      b.   At the time of cash collection.
      c.   At the time of cash collection, using the cost-recovery-first method.
      d.   None of the above.

Exercises

1. On February 1, Year 1, Ketchume Construction Company contracted to build a portion of interstate highway at a contract price of $27 million. A schedule of actual cash collections and contract costs for the 3-year contract is as follows:

Year 1	Cash Collections	Cost Incurred
1	$ 3,600,000	$ 4,800,000
2	13,800,000	10,800,000
3	9,600,000	6,000,000
	$27,000,000	$21,600,000

    Contract costs on the 3-year project totaled $21,600,000 and a $5,400,000 profit was earned on the project.

    Calculate the amount of net income (or profit) for each of the 3 years under the following revenue recognition methods:

    (a) percentage-of-completion method.

    (b) completed contract method.

    (c) installment method.

    (d) cost-recovery-first method.

2. On 12/31, Year 1, Coolidge Company reported the following on its balance sheet:

    Current Assets

Accounts Receivable	$180,000	
Less: Allowance for Uncollectible Accounts	7,875	$172,125

    On 12/31, Year 2, the company reported Accounts Receivable of $213,750 and an Allowance account balance of $9,562.50 (which was based on an aging of accounts receivable). During Year 2, credit sales totaled $1,284,750 and write-offs of uncollectible accounts totaled $20,250.

126

a.   How much cash did Coolidge collect from its credit customers during Year 2?

b.   What did the company report as its "Bad Debts Expense" on its Year 2 income statement?

3. On May 1, Year 1, Geary Co. reported the following accounts on its balance sheet:

    Current Assets

Accounts Receivable	$270,000	
Less: Allowance for Uncollectible Accounts	18,000	$252,000

    Record in journal form the following May transactions:

    a. Gross sales on account for the month of May were $1,300,000. Cash sales were $450,000.

    b. Customers received credit for $10,000 of merchandise purchased on account and returned during May.

    c. Customers' accounts totaling $1,250,000 were collected.

    d. Accounts receivable of $32,000 were written off as uncollectible during the month.

    e. At month-end, an aging of the accounts indicated that $12,000 would be uncollectible.

4. The Earl Company reported sales of $490,000 in Year 2 (of which $140,000 were for cash). It reported the following balances on 12/31/Year 2 before adjustments:

Accounts Receivable	$122,750	
Allowance for Uncollectible Accounts		$7,000

    The accounts written off as uncollectible during Year 2 totaled $21,700. Calculate the Bad Debts Expense for each method below.

    a. The direct write-off method.

    b. The percentage-of-credit-sales method, where experience indicates a 3 percent rate is appropriate.

c. The aging method, where an evaluation of accounts indicates that $11,000 will not be collected.

d. Same as c above except assume that the Allowance for Uncollectible Accounts has a <u>debit</u> balance of $9,000 instead of a <u>credit</u> balance.

Answers to Questions and Exercises

True/False

1.	T	7.	T	13.	T	19.	F	25.	F
2.	T	8.	T	14.	F	20.	T	26.	F
3.	F	9.	T	15.	F	21.	F	27.	T
4.	T	10.	T	16.	F	22.	T	28.	F
5.	F	11.	F	17.	T	23.	F		
6.	F	12.	T	18.	T	24.	T		

Matching

1.	f	4.	a	7.	d	10.	g	13.	k
2.	n	5.	c	8.	l	11.	b	14.	j
3.	m	6.	h	9.	i	12.	e		

Multiple Choice

1.	c	6.	b	11.	b	16.	d	21.	d
2.	d	7.	d	12.	d	17.	d	22.	b
3.	b	8.	c	13.	c	18.	a	23.	d
4.	b	9.	c	14.	b	19.	c	24.	d
5.	c	10.	a	15.	a	20.	a	25.	a

Exercises

1. (a) Percentage-of-completion method:

Year	Incremental Percentage Complete		Revenue Recognized	Expenses Recognized	Net Income
1	4.8/21.6	(.22)	$ 6,000,000	$ 4,800,000	$1,200,000
2	10.8/21.6	(.50)	13,500,000	10,800,000	2,700,000
3	6.0/21.6	(.28)	7,500,000	6,000,000	1,500,000
	21.6/21.6	(1.000)	$27,000,000	$21,600,000	$5,400,000

(b) Completed contract method:

Year	Revenue Recognized	Expenses Recognized	Net Income
1	$ 0	$ 0	$ 0
2	0	0	0
3	27,000,000	21,600,000	5,400,000
	$ 27,000,000	$ 21,600,000	$5,400,000

(c) Installment method:

Year	Cash Collected (= Revenue)	Fraction of Cash Collected	Expense Recognized (Fraction x Total Cost)	Net Income
1	$ 3,600,000	3.6/27	$ 2,880,000	$ 720,000
2	13,800,000	13.8/27	11,040,000	2,760,000
3	9,600,000	9.6/27	7,680,000	1,920,000
	$27,000,000	1.0	$21,600,000	$5,400,000

(d) Cost-recovery-first method:

Year	Cash Collected (= Revenue)	Expenses Recognized	Net Income
1	$ 3,600,000	$ 3,600,000	$ 0
2	13,800,000	13,800,000	0
3	9,600,000	4,200,000	5,400,000
	$27,000,000	$21,600,000	$ 5,400,000

2. a.

Beginning balance, Accounts Receivable	$ 180,000
Credit Sales	1,284,750
Total Accounts Receivable	$1,464,750
Less: Write-offs of uncollectible accounts	(20,250)
Ending Balance, Accounts Receivable	(213,750)
Cash collected from customers during Year 2	$1,230,750

b. Ending balance, Allowance for Uncollectible Accounts $ 9,562.50

Write-offs of uncollectible accounts   20,250.00

Total $29,812.50

Less: Beginning balance, Allowance for Uncollectible

Accounts   7,875.00

Year 2 Bad Debts Expense $21,937.50

3.
  a. Accounts Receivable   1,300,000
     Cash   450,000
       Sales Revenue   1,750,000
     Sales for May.

  b. Sales Returns and Allowances   10,000
       Accounts Receivable   10,000
     Sales returns for May.

  c. Cash   1,250,000
       Accounts Receivable   1,250,000
     Collections on account during May.

  d. Allowance for Uncollectible Accounts   32,000
       Accounts Receivable   32,000
     To write-off uncollectible accounts.

  e. Bad Debts Expense   26,000
       Allowance for Uncollectible Accounts   26,000
     To increase allowance to $12,000 as
     determined by aging process.

     Allowance, May 1 Year 1 $18,000

     Write-offs during May   32,000

     Balance prior to adjustment   ($14,000)

     Required balance, per aging
       of accounts   12,000

     Increase in Allowance $26,000

4.

    a.   <u>$21,700</u>

    b.   .03 x $350,000 = <u>$10,500</u>

	c.		
c.	Total uncollectible	$11,000
	Credit in Allowance Account	<u>7,000</u>
		<u>$ 4,000</u>
d.	Total uncollectible	$11,000
	Debit in Allowance Account	<u>9,000</u>
		<u>$20,000</u>

Chapter 7

Inventories: The Source of Operating Profits

Chapter Highlights

1. The term "inventory" means a stock of goods or other items a firm owns and holds for sale or for processing as part of a firm's business operations. Merchandise inventory refers to goods held for sale by a retail or wholesale business. Finished goods denotes goods held for sale by a manufacturing company. The inventories of manufacturing firms also include work in process (partially completed products) and raw materials (materials which will become part of goods produced).

2. Accounting for inventories includes the process of determining the proper assignment of expenses to various accounting periods. Accounting must allocate the total cost of goods available for sale or use during a period between the current period's usage (cost of goods sold, an expense) and the amounts carried forward to future periods (the end of period inventory, an asset now but an expense later).

3. The following equation aids the understanding of the accounting for inventory. Beginning Inventory + Additions - Withdrawals = Ending Inventory. Beginning Inventory + Additions equal goods available for use or sale. Slightly different terminology applied to the same equation is Beginning Inventory + Purchases - Cost of Goods Sold = Ending Inventory. The valuation for ending inventory will appear on the balance sheet as the asset, merchandise inventory; the amount of cost of goods sold will appear on the income statement as an expense of producing sales revenue.

4. Financial statements report dollar amounts, not physical units such as pounds or cubic feet. The accountant must transform physical quantities for beginning inventory, additions, withdrawals, and ending inventory into dollar amounts in order to measure income for the period as well as financial position at the beginning and end of the period.

5. Some problems of inventory accounting are (a) the costs to be included in acquisition costs, (b) the treatment of changes in the market value of inventories subsequent to acquisition, and (c) the choice of cost flow assumptions used to trace the movement of costs into and out of inventory.

6. The amount on a balance sheet for inventory includes all costs incurred to acquire goods and prepare them for sale. Acquisition cost includes the invoice price less any cash discounts taken for prompt payment. Acquisition cost also includes the cost of purchasing, transporting, receiving, unpacking, inspecting, and shelving as well as any costs for recording purchases.

7. The operating process for a typical manufacturing firm includes (a) acquiring plant and equipment to provide the capacity to manufacture goods, (b) acquiring raw materials for use in production, and (c) converting raw materials into a salable product. The firm holds the finished product in inventory until it sells the goods. At the time the goods are sold, most manufacturing firms recognize revenue because the production activity is completed, a customer has been identified and a sales price has been agreed on. Following the accrual basis, the manufacturing firm matches against the revenue the expense for the manufacturing cost of the items sold.

8. Manufacturing firms incur costs for direct materials, direct labor, and manufacturing overhead to convert raw materials into finished products. Manufacturing overhead includes a variety of indirect costs (depreciation, insurance, supervisory labor, factory supplies) that firms cannot trace directly to products manufactured but which provide a firm with productive capacity. Manufacturing costs are treated as product costs (assets) and are accumulated in various inventory accounts. At the time of sale, the cost of items sold is transferred from the asset account, Finished Goods Inventory, to the expense account, Cost of Goods Sold.

9. A manufacturing firm, like a merchandising firm, incurs various marketing and administrative costs. Both merchandising and manufacturing firms treat selling and administrative costs as period expenses.

10. Manufacturing firms maintain separate inventory accounts for product costs incurred at various stages of completion. The Raw Materials Inventory account includes the cost of raw materials purchased but not yet transferred to production. The Work-in-Process Inventory account accumulates the cost of raw materials transferred from the raw materials storeroom, the cost of direct labor services used in production, and the manufacturing overhead cost incurred. The balance in the Work-in-Process Inventory account indicates the product costs incurred thus far on units not yet finished as of the date of the balance sheet. The Finished Goods Inventory account includes the total manufacturing cost of units completed but not yet sold.

11. GAAP require firms to record inventories initially at acquisition cost. GAAP do not permit firms to revalue inventories above acquisition cost. The benefit of the increase in market value affects net income in the period of sale when the firm realizes the benefit of a higher selling price instead of recognizing the benefit during the periods while market values increased. In contrast, GAAP require firms to write down inventories when their replacement cost, or market value, is less than acquisition cost. GAAP refer to this valuation as the lower-of-cost-or-market valuation method.

12. The lower-of-cost-or-market basis for inventory valuation is a conservative accounting policy. Conservatism in accounting tends to result in higher quality of earnings figures because (a) it recognizes losses from decreases in market value before the firm sells goods, but does not record gains from increases in market value before a sale takes place, and (b) inventory figures on the balance sheet are never greater, but may be less, than acquisition costs. In other words, the lower-of-cost-or-market basis results in reporting unrealized holding losses on inventory items currently in the financial statements through lower net income amounts but delays reporting unrealized holding gains until the firm sells the goods.

13. An inventory valuation problem arises because of two unknowns in the inventory equation. The values of beginning inventory and purchases are known; the values of cost of goods sold and ending inventory are not known. The valuation of the ending inventory may be based on the most recent costs, the oldest costs, the average costs, or some other choice. Once the amount of one unknown is assigned, then the equation automatically determines the amount of the other. The relation between the two unknowns in the inventory equation, cost of goods sold and closing inventory, is such that the higher the value assigned to one of them, the lower must be the value assigned to the other.

14. If the cost of items sold cannot be specifically identified, some assumption must be made as to the flow of cost in order to estimate the acquisition costs applicable to the units remaining in the inventory and to the units sold. Even if a firm finds specific identification feasible, it may choose to make a cost flow assumption. Three principal cost flow assumptions used are first-in, first-out; last-in, first-out; and weighted-average.

15. The first-in, first-out (FIFO) cost flow assumption assigns the costs of the earliest units acquired to the withdrawals and the cost of the most recent acquisitions to the ending inventory.

16. The last-in, first-out (LIFO) cost flow assumption assigns the costs of the most recent acquisitions to the withdrawals and the costs of the oldest units to the ending inventory.

17. The weighted-average method assigns costs to both inventory and withdrawals based upon a weighted average of all merchandise available for sale during the period.

18. When purchase prices change, no acquisition cost-based accounting method for costing inventory and cost of goods sold allows the accountant to show up-to-date costs on both the income statement and the balance sheet. Financial statements can present current cost amounts in the income statement or the balance sheet but not both.

19. Of the three cost flow assumptions, FIFO results in balance sheet figures that are the closest to current cost. The cost of goods sold expense tends to be out-of-date because the earlier purchase prices of beginning inventory and the earliest purchases during the period become expenses. When purchase prices rise, FIFO usually leads to the highest reported net income of the three methods and when purchase prices fall, it leads to the smallest.

20. When purchase prices have been rising and inventory amounts increasing, LIFO produces balance sheet figures usually much lower than current costs. LIFO's cost of goods sold figure closely approximates current costs. LIFO usually results in the smallest net income when purchase prices are rising and the largest when purchase prices are falling.

21. The weighted-average cost flow assumption resembles FIFO more than LIFO in its effect on the financial statements. When inventory turns over rapidly, the weighed-average inventory cost flow provides amounts virtually identical to FIFO's amounts.

22. Differences in cost of goods sold and inventories under the cost flow assumptions relate in part to (a) the rate of change in the acquisition costs of inventory items and (b) the rate of inventory turnover.

23. As the rate of price change increases, the effect of using older versus more recent price increases results in larger differences in cost of goods sold and inventories between FIFO and LIFO.

24. As the rate of inventory turnover increases, purchases during the period make up an increasing proportion of the cost of goods available for sale. Because purchases are the same regardless of the cost flow assumption, cost of goods sold amounts will not vary as much with the choice of cost flow assumptions.

25. LIFO generally results in the deferral of income taxes. If a firm uses LIFO for income tax reporting purposes, it must also use LIFO in its financial report to shareholders. This "LIFO conformity rule" results from the restrictions placed by the Internal Revenue Service on firms using LIFO for income tax reporting.

26. Under LIFO, in any year purchases exceed sales, the quantity of units in inventory increases. This increase is called a LIFO inventory layer.

27. If under LIFO, a firm must reduce end-of-period physical inventory quantities below what they were at the beginning of the period, cost of goods sold will include the current period's purchases plus a portion of the older and lower costs in the beginning inventory. Such a firm will have larger reported income and income taxes in that period than if the firm had been able to maintain its ending inventory at beginning-of-period levels. LIFO results in firms deferring taxes as long as they do not dip into LIFO layers.

28. Because firms often control whether inventory quantities increase or decrease through their purchase or production decisions, LIFO affords firms an opportunity to manage their earnings in a particular year. Analysts view firms who dip into LIFO layers to manage their earnings as having a lower quality of earnings than firms that use FIFO. GAAP require firms that dip into LIFO layers during the period to indicate the effect of the dip on cost of goods sold.

29. Managers of LIFO inventories are often faced with difficult decisions relative to the use of this inventory method. Managers must weigh the purchase decisions at year end with the effect these decisions will have on reported income and income taxes. LIFO can induce firms to manage LIFO layers and Cost of Goods sold in a way that would be unwise in the absence of tax effects. LIFO also gives management the opportunity to manage income. Under LIFO, end-of-year purchases, which the firm can manage, affect net income for the year.

30. The valuation of inventory on the balance sheet under LIFO is understated. As a consequence of the inventory being understated, the computation of a firm's current ratio and inventory turnover is affected. The computed current ratio would tend to underestimate the firm's liquidity and the firm's computed inventory turnover would be overstated. Because the Securities and Exchange Commission is concerned that this out-of-date information might mislead the readers of financial statements, it requires firms using LIFO to disclose, in notes to the financial statements, the amounts by which inventories based on FIFO or current cost exceed their amounts as reported on a LIFO basis.

31. In general, the reported net income under FIFO exceeds that under LIFO during periods of rising prices. The higher reported net income results from including a larger realized holding gain in reported net income under FIFO than under LIFO.

32. The conventionally reported gross margin (sales minus cost of goods sold) consists of (a) an operating margin and (b) a realized holding gain (or loss).

33. Operating margin denotes the difference between the selling price of an item and its replacement cost at the time of sale.

34. The realized holding gain is the difference between the current replacement cost of an item at the time of sale and its acquisition cost. The term inventory profit sometimes denotes the realized holding gain on inventory. The amount of inventory profit varies from period to period as the rate of change in the purchase price of inventories varies. The larger the inventory profit, the less sustainable are earnings and therefore the lower the quality of earnings.

35. The unrealized holding gain is the difference between the current replacement cost of the ending inventory and its acquisition cost. Unrealized holding gains on ending inventory do not appear in a firm's income statement as presently prepared under GAAP.

36. The unrealized holding gain under LIFO is larger than under FIFO since earlier purchases with lower costs are assumed to remain in ending inventory under LIFO.

37. The sum of the operating margin plus all holding gains (both realized and unrealized) is the same under FIFO and LIFO. Most of the holding gain under FIFO is recognized in determining net income each period, whereas most of the holding gain under LIFO is not currently recognized in the income statement. Under LIFO, the unrealized holding gain remains unreported as long as the older acquisition costs appear on the balance sheet as ending inventory.

38. Statement No. 2 of the International Accounting Standards Board supports the use of the lower of cost or market method for the valuation of inventories with market value based on net realizable value. All major industrialized countries require the lower-of-cost-or-market method in the valuation of inventories. Firms in most countries use FIFO and weighted-average cost flow assumptions. Few countries except the United States and Japan allow LIFO as an acceptable cost flow assumption.

39. All transactions involving inventory affect the operations section of the statement of cash flows. An increase in inventory during the year would be deducted from net income in computing cash flows from operations. A decrease in inventory during the year would be added to net income in computing cash flows from operations.

Questions and Exercises

True/False. For each of the following statements, place a T or F in the space provided to indicate whether the statement is true or false.

_____ 1.   When materials are issued to production departments, the Work-in-Process account is debited.

_____ 2.   The Raw Materials account includes the cost of raw materials purchased but not yet transferred to production.

_____ 3.   LIFO gives managers the opportunity to manipulate income.

_____ 4.   A LIFO inventory layer is created when purchases exceed sales therefore increasing inventory.

_____ 5.   The last-in, first-out cost flow method for tax purposes requires that the businesses carry a certain amount of reserve stock units on hand and that current operations and sales can not "dip" into the reserve.

_____ 6.   The balance in the Finished Goods account represents the total manufacturing cost of units completed but not sold.

_____ 7.   The Work-in-Process account is debited for the cost of direct labor services used.

_____ 8.   Reductions in inventory appear in the operating section of the statement of cash flows as an addition to net income in deriving cash flow from operations.

_____ 9.   FIFO, LIFO, and weighted-average cost flow assumptions relate to costs associated with withdrawals from inventory. As a result, income reports vary but balance sheet valuations reflect little difference.

_____ 10.   The LIFO cost flow assumption assigns the cost of the latest units acquired to the withdrawals and the costs of the oldest units to the ending inventory.

_____ 11.   Net income under FIFO is usually smaller than under LIFO when prices are rising.

_____ 12.   The Finished Goods account accumulates the costs incurred in producing units during the period.

_____ 13.   In most cases the total acquisition costs of inventory purchases may be measured accurately by the invoice price of the merchandise.

_____ 14. During periods of rising prices, the unrealized holding gain recognized on the income statement under FIFO is greater than the amount recognized under LIFO.

_____ 15. A conventionally reported gross margin on sales consists of a (1) realized holding gain and (2) an unrealized holding gain.

_____ 16. FIFO has the advantage of reporting up-to-date costs for cost of goods sold on the income statement and inventory on the balance sheet.

_____ 17. The term cost (for merchandise) may include invoice price plus cost of transportation, as well as costs of purchasing, receiving, handling, and storage.

_____ 18. The lower-of-cost-or-market basis refers to valuations using a comparison of acquisition cost and replacement cost.

_____ 19. The "LIFO conformity rule" requires firms which use LIFO for income tax purposes to also use LIFO for its financial reports to shareholders.

_____ 20. The first-in, first-out cost flow assumption assigns the costs of the most recent acquisitions to the inventory and the costs of the earliest units acquired to the withdrawals.

_____ 21. Most industrialized countries require the lower-of-cost-or-market basis for inventory valuation.

_____ 22. Most industrialized countries allow LIFO as an acceptable cost flow assumption.

_____ 23. Analysts view firms who dip into LIFO layers to manage their earnings as having a higher quality of earnings than firms that use FIFO.

_____ 24. Valuation of inventory on the balance sheet under LIFO would tend to lead to an overstatement of the firm's liquidity and an overstatement of the firm's inventory turnover.

_____ 25. In periods of rising prices, reported income under FIFO exceeds that under LIFO because larger realized holding gains are included in net income under FIFO than under LIFO.

_____ 26. The SEC requires firms using LIFO to disclose, in notes to the financial statements, the amounts by which inventories based on FIFO or current cost exceed their amounts as reported on a LIFO basis.

_____ 27. The Finished Goods account is credited for the cost of units completed during the period.

Matching. From the list of terms below, select that term which is most closely associated with each of the descriptive phrases or statements that follows and place the letter for that term in the space provided.

a. Acquisition Cost

b. Cost of Goods Sold

c. FIFO

d. Finished Goods

e. FISH

f. Inventory

g. Inventory Profit

h. LIFO

i. LIFO Conformity Rule

j. LISH

k. Lower-of-Cost-or-Market

l. Operating Margin

m. Purchases

n. Raw Materials

o. Realized Holding Gain

p. Replacement Cost

q. Specific Identification

r. Unrealized Holding Gain

s. Weighted-Average Method

t. Work-in-Progress

_____ 1. The amount a firm would have to pay to acquire a replacement for an inventory item at that particular time.

_____ 2. The difference between the current replacement cost of the ending inventory and its acquisition cost.

_____ 3. The difference between the selling price of an item and its replacement cost at the time of sale.

_____ 4. The difference between cost of goods sold based on replacement cost and cost of goods sold based on acquisition cost.

_____ 5. Inventory cost flow assumption which is physically appropriate for liquid or other types of products for which distinguishing different lots is difficult.

_____ 6. Valuation basis which departs from cost when the utility of the goods is no longer as great as their cost.

_____ 7. This cost flow assumption leads to the deferral of income taxes during periods of rising prices.

_____ 8. The portion of merchandise available for sale or use that is allocated to the current period's usage.

_____ 9. Partially completed products in the factory.

_____ 10. Account title and term designating acquisition of merchandise during the accounting period.

_____ 11. Cost flow assumption that assigns the costs of the earliest units acquired to the withdrawals and the costs of the most recent acquisitions to the ending inventory.

_____ 12. Assignment of cost where a firm can physically match individual units sold with a specific purchase.

_____ 13. Includes invoice price less any cash discounts plus the costs of transporting, receiving, unpacking, inspecting, and shelving.

_____ 14. Goods held for sale by a manufacturing concern.

_____ 15. Materials being stored that will become a part of the goods to be produced.

_____ 16. A stock of goods owned by a firm and held for sale to customers.

_____ 17. LIFO refers to the cost flow for the units sold. This is the parallel description for ending inventory.

_____ 18. This term sometimes denotes the realized holding gain on inventory.

_____ 19. If a firm uses a LIFO assumption in its income tax return, it must also use LIFO in its financial reports to shareholders.

_____ 20. FIFO refers to the cost of the units sold. This is the parallel description for ending inventory.

Multiple Choice. Choose the best answer for each of the following questions and enter the identifying letter in the space provided.

_____ 1. The inventories of a manufacturing company include

    a.   Finished goods.
    b.   Raw materials.
    c.   Work in process.
    d.   All of the above.

_____ 2. The differences between the current replacement cost of the ending inventory and its acquisition cost is the

    a.   Operating margin.
    b.   Realized holding gain.
    c.   Unrealized holding gain.
    d.   Gross margin.

_____ 3. Conventionally, accountants refer to the difference between sales and cost of goods sold as the

    a.   Operating margin.
    b.   Realized holding gain.
    c.   Unrealized holding gain.
    d.   Gross margin.

_____ 4. Characteristics of the use of LIFO include all the following except

     a.   Produces higher balance sheet valuation of inventory than FIFO during periods of rising prices.

     b.   Produces lower net income than FIFO during periods of rising prices.

     c.   Allows managers to manipulate net income.

     d.   All of the above are characteristics.

_____ 5. Under this cost flow assumption, the income statement reports out-of-date cost of goods sold.

     a.   FIFO method.

     b.   LIFO method.

     c.   Weighted-average method.

     d.   Replacement cost method.

_____ 6. In the statement of cash flows, reductions in inventory

     a.   Are treated differently than other reductions in current assets.

     b.   Appear as an addition to net income in deriving cash flow from operations.

     c.   Appear in the financing section.

     d.   Appear in the investing section.

_____ 7. The difference between cost of goods sold based on replacement cost and cost of goods sold based on acquisition cost is the

     a.   Operating margin.

     b.   Realized holding gain.

     c.   Unrealized holding gain.

     d.   Gross margin.

_____ 8. During periods of rising prices, this cost flow assumption produces the highest reported net income

     a.   FIFO method.

     b.   LIFO method.

     c.   Weighted-average method.

     d.   All produce the same net income.

_____ 9. In an international perspective the following statements are accurate except

     a.   Firms in most countries use FIFO and weighted average cost flow assumptions.

     b.   All major developed countries require the lower-of-cost-or-market method.

     c.   Few countries, except the U.S. and Japan allow LIFO.

     d.   All the statements are accurate.

_____ 10. The correct equation that applies to the determination of cost of goods sold is

    a.   Beginning Inventory - Purchases + Ending Inventory = Cost of Goods Sold.
    b.   Beginning Inventory + Purchases - Ending Inventory = Cost of Goods Sold.
    c.   Beginning Inventory + Purchases + Ending Inventory = Cost of Goods Sold.
    d.   None of the above.

_____ 11. Which of the following is not acceptable for determination of inventory cost?

    a.   FIFO method.
    b.   LIFO method.
    c.   Specific identification method.
    d.   All of the above are acceptable.

_____ 12. The amount the firm would have to pay to acquire a replacement for an inventory item at that particular time is the

    a.   Replacement cost.
    b.   Net realizable value.
    c.   Standard cost.
    d.   Market selling value.

_____ 13. The difference between the selling price of an item and its replacement cost at the time of sale is the

    a.   Operating margin.
    b.   Realized holding gain.
    c.   Unrealized holding gain.
    d.   Gross margin.

_____ 14. Under this cost flow assumption, the costs assigned to the ending inventory are the costs of the earliest units acquired

    a.   FIFO method.
    b.   LIFO method.
    c.   Weighted-average method.
    d.   Replacement cost method.

_____ 15. This cost flow assumption conforms to most actual physical inventory flows

    a.   FIFO method.
    b.   LIFO method.
    c.   Weighted-average method.
    d.   Replacement cost method.

_____ 16. If this inventory flow assumption is used for income tax purposes, the Internal Revenue Service requires its use for income determination for financial reports to owners

    a.   FIFO method.
    b.   LIFO method.
    c.   Weighted-average method.
    d.   Replacement cost method.

The following information relates to Questions 17 and 18. At the beginning of the year, FETTIG Company reported balances in Work-in-Process Inventory and Finished Goods Inventory, respectively, of $174,000 and $102,000. During the year, materials, labor, and overhead costs totaling $678,000 were added to production. Products costing $612,000 were transferred to finished goods during the year. At the end of the year, the balance in Finished Goods Inventory is $72,000.

_____ 17. What is the ending balance in the Work-in-Process Inventory account?

    a. $240,000.
    b. $222,000.
    c. $102,000.
    d. $144,000.

_____ 18. What amount should FETTIG report as Cost of Goods Sold for the year?

    a. $714,000.
    b. $582,000.
    c. $678,000.
    d. $642,000.

_____ 19. Which of the following costs would not be included as an element of manufacturing overhead?

    a.   Depreciation on factory machinery.
    b.   Insurance on factory building.
    c.   Raw materials.
    d.   Supervisory labor.

_____ 20. Which of the following is not a product cost?

    a.   Depreciation on plant machinery.
    b.   Salary of the production vice-president.
    c.   Insurance associated with the delivery equipment.
    d.   Property taxes associated with the factory building.

_____ 21. Which of the following is not a period expense?

    a.   Salary of the sales vice-president.
    b.   Salaries of factory custodial employees.
    c.   Salaries of administrative clerical personnel.
    d.   Salaries of employees who deliver the finished product to customers.

_____ 22. Which of the following is the correct sequence of cost flows for a manufacturing firm?

    a.   Work in Process, Finished Goods, Cost of Goods Sold, Raw Materials.

    b.   Raw Materials, Work in Process, Finished Goods, Cost of Goods Sold.

    c.   Cost of Goods Sold, Raw Materials, Work in Process, Finished Goods.

    d.   Finished Goods, Work in Process, Raw Materials, Cost of Goods Sold.

_____ 23. The Work-in-Process account would not be debited for which of the following items?

    a.   Direct labor costs.

    b.   Manufacturing overhead costs.

    c.   Selling and administrative costs.

    d.   Costs of raw materials put into production.

Exercises

1.   The Sheffield Company has completed its first year in business. Given the incomplete information in the four T-accounts below, answer the following questions.

Raw Materials Inventory

Balance 12/31 31,500	

Work-In-Process Inventory

Labor 157,500	
Overhead 75,600	
Balance 12/31 44,100	

Finished Goods Inventory

	252,000
Balance 12/31 31,500	

Cost of Goods Sold

252,000	

a. Determine the amount of goods finished during the period and trans-
    ferred to Finished Goods Inventory.

                        $ _____

b. Determine the amount of raw materials transferred to Work-In-Process
    Inventory during the period.

                        $ _____

c. Determine the amount of raw materials purchased during the period.

                        $ _____

d. Record all journal entries for the company's manufacturing activities during the period. Assume that the $75,600 overhead cost relates to depreciation on the factory building.

2. Place the correct number in the space provided for each of the following.

Beginning Inventory	$ 40,000	$ (c)	$ (e)	$ 22,500	$ (i)
Net Purchase	(a)	20,000	47,500	(g)	137,500
Total Goods Available	$440,000	$22,500	$47,500	$122,500	$175,000
Ending Inventory	36,000	(d)	-0-	(h)	45,000
Cost of Goods Sold	$ (b)	$19,000	$ (f)	$107,500	$ (j)

a. _____   f. _____

b. _____   g. _____

c. _____   h. _____

d. _____   i. _____

e. _____   j. _____

3. Natasha Company uses LIFO inventory costing. Certain items of information relating to the current inventory operations are listed below:

Replacement cost of goods sold $ 9,600

Acquisition cost of goods sold $ 9,000

Replacement cost of ending inventory $21,000

Acquisition cost of ending inventory $16,200

Sales Revenue $16,500

Determine   a.   Operating Margin on Sales

b.   Realized Holding Gain

c.   Conventionally Reported Gross Margin

d.   Unrealized Holding Gain

4.   The following data were obtained from the inventory records of James
      Company for the month of June:

June 1	Beginning Inventory	3,000 units @ $6 each
June 5	Issued	750 units
June 8	Purchased	1,500 units @ $8 each
June 12	Purchased	450 units @ $9 each
June 15	Issued	600 units
June 20	Issued	1,200 units
June 25	Issued	750 units
June 30	Purchased	750 units @ $10 each

a.   Calculate the cost of June ending inventory assuming James uses a:

      1.   FIFO cost flow assumption.

2.   LIFO cost flow assumption.

3.   Weighted-average flow assumption.

b.   Calculate the cost of goods sold for June assuming James uses a:

1.   FIFO cost flow assumption.

2.   LIFO cost flow assumption.

5.   The following data were obtained from the inventory records of Brian Company for the months of May, June, and July:

	Units	Unit Cost	Total Cost
Beginning Inventory, May 1..............	-	-	-
Purchases, May 3......................	50	$5.00	$ 250
Purchases, May 23.....................	75	6.00	450
Total Goods Available for Sale......	125		$ 700
Withdrawal during May.................	100		?
Ending Inventory, May 31, and Beginning Inventory, June 1.........	25		?
Purchases, June 15....................	100	6.50	650
Purchases, June 19....................	150	7.00	1,050
Total Goods Available for Sale......	275		?
Withdrawals during June...............	225		?
Ending Inventory, June 30, and Beginning Inventory, July 1.........	50		?
Purchases, July 3.....................	225	8.00	1,800
Total Goods Available for Sale......	275		?
Withdrawals during July...............	245		?
Ending Inventory (July 31)...........	30		?

a. Compute the cost of goods sold (withdrawals) for May, June and July, using a (1) FIFO and (2) LIFO, cost flow assumption.

b. Assume the following:

	June 30	July 31
Current assets excluding inventories...	$650	$730
Current Liabilities	715	712

    1.   Compute the current ratio for June 30 and July 31 using (a) FIFO and (b) LIFO cost flow assumption.

    2.   Compute the inventory turnover ratio for June and July using (a) FIFO and (b) LIFO cost flow assumption.

c. Comment on the results determined in b-1 and b-2 above.

6.   Trey Company values its inventory using the LIFO cost flow assumption. The beginning inventory on 1/1/2005 consisted of 530 units in the following layers:

300 units from 2002 @ $ 6.00 each	$1,800
140 units from 2003 @ $ 8.25 each	1,155
90 units from 2004 @ $ 9.30 each	837
530 units	$3,792

Trey purchased 1,150 units @ $10.00 each in 2005 and sold 1,500 units @ $17.00 each during 2005.

a. Compute the Cost of Goods Sold in 2005 using the LIFO cost flow assumption.

b. Compute the 12/31/2005 inventory using the LIFO cost flow assumption.

c. Now assume that Trey purchased 1,520 units @$10.00 each during 2005.

    1.   Compute the Cost of Goods Sold in 2005 using the LIFO cost flow assumption.

    2.   Compute the 12/31/2005 inventory using the LIFO cost flow assumption.

d. Why is the computed Cost of Goods Sold in parts (a) and (c-1) different?

e. Prepare the relevant portion of an income statement for 2005 (1) assuming that 1,150 units were purchased during 2005 and (2) assuming that 1,520 units were purchased during 2005.

f. What are the earnings and tax implications of Trey dipping into its LIFO layers in 2005?

g. What should Trey report in the notes to its 2005 financial statements relative to its inventory (assuming that the ending inventory consisted of 180 units and the beginning inventory consisted of 530 units)?

Answers to Questions and Exercises

True/False

1. T	7. T	13. F	19. T	25. T
2. T	8 T	14. F	20. T	26. T
3. T	9. F	15. F	21. T	27. F
4. T	10. T	16. F	22. F	
5. F	11. F	17. T	23. F	
6. T	12. F	18. T	24. F	

Matching

1. p	5. s	9. t	13. a	17. e
2. r	6. k	10. m	14. d	18. g
3. l	7. h	11. c	15. n	19. i
4. o	8. b	12. q	16. f	20. j

Multiple Choice

1. d	5. a	9. d	13. a	17. a	21. b
2. c	6. b	10. b	14. b	18. d	22. b
3. d	7. b	11. d	15. a	19. c	23. c
4. a	8. a	12. a	16. b	20. c	

Exercise

1.

Raw Materials Inventory	
Purchased 126,000	
	94,500
Balance 12/31 31,500	

Work-in-Process Inventory	
Materials 94,500	
Labor 157,500	
Overhead 75,600	283,500
Balance 12/31 44,100	

Finished Goods Inventory	
283,500	252,000
Balance 12/31 31,500	

Cost of Goods Sold	
252,000	

a. $283,500.
b. $ 94,500.
c. $126,000.
d. Journal entries:

		Dr.	Cr.
(1)	Raw Materials Inventory	126,000	
	Cash or Accounts Payable		126,000
	To record purchase of raw materials.		
(2)	Work-In-Process Inventory	94,500	
	Raw Materials Inventory		94,500
	To record cost of raw materials transferred to work-in-process inventory.		
(3)	Work-In-Process Inventory	157,500	
	Cash or Salaries Payable		157,500
	To record salaries of factory workers.		
(4)	Work-In-Process Inventory	75,600	
	Accumulated Depreciation		75,600
	To record depreciation on factory building.		
(5)	Finished Goods Inventory	283,500	
	Work-In-Process Inventory		283,500
	To record cost of completed units transferred to finished goods storeroom.		
(6)	Cost of Goods Sold	252,000	
	Finished Goods Inventory		252,000
	To record cost of goods sold.		

2.
   a. $400,000
   b. $404,000
   c. $ 2,500
   d. $ 3,500
   e.   -0-
   f. $ 47,500
   g. $100,000
   h. $ 15,000
   i. $ 37,500
   j. $130,000

3.

   a. Sales Revenue $16,500
      Less Replacement Cost of Goods Sold   9,600
      Operating Margin on Sales $ 6,900

   b. Replacement Cost of Goods Sold $ 9,600
      Less Acquisition Cost of Goods Sold   9,000
      Realized Holding Gain $ 600

   c. Sales Revenue $16,500
      Less Acquisition Cost of Goods Sold   9,000
      Conventionally Reported Gross Margin $ 7,500
        (Sum of a. + b. above)

   d. Replacement Cost of Ending Inventory $21,000
      Less Acquisition Cost of Ending Inventory   16,200
      Unrealized Holding Gain $ 4,800

4.

a. 1.

			Available	Issued
June 1 Beginning			3,000	
June 5				750
June 8			1,500	
June 12			450	
June 15				600
June 20				1,200
June 25				750
June 30			750	
Total Available Units			5,700	3,300
Issued Units			3,300	
Units in Ending Inventory			2,400	

	Units	Unit Cost	Total
	750	$10	$ 7,500
	450	9	4,050
	1,200	8	9,600
FIFO Ending Inventory	2,400		$21,150

2.	Units	Unit Cost	Total
LIFO Ending Inventory	2,400	$ 6	$14,400

3.	Units	Unit Cost		Total
	3,000	$ 6	=	$18,000
	1,500	8	=	12,000
	450	9	=	4,050
	750	10	=	7,500
	5,700			$41,550

$41,550/5,700 = $7.29*/unit

Weighted-Average
 Ending Inventory 2,400 @ $7.29   = $17,496
*Rounded to the nearest cent.

b. 1.

	Units Sold	Unit Cost	Total
	3,000	$6	$18,000
	300	8	2,400
FIFO Cost of Goods Sold	3,300		$20,400

2.			
	750	$10	$ 7,500
	450	9	4,050
	1,500	8	12,000
	600	6	3,600
LIFO Cost of Goods Sold	3,300		$27,150

154

5.

a.

	Units	Unit Costs	Total Cost FIFO	Total Cost LIFO
Beginning Inventory May 1				
Purchases, May 3	50	$5.00	$ 250	$ 250
Purchases, May 23	75	6.00	450	450
Total Good Available for Sale	125		$ 700	$ 700
May Withdrawals	100		550a	575c
Ending Inventory, May 31, and Beginning Inventory June 1	25		$ 150b	$ 125d
Purchases, June 15	100	6.50	650	650
Purchases, June 19	150	7.00	1050	1050
Total Goods Available for Sale	275		$1850	$1825
June Withdrawals	225		1500e	1538g
Ending Inventory, June 30, Beginning Inventory, July 1	50		$ 350f	$ 287h
Purchases, July 3	225	8.00	1800	1800
Total Goods Available for Sale	275		$2150	$2087
July Withdrawals	245		1910i	1930k
Ending Inventory, July 31	30		$ 240j	$ 157l

a. (50 @ $5.00) + (50 @ $6.00) = $550

b. 25 x $6.00 = $150

c. (75 @ $6.00) + (25 @ $5.00) = $575

d. 25 x $5.00 = $125

e. (25 @ $6.00) + (100 @ $6.50) + (100 @ $7.00) = $1500

f. 50 @ $7.00 = $350

g. (150 @ $7.00) + (75 @ $6.50) = $1,538 (rounded)

h. (25 @ $5.00) + (25 @ $6.50) = $287 (rounded)

i. (50 @ $7.00) + (195 @ $8.00) = $1,910

j. 30 @ $8.00 = $240

k. (225 @ $8.00) + (20 @ $6.50) = $1930

l. (25 @ $5.00) + (5 @ $6.50) = $157 (rounded)

b. 1. Current Ratio = $\dfrac{\text{Current Assets}}{\text{Current Liabilities}}$

June 30	FIFO	LIFO
($650 + $350)/$715	1.40	
($650 + $287)/$715		1.31

July 31	FIFO	LIFO
($730 + $240)/$712	1.36	
($730 + $157)/$712		1.25

b. 2. Inventory Turnover Ratio = $\dfrac{\text{Cost of Goods Sold}}{\text{Average Inventory}}$

June	FIFO	LIFO
$1,500/.5($150 + $350)	6.00	
$1,538/.5($125 + $287)		7.47

July	FIFO	LIFO
$1,910/.5($350 + $240)	6.47	
$1,930/.5($287 + $157)		8.69

c. The current ratio computed for LIFO in b-1 may lead the user to underestimate the short-term liquifidity of Brian Company because the amount of inventory included in the numerator (Current Assets) is smaller than it would be if Brian valued inventory using FIFO.

The inventory turnover ratio under LIFO in b-2 is misleading because it uses relatively current cost in the numerator (Cost of Goods Sold) and the older cost of LIFO layers in the denominator (Average Inventory). The inventory turnover ratio under FIFO is a better measure of actual turnover of inventory because it uses relatively current cost data in both the numerator and the denominator.

6. a. Cost of Goods Sold computed on a LIFO cost flow:

1,150 units @ $10.00 each	$11,500
90 units @ $ 9.30 each	837
140 units @ $ 8.25 each	1,155
120 units @ $ 6.00 each	720
1,500	14,212

b. 12/31/2005 inventory computed on a LIFO cost flow:

180 units @ $6.00	$ 1,080

c. 1. Cost of Goods Sold computed on a LIFO cost flow:

1,500 units @ $10 each	$15,000

2. 12/31/2005 inventory computed on a LIFO cost flow:

300 units from 2002 @ $ 6.00 each	$1,800
140 units from 2003 @ $ 8.25 each	1,155
90 units from 2004 @ $ 9.30 each	837
20 units from 2005 @ $10.00 each	200
550 units	$3,992

d. In part (a), it was assumed that units sold (1,500) exceeded units purchased (1,150) during 2005. As a result, the company dipped into its LIFO layers for the difference (350 units). Since inventory costs have been increasing (and therefore the earlier costs are lower), the company reports a lower Cost of Goods Sold and a correspondingly higher Gross Margin than it would have reported if the units purchased had exceeded the units sold in 2005 and the company had not dipped into its LIFO layers (the assumption in part c-1).

e.

	(1) Assumption: 1,150 units purchased @ $10 ea.		(2) Assumption: 1,520 units purchased at $10 ea.	
Sales (1500 x $17)		$25,500		$25,500
Cost of Goods Sold:				
Beginning Inventory	$ 3,792		$ 3,792	
Purchases	11,500		15,200	
Goods Available	$15,292		$18,992	
Ending Inventory	1,080*		3,992**	
Cost of Goods Sold		14,212		15,000
Gross Margin		$11,288		$10,500

*   part b
** part c-2

f. Trey's earnings in 2005 will be higher by $788 because its Cost of Goods Sold of $14,212 in 2005 is less than what it would have been ($15,000) if Trey had not dipped into its LIFO layers. Since the company reported higher earnings, its income taxes would be higher. In effect, taxes that were deferred in previous years when units purchased exceeded units sold (and inventory quantities increased) now become due and must be paid.

g. The SEC requires firms using LIFO to disclose the amounts by which inventories based on FIFO or current cost exceed their amounts as reported on a LIFO basis. In part, Trey would report in the notes to its 2005 financial statements:

"If inventories had been valued at current cost, they would have been $720* higher than reported at year end and $1,137** higher than reported at the beginning of the year."

*[$10-$6] X 180 = $720 or [$10 X 180] - $1,080 = $720

**[$9.30 X 530] - $3,792 = $1,137

Chapter 8

Long-Lived Tangible and Intangible Assets:
The Source of Operating Capacity

Chapter Highlights

1. Long-lived tangible assets, sometimes labeled plant assets, or fixed assets, are assets with benefits beyond the current year used in operations of trading, service, and manufacturing enterprises and include land, buildings, machinery, and equipment.

2. The cost of a plant asset includes all charges necessary to prepare it for rendering services. For an asset such as equipment, the total cost would include the invoice price (less any discount), transportation costs, installation charges, and any other costs before the equipment is ready for use.

3. When a firm constructs its own building or equipment, the asset's costs include the costs of material, labor, and overhead during construction. In addition FASB Statement No. 34 requires the firm to capitalize interest paid during construction. The amount capitalized is the portion of interest cost incurred during the asset's construction periods that theoretically could have been avoided if the asset had not been constructed.

4. If there are specific borrowings in connection with a self-constructed asset, the interest rate on that borrowing is used. If expenditures on plant exceed the specific borrowing, the interest rate to be applied to the excess is a weighted average of rates applicable to other borrowings of the enterprise. The total amount of interest to be capitalized cannot exceed the total interest costs for the period.

5. The cost of an asset with a limited life is the price paid for a series of future benefits--a purchase of so many hours or units of service. The plant asset accounts, other than land, are therefore similar in many respects to prepaid rent or insurance--payments in advance for benefits to be received in the future. As the firm uses assets in each period, it treats a portion of the investment in the assets as a cost of the benefits received.

6. Depreciation refers to periodic write-off of the acquisition cost of tangible long-lived assets (other than land). Amortization refers to the process of writing off the cost of all intangible assets.

7. The determination of the amount of depreciation for any year is not an exact process, since the cost of the plant asset is a joint cost of several periods. Each period of the asset's use benefits from the services, but there is usually no single correct way to allocate a joint cost. Depreciation accounting attempts to assign reasonable periodic charges that reflect systematic calculations.

8. Basing depreciation on acquisition costs will enable a business to expense an amount equal to its initial cash investment. Because prices of the services generally increase over time depreciation will not necessarily provide an expense equal to the cost of replacing the physical productive capacity initially purchased with the cash.

9. Depreciation is frequently characterized as a decline in the market value of assets. While there is certainly a decline in value of an asset from the time it is acquired until it is retired from service, the yearly decline in value is an unsatisfactory description of the charge for depreciation made to the operations of each accounting period. Depreciation is a process of cost allocation and not one of valuation.

10. There are three principal accounting issues in allocating the cost of an asset over time. They are: (a) measuring the depreciable or amortizable basis of the asset; (b) estimating its useful service life; and (c) deciding on the pattern of expiration of asset cost over the useful service life.

11. Historical cost accounting bases depreciation and amortization charges on the difference between acquisition cost and the asset's estimated salvage value (or net residual value). Salvage value represents the estimated proceeds on disposition of an asset less all removal and selling costs.

12. The causes of the process requiring depreciation are the same causes of decline in service potential. The decline results from either physical or functional causes. Physical factors include the normal wear and tear, decay, and deterioration from use. The most important functional cause is obsolescence. Identification of specific causes of depreciation can help when estimating the useful life of an asset. The estimate of service life must take into consideration both the physical and functional causes of depreciation. Past experience with similar assets, corrected for differences in the planned intensity of use or alterations in maintenance policy, is usually the best guide for the estimate.

13. Income tax laws allow shorter lives to be used in computing depreciation for tax reporting. For income tax reporting, firms generally use the Modified Accelerated Cost Recovery System (MACRS). MACRS specifies accelerated depreciation charges based on the class of asset. Under MACRS, almost all assets are grouped in one of seven classes of write-off periods. They are:
    (a) 3 years   -- Some racehorses; almost no others.
    (b) 5 years   -- Computers, cars, trucks, some manufacturing equipment, research and development property.
    (c) 7 years   -- Office equipment, railroad cars, locomotives.
    (d) 10 years -- Vessels, barges, land improvements.
    (e) 20 years -- Municipal sewers.
    (f) 27.5 years -- Residential rental property.
    (g) 39 years -- Nonresidential buildings acquired after 1993; otherwise 31.5 years.

160

14. However, when these lives are shorter than the economic service lives of the assets, the estimated service lives must be used for financial reporting.

15. There are five basic patterns for the allocation of the total depreciation and amortization charges to specific years when the allocation is based on the passage of time. They are:
    (a) Straight-line method;
    (b) Accelerated method;
    (c) Decelerated method;

    Accelerated and decelerated are terms describing depreciation patterns in comparison with straight-line depreciation. Decelerated depreciation is not allowed for generally accepted accounting principles. No depreciation is taken on land since it has unlimited life. Amortization of intangible assets follows the straight-line method in usual practice.

16. The GAAP acceptable depreciation methods to be discussed are:
    (a) Straight-line (time) method;
    (b) Production or use (straight-line use) method;
    (c) Accelerated depreciation methods:
        (1) Declining-balance methods;
        (2) Sum-of-the-years'-digits method; and
        (3) Modified Accelerated Cost Recovery System (MACRS).

17. Financial reporting most commonly uses the straight-line method, which provides a uniform pattern of depreciation per year. The annual depreciation is determined in the following manner:

$$\text{Annual Depreciation} = \frac{\text{Cost Less Estimated Salvage Value.}}{\text{Estimated Life in Years}}$$

18. Many assets are not used uniformly over time, as straight-line depreciation implies. Where assets are not likely to receive the same amount of use in each month or year of their lives, the straight-line method may result in an illogical charge for such assets. Instead, a depreciation charge based on actual usage during the period may be justified. The production method uses a uniform cost per unit of activity that is multiplied by the units of production for the period. The depreciation cost per unit of activity is:

$$\text{Depreciation Cost Per Unit} = \frac{\text{Cost Less Estimated Salvage Value.}}{\text{Estimated Number of Units}}$$

19. The efficiency and earning power of many plant assets decline as the assets grow older. These assets provide more and better services in early years, with increasing amounts of maintenance as the assets grow older. These cases justify an accelerated method in which depreciation charges in early years are greater than in later years. Declining balance, sum-of-the-years'-digits, and MACRS are three types of accelerated methods.

20. In the declining-balance method, the depreciation charge results from multiplying the net book value of the asset at the start of each period (cost less accumulated depreciation) by a fixed rate. The depreciation charge is then subtracted from the net book value in determining the depreciation base for the subsequent year. The salvage is not subtracted from the cost in making this depreciation calculation. However, the total depreciation taken over an asset's useful life cannot exceed the asset's cost less salvage value. Firms sometimes use the 200-percent declining-balance method, in which the rate multiplied times the net book value is 200 percent of the straight-line rate. Under declining-balance methods, the firm switches to straight-line depreciation of the remaining book value when the straight-line depreciation charge is higher than the declining-balance charge for depreciation.

21. Another accelerated method is sum-of-the-years' digits. Under this method, the depreciation charge results from applying a fraction, which diminishes from year to year, to the cost less salvage value of the asset. The numerator of the fraction is the number of periods of remaining life at the beginning of the year for which depreciation is being computed. Thus, the numerators for years 1-5 of an asset with a 5-year life would be 5, 4, 3, 2, 1, respectively. The denominator of the fraction, which remains the same for each year, is the sum of all such numbers. For an asset with a 5-year life, the denominator would be 15 (=1 + 2 + 3 + 4 + 5). The formula n(n+1)/2, where n is the asset's depreciable life, is useful in determining the sum-of-the year's digits denominator.

22. MACRS, used for tax purposes, is an accelerated method for three reasons. First, the depreciable lives specified by class of asset are generally shorter than the economic lives. Second, the rates employed for assets other than buildings are similar to the 150-percent and 200-percent declining-balance method which are more rapid than straight-line. Third, MACRS allows salvage to be ignored in calculating depreciation, therefore the entire depreciable basis can be written off. Firms rarely judge MACRS appropriate for financial reporting.

23. The goal in depreciation accounting for tax purposes should be to maximize the present value of the reductions in tax payments from deducting depreciation. Earlier deductions are worth more than later ones (if tax rates do not change) because a dollar saved today is worth more than a dollar saved later. For tax purposes, the asset should be written off as soon as possible. Use of MACRS will accomplish this purpose.

24. The goal in financial reporting for long-lived assets is to provide a statement of income that is realistic in measuring the expiration of these assets. In order to accomplish this purpose, the depreciation reported and the method selected should report depreciation charges based upon reasonable estimates of asset expirations. Most U.S. firms use the straight-line method for financial reporting.

25. The journal entry to record depreciation involves a debit either to Retained Earning (Depreciation or Administration Expense) (Shareholders' Equity Decrease), or, in the case of a manufacturer, to a product cost account and a credit to a contra asset account, Accumulated Depreciation (asset decrease). The Accumulated Depreciation account is shown on the balance sheet as a deduction from the asset account to which it relates. The term book value refers to the difference between the balance of the asset account and the balance of its accumulated depreciation account.

26. The original depreciation schedule for a particular asset may require changing due to previously incorrect estimates of the asset's useful life or salvage value. If the misestimate is material, corrective action must be taken. The generally accepted procedure for handling this problem is to make no adjusting entry for the past misestimate but to spread the undepreciated balance less the revised estimate of the salvage value over the revised estimate of the remaining service life of the asset.

27. Depreciation is not the only cost of using a depreciating asset. There will almost always be some repair and maintenance costs incurred during the life of the asset. Repairs include the costs of restoring an asset's service potential after breakdowns or other damage. Maintenance includes routine costs such as cleaning and adjusting. Repair and maintenance costs are charged to expense as costs are incurred.

28. Improvements involve making an asset subsequently better by improving its productive capacity. Whereas repairs maintain or restore service potential, improvements extend service beyond what was originally anticipated. Expenditures for improvements are sometimes called betterments. Accountants treat costs of improvements as an asset acquisition.

29. Firms incur research and development costs to develop a new product or process, to improve present products or processes, or to develop new information that may be useful at some future date. Whatever the reason, nearly all research costs will yield their benefits, if any, in future periods. The accounting issue, therefore, is whether to expense these costs immediately when incurred, or to capitalize them and amortize them over future periods. Theoretically, the research costs should be matched with the benefits produced by their expenditure through the capitalization procedure with amortization over the benefited periods. Generally accepted accounting principles, however, require immediate expensing in all cases because of the uncertainty of future benefits and conservatism.

30. A patent is a right obtained from the federal government to exclude others from the use of the benefits of an invention. A firm amortizes purchased patent costs over the shorter of (a) the remaining legal life (as long as 20 years), or (b) the estimated economic life. A firm expenses internally developed patent costs as required for all research and development costs.

31. Intangible assets provide future benefits without having physical form. Examples are research costs, advertising costs, patents, trade secrets, know-how, trademarks, and copyrights. The first problem with intangibles is to decide whether the expenditures have future benefits and should be capitalized and amortized over time or whether they have no measurable future benefits and should be expensed in the period incurred. The second problem is how to amortize the cost if they are capitalized. Amortization of capitalized intangibles usually uses the straight-line method, but other methods can be used if they seem appropriate.

32. Firms incur advertising expenditures to increase sales of the period in which they are made. There is a lag, however, between the incurrence of these costs and their impact, probably extending into subsequent periods. Even though advertising often benefits more than merely the period of expenditure, GAAP requires firms to immediately expense almost all advertising costs.

33. Goodwill is an intangible asset that arises from the purchase of one company by another company and is the difference between the amount paid for the acquired company as a whole and the current value of its individual identifiable net assets. The amount of goodwill acquired is recognized only on the books of the company making the acquisition. Goodwill is not recognized by a company that has internally developed goodwill. Generally taxpayers cannot deduct goodwill amortization on their tax returns.

34. The expected future benefits of an asset change, sometimes increasing and sometimes decreasing. GAAP do no permit firms to write up the book value of their tangible and intangible le long-lived assets when market values increase. GAAP on the other hand do not allow assets whose values have declined substantially to remain on the balance sheet at amortized acquisition cost. GAAP distinguishes three categories of assets for purposes of measuring and recognizing impairment losses:
   a. All assets except intangibles that do not require amortization.
   b. Intangibles other than goodwill that do not require amortization.
   c. Goodwill.

35. The test for an impairment loss on all assets except intangibles that do not require amortization (a. above) compares the undiscounted cash flows from the assets with their book values. Asset impairment occurs when the current book value exceeds the sum of remaining expected undiscounted cash flows. Accounting requires a firm to write down the book value of an impaired asset to its then-current fair value (market value) or, if the firm cannot assess the market value, the expected net present value of the future cash flows. The test for impairment loss of intangibles that do not require amortization other than goodwill (b. above) compares the book values of the assets to their market value. The loss is the excess of the book values over their market values. Firms are not required to amortize goodwill in measuring net income each period. However, firms must test annually for impairment in the value of goodwill and write down goodwill and recognize an impairment loss should one occur.

164

36. When an asset is retired, an entry should be made to bring depreciation up to date. Then the cost of the asset and its related accumulated depreciation must be removed from the books. The difference between the proceeds received on retirement and the book value (cost less accumulated depreciation) is either a gain (Shareholders' equity increase) or a loss (Shareholders' equity decrease).

37. Instead of selling an asset, a firm may trade it in on a new one. The trade-in transaction can be viewed as a sale of an old asset followed by the purchase of a new asset. The accounting for trade-in transactions determine simultaneously the gain or loss (Shareholders' equity increase or decrease) on disposal of the old asset and the acquisition costs recorded for the new asset.

38. Property, plant, and equipment accounts appear in the balance sheet among the noncurrent assets. Firms generally disclose the assets' cost and accumulated depreciation in one of three ways: (a) the balance sheet contains the original cost less accumulated depreciation; (b) the balance sheet omits the original costs, presenting the accumulated depreciation and book value; and (c) the balance sheet omits the original cost and accumulated depreciation, presenting only the book value (details appear in notes).

39. Depreciation expense appears in the income statement, sometimes disclosed separately and sometimes, particularly for manufacturing firms, as part of cost of goods sold expense.

40. In most developed countries accounting for plant assets, depreciation, and intangible assets parallels that in the United States. In Great Britain firms now place a valuation on their brand names and include this item among the assets on the balance sheet. Independent appraisers might base their brand names valuation on premium prices charged customers for a branded over a nonbranded product, or the promotion and other costs likely to be incurred in launching a new branded product, or on the price paid in recent mergers and acquisitions for branded product firms.

41. The statement of cash flows reports the cash used for acquisition of plant and intangible assets and cash provided by their retirement among the investing activities. The investing section of the statement shows all the proceeds from the sale of plant and intangible assets. On the statement of cash flows using the indirect approach the net income is the starting point in computing cash flow from operations. If plant or intangible assets are sold for an amount different from their book value then a gain or loss results. Since this sale is nonoperating any loss is added back and any gain is deducted from net income in deriving operating cash flows. The statement shows adjustments for depreciation and amortization in deriving cash from operations. Depreciation and amortization are added back to net income in deriving cash from operations. Acquisition of plant and intangible assets by obtaining new financing is presented as an investing activity and a financing activity on the statement of cash flows. Acquisitions by bartering (not involving cash exchange) for financing with the seller are disclosed in a supplemental schedule or note.

Questions and Exercises

True/False. For each of the following statements, place a T or F in the space provided to indicate whether the statement is true or false.

_____ 1. Declines in the service potential of an asset are due to both physical and functional factors.

_____ 2. Amortization of intangible assets is called depletion.

_____ 3. The book value of an asset is the difference between the balance of the asset account and its salvage value.

_____ 4. Accumulated depreciation is a contra asset account used to house the total amount written off through depreciation.

_____ 5. An asset impairment occurs when the current book value of the asset exceeds the sum of the asset's expected undiscounted cash flows.

_____ 6. When the proceeds from the sale of an asset exceed the net book value, there is a gain (Shareholders' Equity Increase) on the sale.

_____ 7. The cost of testing a newly acquired piece of equipment, prior to initial use, should be expensed.

_____ 8. The depreciation method most commonly used for financial statement purposes is the straight-line method.

_____ 9. When the rate of usage of an asset varies from period to period, a depreciation charge based upon actual usage during the period may be justified.

_____ 10. Expenditures made to repair an asset should be capitalized.

_____ 11. The amount of expenses in any one year is the same whether interest during construction is capitalized or not.

_____ 12. Identifying the specific cause of depreciation is not essential for measuring it.

_____ 13. Salvage value can never be negative.

_____ 14. Interest costs incurred during construction of a plant asset should be capitalized.

_____ 15. When one company purchases another company, the acquiring firm must immediately write off the newly recorded value of R&D assets unless those R&D assets have already provided commercially feasible results.

_____ 16. Property, plant, and equipment accounts appear in the balance sheet among the financing items.

_____ 17. When the efficiency and earning power of assets decline as the assets grow older, it may be appropriate to employ an accelerated depreciation method.

_____ 18. Firms expense all research and development costs when incurred for financial accounting purposes.

_____ 19. The usual entry to record depreciation on a building is to debit Depreciation Expense and credit Building.

_____ 20. Expenditures made on an asset to maintain the service level anticipated should be expensed when incurred, but costs to improve an asset should be capitalized.

_____ 21. The main purpose underlying depreciation accounting is to record the decline in market values of assets over their useful life.

_____ 22. Since the investment in a depreciable asset is the price paid for a series of future benefits, the asset is similar in many respects to prepayments for rent or insurance.

_____ 23. Theoretically, research and development costs should probably be capitalized and amortized over future periods.

_____ 24. The sum-of-the-years' digits depreciation method applies a constant rate per year times the declining book value of the asset.

_____ 25. Since the cost of a plant asset is a joint cost of many benefitted periods, there is no single correct way to determine the amount of periodic depreciation charge.

_____ 26. The 150-percent declining-balance method is one of several decelerated methods.

_____ 27. Since 1981, firms generally use MACRS method of depreciation for financial reporting.

_____ 28. Intangible assets lack physical substance.

_____ 29. When calculating depreciation for tax reporting, salvage is ignored.

_____ 30. A major difficulty in MACRS depreciation is determining the useful life of the asset.

_____ 31. The production method is a type of straight-line method.

_____ 32. The recognition of goodwill when one company acquires another should be made on the books of the company that developed the goodwill.

_____ 33. Patent costs must be amortized over the legal life of the patent--20 years.

_____ 34. When a depreciable asset is disposed of, an entry should be made to bring depreciation up to date before making the entry to remove the asset from the books.

_____ 35. When the estimated useful life of an asset is revised, it is necessary to correct the books for misstated depreciation in previous years.

_____ 36. When one company purchases another company, the acquiring firm accounts for newly recorded R&D assets similarly to Goodwill recorded in the same acquisition.

_____ 37. In the depreciation calculation, the task of estimating service lives is no problem due to the abundant data from experience.

_____ 38. If the current value of a depreciable asset rises instead of falls over a year, the income statement would report an appreciation gain rather then depreciation expense.

_____ 39. The term, accelerated depreciation method, implies that the amount of depreciation per year decreases as the asset becomes older.

_____ 40. A firm is not required to use the same method of depreciation for financial accounting and income tax purposes.

_____ 41. The goal of a firm when choosing a depreciation method for tax purposes should be to maximize the present value of the tax savings attributable to the depreciation charge.

_____ 42. Depreciation can be recorded as a product cost or an expense.

_____ 43. The goal for computing depreciation is the same for tax purposes and financial accounting even though different methods may be used.

_____ 44. Common practice is to expense advertising costs even though the benefits extend beyond the period of expenditure.

_____ 45. The useful life of an asset for computing depreciation should be the total number of years for which the asset is physically capable of performing.

_____ 46. When an asset impairment occurs accounting requires the firm to write down the book value of the asset to zero.

Matching. From the following list of terms, select that term which is most closely associated with each of the descriptive phrases or statements that follows and place the letter for that term in the space provided.

a. Accelerated Methods
b. Accumulated Depreciation
c. Advertising
d. Amortization
e. Book Value
f. Building Under Construction
g. Cost Allocation
h. Depreciation
i. Expense
j. Goal of Depreciation Accounting for Financial Statement Purposes
k. Goodwill

l. Impairment
m. Improvements
n. Intangible Assets
o. Modified Accelerated Cost Recovery System
p. n(n+1)/2
q. Obsolescence
r. Repairs
s. Salvage Value
t. Trade-In Allowance
u. Self-Constructed Assets
v. Work-in-Process Inventory

_____ 1. Occurs when the then-current book value exceeds the sum of expected undiscounted cash flow.

_____ 2. An intangible that appears on the balance sheet only when one company is acquired by another.

_____ 3. Accountants use the term to refer to the periodic write-off of intangible assets.

_____ 4. Cost less accumulated depreciation.

_____ 5. Proper accounting for all research and development costs when incurred.

_____ 6. Assets that can provide future benefits without having physical form.

_____ 7. Groups assets into one of seven classes for tax depreciation.

_____ 8. Account debited if depreciation is a production cost.

_____ 9. Interest is capitalized for these items.

_____ 10. Depreciation is not a decline in value; it is a process of __?__ .

_____ 11. Small adjustments and replacement to plant assets with little or no effect on useful life.

_____ 12. Proceeds upon disposition of an asset at the end of its useful life.

_____ 13. Matching of costs with the benefits derived from the use of an asset.

_____ 14. A cost normally expensed when incurred even though future benefits exist.

_____ 15. A functional factor in determining depreciation.

_____ 16. Sum-of-the-years'-digits is an example of one.

_____ 17. The account credited for depreciation.

_____ 18. Denominator of the sum-of-the-years'-digits fraction.

Multiple Choice. Choose the best answer for each of the following questions and enter the identifying letter in the space provided.

_____ 1. An asset impairment occurs when the then-current book value of an asset exceeds

    a. The sum of expected undiscounted cash flows of the asset.
    b. The market value of the asset.
    c. The discounted future cash flows of the asset.
    d. None of the above.

_____ 2. The generally accepted procedure for corrective action for material misestimates involving depreciation is

    a. To spread the remaining undepreciated balance less the new estimate of salvage value over the new estimate of remaining service life of the asset.
    b. To make an adjustment for the past misestimate.
    c. Either (a) or (b).
    d. Neither (a) or (b).

_____ 3. The text describes five basic patterns for cost allocations of fixed assets. They are:
        E - Expense immediately.
        S - Straight-Line depreciation/amortization.
        A - Accelerated depreciation/amortization.
        D - Decelerated depreciation/amortization.
        N - No depreciation/amortization.

    Which basic pattern would be appropriate for land?

    a. E.
    b. S.
    c. D.
    d. N.

_____ 4. Referring to the question above, which pattern would be appropriate for most intangibles?

    a.   E.
    b.   S.
    c.   A.
    d.   N.

_____ 5. When an asset impairment occurs a firm writes down the asset to

    a.   The sum of its undiscounted cash flows.
    b.   Its then-current fair value.
    c.   Zero.
    d.   None of the above.

_____ 6. In the statement of cash flows using the indirect method, the following would be added to net income in deriving operating cash flows

    a.   Amortization.
    b.   Depreciation.
    c.   Loss on retirement of a plant asset.
    d.   All of the above.

_____ 7. Which of the costs listed below would not be included in the cost of the machinery?

    a.   Invoice price.
    b.   Installation costs.
    c.   Testing of machinery prior to its intended use.
    d.   All of the above would be included.

_____ 8. Grouping assets into one of seven life classes is a characteristic of which of the following

    a.   Sum-of-the-Years' digits method.
    b.   Modified Accelerated Cost Recovery System.
    c.   Declining-balance method.
    d.   None of the above.

_____ 9. Which of the factors listed below is an example of a functional cause of depreciation?

    a.   Wear and tear.
    b.   Inadequate size to meet current needs of the company.
    c.   Rust or decay.
    d.   Deterioration from wind and rain.

_____ 10. In the statement of cash flows using the indirect method, the following would be deducted from net income in deriving operating cash flows

    a.   Gain on retirement of a plant asset.
    b.   Depreciation.
    c.   Loss on retirement of a plant asset.
    d.   None of the above.

_____ 11. The Siegfried Co. owns machinery having a cost of $100,000 and accumulated depreciation of $60,000 on January 1, 2005. On July 1, 2005, the machinery is sold for $43,000. The straight-line depreciation method has been used during the previous six years of life. How much gain or loss will be recorded on the sale?

   a. $ 3,000 gain.
   b. $13,000 gain.
   c. $22,000 loss.
   d. $ 8,000 gain.

_____ 12. All else equal, analysts

   a.   Prefer that firms have high recurring earnings.
   b.   Will give a higher valuation to a firm with a one-time charge than a firm that reports an expense that continues year to year.
   c.   Regard recurring earnings as higher quality than one-shot earnings.
   d.   All of the above.

_____ 13. Nancy Co. acquired a machine for $20,000 in 2004 and has depreciated it on the straight-line basis (no salvage value) for 2 years based upon an estimated 10-year life. In 2006 it was determined that the remaining life was only 4 years instead of 8. What amount of depreciation should be recorded for 2006, based upon generally accepted accounting principles?

   a. $5,000.
   b. $4,000.
   c. $3,333.
   d. $2,000.

_____ 14. Which cost below is capitalized for a self-constructed asset?

   a.   Interest prior to construction.
   b.   Interest during construction.
   c.   Interest after construction.
   d.   All of the above.

_____ 15. For which method below may salvage be ignored in calculating depreciation?

   a.   Straight-line.
   b.   Sum-of-the-years'-digits.
   c.   Production method.
   d.   MACRS.

_____ 16. For which depreciation method below is the estimate of useful life not required?

   a.   Straight-line.
   b.   Sum-of-the-years'-digits.
   c.   200-percent declining-balance.
   d.   MACRS.

_____ 17. Tiny Tim Co. purchased a machine that cost $20,000 and has a $2,000 salvage value and a 5-year life. The depreciation charge for the first year under the sum-of-the-years'-digits method should be

    a. $1,200.
    b. $6,000.
    c. $6,667.
    d. $8,000.

_____ 18. Anna Co. buys a building on April 1, 2005, for $100,000. The building has a physical life of 50 years, but Anna anticipates using the building for 30 years. At the end of 50 years, the building will have no disposal value, but it will have a disposal value of $5,000 in 30 years. How much depreciation would be recorded on December 31, 2005, if the straight-line method is used?

    a. $3,167.
    b. $2,000.
    c. $1,500.
    d. $2,375.

_____ 19. The Allison Company on January 1, 2006, has machinery on the books that originally cost $200,000. During 2006, the following expenditures were made:

Minor Repairs	$ 5,000
Improvements	10,000
Additions	37,000

How much would be recorded in the machinery account on December 31, 2006?

    a. $252,000.
    b. $247,000.
    c. $235,000.
    d. $225,000.

_____ 20. Shamaine Co. purchases a piece of equipment on January 1, 2005, at a cost of $100,000. The equipment has a 5-year useful life and can be sold for $10,000 at the end of five years. How much depreciation would be recorded in the second year if Shamaine Co. uses the 200-percent declining-balance depreciation method.

    a. $12,000.
    b. $20,000.
    c. $15,900.
    d.   None of the above.

_____ 21. Michelle Co. has spent $250,000 on research and development during 2005 to generate new product lines. Of the five projects being worked on, one resulted in a patented item while the other four were considered unsuccessful. According to GAAP, how much of the $250,000 should be recognized as an expense in 2005?

    a. $250,000.
    b. $ -0-.
    c. $200,000.
    d. $ 50,000.

_____ 22. When the MACRS method of depreciation is employed, which life would be used for automobiles?

    a.   3 years.
    b.   5 years.
    c.   10 years.
    d.   15 years.

_____ 23. Which statement is not true concerning MACRS depreciation?

    a.   It is an accelerated method.
    b.   It is used for tax reporting.
    c.   Salvage cannot be ignored.
    d.   It assumes that all purchases take place at midyear.

_____ 24. When the rate of usage for an asset varies greatly from period to period, the depreciation method that would best match the cost with expected benefits would be which of the following?

    a.   Straight-line method.
    b.   Production method.
    c.   Declining-balance method.
    d.   Sum-of-the-years'-digits method.

_____ 25. Volley Co. reports its net assets at a book value of $150,000. Recent investigation revealed that the net assets had a market value of $175,000. In addition, Volley had been offered $220,000 for the company by Conglomerate Corp. What is the amount of goodwill that should be recorded on the books of Volley?

    a. $ -0-.
    b. $25,000.
    c. $45,000.
    d. $70,000.

_____ 26. Firms generally disclose in the balance sheet property, plant, and equipment, and related accumulated depreciation by displaying:

    a.   The original cost less accumulated depreciation.
    b.   The accumulated depreciation and the book value.
    c.   The book value and by providing the detail of cost and accumulated depreciation in the notes.
    d.   All of the above are used.

_____ 27. In the statement of cash flows using the indirect method, the following would be included in the cash flows from investing activities

a. Proceeds from the retirement of plant assets.
b. Amortization.
c. Depreciation.
d. Net Income.

_____ 28. Which term below is used when referring to the write-off of intangible assets?

a. Amortization.
b. Depreciation.
c. Depletion.
d. Write-off.

_____ 29. In selecting the best depreciation method for tax purposes, which statement below would not be correct?
a. The goal should be to maximize the present value of the tax savings from the depreciation deductions.
b. The asset should be written off as soon as possible
c. Earlier depreciation deductions are more valuable than later ones.
d. A decelerated depreciation method should be employed.

Exercises

1. The Williams Corp. purchased some equipment on April 1, 2007, for $78,000. The freight costs were $1,500. Upon receipt, the following expenditures were incurred:

Major repair prior to use	$ 2,300
Rearrangement of other machinery to accommodate new machine	2,000
Rewiring for new machine	500
Installation	650
Testing prior to productive use	
Labor	500
Materials	200
Operating costs after start of productive operations	29,000
Minor repair during operational period	820
Depreciation in first year of use	1,500

Determine the costs that should be assigned to the equipment account. Include how any items excluded from this account would be properly handled.

2. The Lois Company has the following relevant debt and equity structure:

Long-term debt, at 13%	$5,000,000
Capital Stock	6,000,000
Retained Earnings	2,500,000

Lois is constructing a building for its own productive use, which is being financed with long-term debt. During the year the average balance in the construction accounts was $6,000,000. A construction loan for $4,000,000 was taken out at the beginning of the year, requiring the payment of interest at 14 percent.

Determine the amount of interest to be capitalized for the year.

3. Elizabeth Corp. owns an apartment building which cost $40 million and at the end of the current period has accumulated depreciation of $16 million, with net book value of $24 (= $40 - $16) million. Elizabeth Corp. had originally expected to collect $64 million over 30 years of expected rentals before selling the building for $16 million. Economic circumstances caused Elizabeth Corp. to re-assess the future rentals. Elizabeth Corp. expects the building to provide rentals for only 15 more years before Elizabeth will sell it. Elizabeth Corp. uses an appropriate discount rate in discounting expected rentals for the building. Determine the asset impairment entry associated with the three independent cases below.

a. Elizabeth Corp. expects annual rentals of $1.6 million per year for 15 years and to sell the building for $8 million after 15 years, which, discounted at an appropriate discount rate has a present value of $16.3 million. The building has market value of $16 million.

b. Elizabeth Corp. expects annual rentals of $800 thousand per year for 15 years and to sell the building for $8 million after 15 years, which, discounted at an appropriate discount rate per year, has a present value of $13.6 million. The building has market value of $8 million.

c. As in the preceding case, Elizabeth Corp. expects annual rentals of $800 thousand per year for 15 years and to sell the building for $8 million after 15 years, which, discounted at an appropriate interest rate, has present value of $13.6 million. Because of new housing code regulation, Elizabeth Corp. cannot readily find a buyer nor even anyone who will quote a market value.

4. Journalize the following transactions. All of the transactions are related to the same machine.

   a. A machine is purchased for $4,000 on account.
   b. Depreciation of $500 for one year is recorded.
   c. The machine is sold for $800 cash. At the time of the sale, the Accumulated Depreciation account shows a balance of $2,500. Depreciation of $500 for the current year (asset is sold at the end of the year) has not been recorded.

5. A truck is purchased for $8,000 and is expected to have a 5-year useful life and a $1,000 salvage value at the end of that time. The truck is further expected to be operable for a total of 1,400 hours during the five years. Calculate the depreciation expense in each of the five years for the following depreciation methods.

   a.   The straight-line method.
   b.   The sum-of-the-years'-digits method.
   c.   The 150-percent declining-balance method.
   d.   The hours of production method, if the production hours in years 1-5 were 240, 280, 360, 320, and 200, respectively.
   e.   The MACRS method (for tax purposes).

6. Prince Company purchased land with a building on it as a site for a new plant it planned to construct. Classify the expenditures listed below into either the Land account, the Plant account, or neither Land nor Plant.

   a.   Cost of building permit.
   b.   Cost of property taxes assumed by Prince accrued to date of purchase of land.
   c.   Proceeds from sale of salvage material from old building.
   d.   Interest incurred to finance construction.
   e.   Property taxes accrued since date of land acquisition.
   f.   Cost of land and old building.
   g.   Legal fees in connection with land purchase.
   h.   Cost of construction of plant by independent contractor.
   i.   Cost of repairing a construction truck damaged in an accident by a careless worker.

7. On July 1, 2005, the Phylis Company purchased a machine for $20,000, having an estimated life of eight years and a salvage value of $2,000.

   In early 2006, a major improvement to the machine took place, costing $2,500. As a result the annual capacity was expanded, but its estimated life remained unchanged.

   During 2007, Phylis revised its estimated useful life to be only three remaining years and its salvage value to be $1,000.

   Calculate the depreciation for 2005, 2006, and 2007 using the straight-line method.

8. Give correcting journal entries for the following situation. Assume each case is independent and the firm uses straight-line depreciation. You are making the correction at year end prior to the company closing its books.
   a.   A piece of store equipment was purchased for $1,000 at the beginning of the year. The equipment had an estimated life of five years, with no salvage value. The bookkeeper made the following entry to record the transaction:

         Retained Earnings (Supplies Expense)....... 1,000
               Cash   1,000

b. A used truck was sold for $4,000. At the time of the sale, the truck's related accumulated depreciation (properly recorded) was $5,000. Its original cost was $8,000. The bookkeeper made the following entry to record the transaction:

```
Cash ................................. 4,000
     Truck .............................       4,000
```

9. On January 1, year 1, Heather Corp. pays cash for Edward Company at the time when Edward Company's assets and liabilities have book and market values as shown below. At the time of the purchase, Edward Company has recorded book values of shareholders' equity of $58,000 and market value of shareholders' equity of $124,000.

Edward Company Purchased by Heather Corp
Book and Market Values of Assets and Liabilities at the Time of Purchase

	Book Values On Edward's Balance Sheet	Market Values at the time of Purchase by Heather
Cash	$ 8,000	$ 8,000
Patent Developed By Edward		25,000
Patent Purchased By Edward	10,000	8,000
R&D in Process		15,000
Other Assets	70,000	100,000
Less:		
Liabilities	(30,000)	(32,000)
Totals	$ 58,000	$ 124,000

a. Indicate the new asset and liability valuations on Heather Corp.'s balance sheet if it pays $124,000 for Edward Company. What assets, if any, will Heather Corp write off after recording these items?

b. Indicate the new assets and liability valuation on Heather Corp.'s balance sheet if it pays $140,000 for Edward Company. What assets, if any, will Heather Corp write off after recording these items?

c. Assume immediately after the acquisition in b. one of Heather's competitors makes an announcement substantially affecting the evaluation of Edwards assets acquired. Assuming all of Edwards' identifiable assets are valued the same as in b except the other assets now have an undiscounted cash flow expectation of $98,000 and a fair market value of $95,000. Also assume the now current fair market value of the entire operations acquired from Edwards is $128,000. What impairment loss if any would Heather recognize?

Answers to Questions and Exercises

True/False

1.	T	11.	F	21.	F	31.	T	41.	T
2.	F	12.	T	22.	T	32.	F	42.	T
3.	F	13.	F	23.	T	33.	F	43.	F
4.	T	14.	T	24.	F	34.	T	44.	T
5.	T	15.	T	25.	T	35.	F	45.	F
6.	T	16.	F	26.	F	36.	F	46.	F
7.	F	17.	T	27.	F	37.	F		
8.	T	18.	T	28.	T	38.	F		
9.	T	19.	F	29.	T	39.	T		
10.	F	20.	T	30.	F	40.	T		

Matching

1.	l	5.	i	9.	u	13.	j	17.	b
2.	k	6.	n	10.	g	14.	c	18.	p
3.	d	7.	o	11.	r	15.	q		
4.	e	8.	v	12.	s	16.	a		

Multiple Choice

1.	a	7.	d	13.	b	19.	b	25.	a
2.	a	8.	b	14.	b	20.	d	26.	d
3.	d	9.	b	15.	d	21.	a	27.	a
4.	b	10.	a	16.	d	22.	b	28.	a
5.	b	11.	d	17.	b	23.	c	29.	d
6.	d	12.	d	18.	d	24.	b		

Exercises

1. The Cost of Equipment:

Purchase price	$78,000
Freight	1,500
Major repair	2,300
Rearrangement of machinery	2,000
Rewiring	500
Installation	650
Testing	700
	$85,650

The operating expenses, minor repair and depreciation, would be in the operating expense section of the 2007 income statement.

2. The interest capitalized for Lois Company is:

.14 x $4,000,000 = $560,000
.13 x 2,000,000 = 260,000
                   $820,000

3. a. No impairment has occurred because the expected undiscounted future cash flows of $32 [= ($1.6 x 15) + $8] million exceed the book value of $24 million. Elizabeth Corp. has experienced an economic loss but will not recognize any loss in its accounts.

    b. An asset impairment has occurred because book value of $24 million exceeds the expected undiscounted future cash flows, $20 [=($800,000 x 15) + $8 million] million. Therefore, Elizabeth Corp. records (with amounts in millions) the impairment by recognizing the loss and recording the market value.

	Dr.	Cr.
Accumulated Depreciation	$16	
Building - Apartment (new valuation)	8	
Retained Earnings (Loss on Impairment)	16	
Building - Apartment (original cost)		40

    c. An asset impairment has occurred because the book value of $24 million exceeds the undiscounted future cash flow, $20 [=($800,000 x 15) + $8 million] million. Where no market value can be determined the net present value of the discounted future cash flow will be to establish the new cost basis of the asset.

	Dr.	Cr.
Accumulated Depreciation	$16	
Building - Apartment (new valuation)	13.6	
Retained Earnings (Loss on Impairment)	10.4	
Building - Apartment (original cost)		40

4.

		Dr.	Cr.
a.	Machinery	4,000	
	Accounts Payable		4,000
	Purchased machine on account.		
b.	Retained Earnings (Depreciation Expense)	500	
	Accumulated Depreciation		500
	To record annual depreciation.		
c.	Depreciation Expense	500	
	Accumulated Depreciation		500
	To record annual depreciation.		
	Cash	800	
	Accumulated Depreciation	3,000	
	Retained Earnings (Loss on Sale of Machine)	200	
	Machinery		4,000
	To record sale of machine.		

5. a. Depreciation per year = $\dfrac{\$8,000 - \$1,000}{5}$ = $1,400

b.

Year	Depreciation Fraction		Cost Less Salvage	Depreciation
1	5/15*	x	$7,000	$2,333
2	4/15	x	7,000	1,867
3	3/15	x	7,000	1,400
4	2/15	x	7,000	933
5	1/15	x	7,000	467
				$7,000

*(1 + 2 + 3 + 4 + 5 = 15)

c.

Year	Book Value at Beginning of Year		Depreciation Rate	Depreciation
1	$8,000	x	.30	$2,400
2	5,600	x	.30	1,680
3	3,920	x	.30	1,176
4	2,744	x	.30	823
5	1,921	x	.30	576*
End	1,345			
				$6,655

*Since the book value was still $1,345 at the end of year 5, an additional depreciation of $345 may have been taken to reduce the book value to the $1,000 salvage value.

d.

Year	Hours Produced	Depreciation Rate*	Depreciation
1	240	$5	$1,200
2	280	5	1,400
3	360	5	1,800
4	320	5	1,600
5	200	5	1,000
			$7,000

*($8,000 - $1,000)/1,400 = $5/hour.

e.

Year*	MACRS %		Cost	Depreciation
1	20.0%	x	$8,000	$1,600
2	32.0	x	8,000	2,560
3	19.2	x	8,000	1,536
4	11.5	x	8,000	920
5	11.5	x	8,000	920
6	5.8	x	8,000	464
				$8,000

*An asset in the 5-year property class for MACRS will have depreciation charges in six calendar years.

6. a. Plant
    b. Land
    c. Land (deduction)
    d. Plant
    e. Other (Retained Earnings [Expense]
    f. Land
    g. Land
    h. Plant
    i. Other (Retained Earnings [Loss or Expense]

7. 2005: Depreciation = $\dfrac{\$20,000 - \$2,000}{8} = \dfrac{\$18,000}{8}$ x ½ year = $\underline{\$1,125}$

    2006:

Original Cost	$20,000
Less: Depreciation in 2005	(1,125)
Plus: Improvement	2,500
Book Value, Before 2006 Depreciation	$21,375
Less: Salvage	2,000
Depreciable Basis	$19,375
Remaining Life	÷ 7.5 years
Depreciation, 2006	$ 2,583

    2007:

Book Value, Before 2006 Depreciation	$21,375
Less: Depreciation in 2006	2,583
Book Value, 1/1/07	$18,792
Less: Revised Salvage	1,000
Depreciable Basis	$17,792
Remaining Life (Revised)	÷ 3
Depreciation, 2007	$ 5,931

8.

	Dr.	Cr.
a. Equipment	1,000	
Retained Earnings (Depreciation Expense)	200	
Retained Earnings (Supplies Expense)		1,000
Accumulated Depreciation		200
To correct error in recording equipment purchase.		
b. Accumulated Depreciation	5,000	
Truck		4,000
Retained Earnings (Gain on Sale of Truck)		1,000
To correct error in recording sale of truck.		

9. a. The assets and liabilities will appear on Heather Corp.'s balance sheet at the exact amounts appearing in the market values column except for the R&D in progress. Heather Corp will expense this $15,000. GAAP require firms to expense in the year of acquisition "in-process" technologies because of the uncertainty of future benefits.

    b. The answer is the same as in a. except goodwill would be recognized by Heather Corp for the amount ($16,000) paid in excess of the identifiable assets.

c. Heather would recognize an impairment loss on the Other Assets and an impairment loss on the Goodwill. Since the undiscounted cash flow expectation ($98,000) is less than the book value ($100,000) of Other Assets an impairment loss should be recognized. The loss would be $5,000, the amount necessary to write Other Assets down to its fair market value ($95,000). An impairment loss on Goodwill of $7,000 would be recognized. The market value of the entire operations is now $128,000, a decline of $12,000 (from the original fair market value of $140,000). Since $5,000 of the $12,000 decline can be attributed to Other Assets, the remainder, $7,000 is attributed to Goodwill.

Chapter 9

Liabilities: Introduction

Chapter Highlights

1. Firms recognize an obligation as a liability if it has three essential characteristics: (a) the obligation involves a probable future sacrifice of resources -- a future transfer of cash, goods, or services or the foregoing of a future cash receipt -- at a specified or determinable date. The firm can measure with reasonable precision the cash-equivalent value of resources to be sacrificed; (b) the firm has little or no discretion to avoid the transfer; (c) the transaction or event giving rise to the obligation has already occurred.

2. Accounting recognizes the following obligations as liabilities: (a) obligations with fixed payment dates and amounts, such as notes payable; (b) obligations with fixed payment amounts but estimated payment dates, such as accounts payable; (c) obligations for which both timing and amount of payment must be estimated, such as warranties payable; and (d) obligations arising from advances from customers on unexecuted contracts and agreements, such as rental fees received in advance.

3. Obligations under mutually unexecuted contracts (such as purchase commitments) are generally not recognized as liabilities. Accounting does not recognize assets or liabilities for executory contracts -- the mere exchange of promises where there is no mutual performance.

4. A contingent liability is a potential future obligation that arises from an event that has occurred in the past but whose outcome is not now known. A future event will determine whether or not the item becomes an obligation. An estimated loss from a contingency should be recognized in the accounts if "Information available prior to the issuance of the financial statements indicates that it is probable that an asset had been impaired or that a liability had been incurred..." and "The amount of the loss can be reasonably estimated." The term "contingent liability" is used only when the item is not recognized in the accounts. Contingent liabilities are disclosed in the footnotes to the financial statements.

5. Liabilities appear on the balance sheet at the present value of payments a firm expects to make in the future. The historical interest rate (the interest rate that the borrower was required to pay at the time the liability was incurred) is used in computing the present value of the liability.

6. Liabilities are generally classified on the balance sheet as current or noncurrent. Current liabilities fall due within the operating cycle, usually one year. Noncurrent liabilities fall due later.

7. Most current liabilities are shown on the balance sheet at the undiscounted amount payable because of the immaterially small difference between the amount ultimately payable and its present value. Examples of current liabilities include accounts payable, short-term notes payable, and taxes payable.

8. Businesses organized as corporations must pay federal income tax based on their taxable income from business activities. In contrast, the income earned by a partnership or sole proprietorship is taxed to the individual partners or the sole proprietor.

9. Some current liabilities arise from advance payments by customers for goods or services to be delivered in the future. In other words, cash is received before the goods or services are furnished to the customer. Examples of this type of transaction include the advance sale of theater tickets and the collection in advance for magazine subscriptions. Another type of deferred performance liability arises when a firm provides a warranty for service or repairs for some period after a sale.

10. The differences between current and noncurrent liabilities, in addition to their maturity dates, are that: (a) interest on long-term liabilities is ordinarily paid at regular intervals during the life of the long-term obligation, and (b) either the principal of long-term obligations is paid back in installments or special funds are accumulated by the borrower for retiring the liability.

11. Long-term liabilities are recorded at the present value of all payments to be made using the historical market interest rate at the time the liability is incurred. For most long-term liabilities, the borrower knows the amount of cash received as well as the amounts and due dates of cash repayments, but the loan does not explicitly state the market interest rate or, perhaps, states it incorrectly. Finding the market interest rate implied by the receipt of a given amount of cash now in return for a series of promised future repayments requires a process called "finding the internal rate of return." The internal rate of return is the interest rate that discounts a series of future cash flows to its present value.

12. The borrower uses the original market rate, either specified or computed at the time the borrower receives the loan, throughout the life of the loan to compute interest expense. When the borrower makes a cash payment, a portion (perhaps all) of the payment represents interest. Any excess of cash payment over interest expense reduces the borrower's liability for the principal amount. If a given payment is too small to cover all the interest expense accrued since the last payment date, then the liability principal increases by the excess of interest expense over cash payment.

13. An example of a long-term liability is a mortgage contract in which the lender (mortgagee) is given legal title to certain property of the borrower (mortgagor), with the provision that the title reverts to the borrower when the loan is repaid in full. The mortgaged property is collateral for the loan.

14. Firms often finance the acquisition of buildings, equipment, and other fixed assets using interest-bearing notes. If the borrowing arrangement does not state an explicit interest rate, the principal of the note includes implicit interest.

15. Generally accepted accounting principles require that all long-term monetary liabilities, including those carrying no explicit interest, appear on the balance sheet at the present value of the future cash payments. To determine the present value of the future cash payments, an imputed interest rate is used in the discounting process. The imputed interest rate is the interest rate appropriate for the particular borrower at the time it incurs the obligation, given the amount and terms of the borrowing arrangement and the borrower's risk of defaulting on its obligations.

16. The computation of the present value of the liability and the amount of imputed interest can be based on the market value of the asset acquired. If the asset's current market value is not known, the present value of the liability can be computed by discounting the payments using the interest rate the firm would have to pay for a similar loan in the open market at the time that it acquired the asset. Regardless of how the present value of the liability and the imputed interest is computed, the total expense over the combined lives of the liability and the asset-interest plus depreciation plus gain or loss on sale-is the same.

17. A borrower's long-term payable is the lender's long-term asset. GAAP require the lender to show the asset in the Long-Term Receivable account at its present value.

18. When large amounts of funds are needed, a firm may borrow from the general investing public through the use of a bond issue. The distinctive features of a bond issue are: (a) A bond indenture, or agreement, is drawn up that shows in detail the terms of the loan; (b) Bond certificates are issued, each one representing a portion of the total loan; (c) A trustee is named to hold title to any property serving as collateral for the loan and to act as the representative of the bondholders; (d) An agent is appointed to act as registrar and disbursing agent; (e) Some bonds have coupons for the interest payments attached to the bond certificate. However, in recent years, most bonds are registered, which means that the borrower records the name and address of the bondholder and sends the periodic payments to the registered owner who need not clip coupons and redeem them. (f) The entire bond issue is usually sold by the borrower to an investment banking firm, or a group of bankers, which assumes the responsibility of reselling the bonds to the investing public.

19. The most common type of corporate bond is the debenture bond, which carries no special collateral; instead, it is issued on the general credit of the business. To give added protection to the bondholders, the bond indenture usually includes provisions that limit the dividends that the borrower can declare, or the amount of subsequent long-term debt that it can incur. Mortgage bonds and collateral trust bonds are examples of bonds collateralized by property of the issuer. Convertible bonds are debentures that the holder can exchange, after some specified period of time has elapsed, for a specific number of shares of common or, perhaps, preferred stock.

20. Most bonds provide for the payment of interest at regular intervals, usually semiannually. The amount of interest is usually expressed as a percentage of the principal or face value of the bond.

21. The amount of funds received by the borrower may be more or less than the par (face) value of the bonds issued. The price at which a firm issues bonds depends on (a) the future cash payments that the bond indenture requires the firm to make and (b) the discount rate that the market deems appropriate given the risk of the borrower and the general level of interest rates in the economy. If the coupon (or stated)` rate is less than the market interest rate, the bond will sell at a discount (the bond will sell for less than its face amount). If the coupon rate is higher than the market interest rate, the bond will sell at a premium (the bond will sell for more than its face amount). If the coupon rate equals the market interest rate, the bond will sell at its face amount.

22. When a bond is issued for less than par, the difference between the face value and the amount of the proceeds represents additional interest, which will be paid as a part of the face value at maturity. This additional interest plus the periodic payments of interest will be charged to the periods during which the bond is outstanding. Therefore, the periodic interest expense includes the interest payment plus a portion of the discount. The process of allocating the discount as additional interest expense over the life of the bond is called amortization. The Discount on Bonds Payable account is a contra liability account and should be shown on the balance sheet as a deduction from the liability account (or shown as a net amount), Bonds Payable.

23. A premium on bonds, like a discount on bonds, represents an adjustment of the cost of borrowing. The effect of amortizing the premium will be to reduce the interest expense below the cash actually paid for interest. Over the life of the bonds, the interest expense will be less than the amount of cash actually paid for interest by the principal lent but not repaid at maturity. The Premium on Bonds Payable is an adjunct to a liability account and should be shown on the balance sheet as an addition to (or shown as a net amount) Bonds Payable.

24. Generally accepted accounting principles require the effective-interest method of recognizing interest expense. Under the effective-interest method (a) interest expense each period is equal to the market interest rate at the time the bonds were issued (the historical interest rate) multiplied by the book value of the liability at the beginning of the interest period; (b) the interest expense on the income statement will equal a constant percentage (historical interest rate) of the recorded liability at the beginning of each interest period (for a bond issued at a discount, interest expense on the income statement will be an increasing amount each period because the book value amount of the liability increases each period and for a bond issued at a premium, interest expense on the income statement will be a decreasing amount each period because the book value amount of the liability decreases each period); and (c) the bonds will be stated on the balance sheet at the present value of the remaining cash outflows discounted at the market rate of interest when the bonds were issued (historical interest rate).

25. Bonds may remain outstanding until their stated maturity date or a firm may enter the marketplace and purchase its own bonds before they mature. As market interest rates change, the market price of a bond issue will change. For example, assume that a company issues a 6 percent bond at par (the market rate of interest is also 6 percent). The issuing company records the bonds at par, using the historical cost convention. If market interest rates rise, the market price of the bond issue will decrease. If market interest rates drop, the market price of the bond issue will increase. In other words, there is an inverse relationship between the market interest rate and the market price of the bond. If market interest rates rise and the market price of the bond issue decreases, the issuing company can go into the marketplace and repurchase its bonds and record a gain from the retirement of the bonds. The gain actually occurred as interest rates increased. Under historical cost accounting, the gain is realized in the period the bond is retired.

26. The FASB requires that all gains and losses on bond retirements be reported in the income statement as extraordinary items. Such a gain or loss results because the bond issue is recorded at historical cost amounts and changes in the bond's market price are not recorded.

27. Two types of provisions for bond retirements are frequently encountered. One provides that certain portions of the principal amount will come due on a succession of maturity dates; the bonds of such issues are known as serial bonds. The other major type of retirement provision stipulates that the firm must accumulate a fund of cash or other assets (commonly known as a sinking fund) that will be used to retire the bonds. The sinking fund appears on the balance sheet of the borrower as a noncurrent asset in the Investments section.

28. Some bond issues make no provision for installment repayment or for accumulating funds for the payment of the bonds when they come due. In such situations, the bond liability either may be paid at maturity out of cash available at that time, or the bond issue may be refunded (new bonds issued to obtain the funds to retire the old ones when they come due). A common provision gives the company that issued the bonds the right to retire (call) portions of the bond issue before the bond's maturity date. The bond indenture usually provides that the bonds shall be callable at specified prices. The call price is usually set a few percentage points above the par and declines as the maturity date approaches.

30. When a firm uses the indirect method of deriving cash flows from operations, the statement of cash flows (a) must, for bonds issued at a discount, add back to net income the difference between the interest expense recorded and the interest paid in cash and (b) must, for bonds issued at a premium, subtract from net income the difference between the interest expense recorded and the interest paid in cash.

31. When a firm retires a bond for cash, it reports that cash in the financing section of the statement of cash flows. If there is a gain or loss on the bond retirement transaction, the gain must be subtracted or the loss added back to net income in the operations section of the statement of cash flows to derive operating cash flows.

Questions and Exercises

True/False. For each of the following statements, place a T or F in the space provided to indicate whether the statement is true or false.

_____ 1. A manufacturing company guarantees its product against defects for one year. Since the amount due and the due date are not known with certainty, the liability for the warranty need not be disclosed.

_____ 2. Under the effective-interest method of recognizing interest expense, a bond liability would be shown on the balance sheet at the present value of future cash outflows discounted at the historical market rate of interest.

_____ 3. Obligations under mutually unexecuted contracts are generally not recognized as liabilities.

_____ 4. Contingent liabilities are presented on the balance sheet at their present value between current liabilities and noncurrent liabilities.

_____ 5. Long-term liabilities are recorded initially at the present value of all payments.

_____ 6. The effective-interest method results in a changing rate of interest each period.

_____ 7. Under the effective-interest method, interest expense each period is equal to the historical interest rate times the recorded book value of the liability at the beginning of the interest period.

_____ 8. Bonds sold at a discount (less than par) have a higher effective rate of interest than bonds sold at a premium.

_____ 9. The premium (more than par) on bonds payable represents additional interest that will be paid at the bond's maturity.

_____ 10. The effect of amortizing the discount (the amount less than par) on bonds payable is to increase the interest expense over the amount actually paid as interest.

_____ 11. The terms "face value" and "par value" are synonymous and refer to the principal amount of a bond.

_____ 12. When a company has the right to retire portions of a bond issue before the bond's maturity date, the bond is said to be callable.

_____ 13. For a bond issued at a discount (less than par), the amount of interest expense reported on the income statement each period will be decreasing under the effective-interest method of recognizing interest expense.

_____ 14. When the market rate of interest exceeds the interest rate stated on a bond, the bond will sell at a premium (more than par).

_____ 15. The historical interest rate is the market interest rate at the time the debt was initially issued.

_____ 16. If a liability can be retired for an amount that is less than the amount owed, a loss would be reported by the party paying off the liability.

_____ 17. A debenture is a bond contract that shows in detail the terms of the loan.

_____ 18. Footnotes to the financial statements may be employed to report contingent liabilities.

_____ 19. Contingent liabilities are liabilities that are known to exist, but that are uncertain in amount.

_____ 20. For a bond sold at a premium (more than par), the annual cash payment for interest exceeds the annual interest expense.

_____ 21. One difference between current and noncurrent liabilities is that either the principal of long-term obligations is paid back in installments or special funds are accumulated by the borrower for retiring the liability.

_____ 22. Another difference between current and noncurrent liabilities is that interest on short-term liabilities is ordinarily paid at regular intervals during the life of the short-term obligation.

_____ 23. A fund of cash or other assets that will be used to retire bonds is commonly known as a sinking fund.

_____ 24. When bonds are sold at a discount (less than par), the difference between the face value and the amount of the proceeds represents additional interest, which will be paid as a part of the face value at maturity.

_____ 25. The balance in the Warranty Liability account represents an estimate of the cost of repairs to be made under outstanding warranties.

_____ 26. Bond indentures usually limit the borrower's right to declare dividends.

_____ 27. For a bond, the contractual amount of interest payable is the product of the bond's interest rate and the bond's principal amount.

_____ 28. Upon retiring bonds that were originally issued at a discount (less than par), the appropriate portion of the unamortized discount (less than par) also must be retired.

_____ 29. When bonds are issued at a premium (more than par), the dollar amount of interest expense will remain constant each period.

_____ 30. The allowance method of accounting for warranties may be used for tax reporting purposes.

_____ 31. The process of issuing new bonds to obtain funds to retire old bonds as they come due is known as calling the old bond issue.

_____ 32. Discount (less than par) on Bonds Payable should be classified as a contra account to Bonds Payable.

_____ 33. If a bond's interest rate is higher than the market interest rate, the bond will sell at a discount (less than par).

_____ 34. Coupon bonds have coupons for the interest payments attached to the bond certificate.

_____ 35. Current liabilities are those due within the current operating cycle, normally one year.

_____ 36. Bonds that are due on a succession of maturity dates are known as serial bonds.

_____ 37. For a bond sold at a discount (less than par), the amount of cash paid annually for interest will be more than the amount of interest expense recorded.

_____ 38. In mortgage contracts, the lender is known as the mortgagee, and the borrower is known as the mortgagor.

_____ 39. Liabilities are generally classified on the balance sheet as current or indeterminate term.

_____ 40. Current liabilities are valued on the balance sheet at their present value at that date and not at the amount that will be paid.

Matching. From the list of terms below, select the term which is most closely associated with each of the descriptive phrases or statements that follows and place the letter for that term in the space provided.

a. Bond Principal

b. Contingent Liability

c. Debenture Bond

d. Discount on Bonds Payable

e. Effective-Interest Method

f. Executory Contracts

g. Historical Interest Rate

h. Implicit Interest Rate

i. Liability

j. Mortgage

k. Partially Executed Contracts

l. Premium on Bonds Payable

m. Refunding

n. Serial Bonds

o. Sinking Funds

p. Take-or-pay contract

q. Throughput Contract

_____ 1. Cash or other assets are accumulated and used to pay the bonds when they mature.

_____ 2. This method of interest expense recognition results in an interest charge each period that results in a constant interest rate.

_____ 3. A situation in which there has been an exchange of promises but no mutual performance.

_____ 4. An interest rate appropriate for a borrower at the time it incurs an obligation, given the amount and terms of the borrowing arrangement.

_____ 5. An obligation arising from a transaction with a customer, such as rental fees received in advance.

_____ 6. A situation in which a company has agreed to pay for shipping services whether or not the company actually ships any of its product.

_____ 7. A potential future obligation that arises from an event that has occurred in the past but whose outcome is not now known.

_____ 8. Face value or par value.

_____ 9. When allocated over the life of the bond, interest expense is increased.

_____ 10. An obligation that involves a probable future sacrifice of resources, results from a past transaction or event, and for which the entity has little or no discretion to avoid the transfer.

_____ 11. Contract in which the lender is given legal title to certain property of the borrower, with the provision that the title reverts to the borrower when the loan is repaid in full.

_____ 12. New bonds are issued to obtain the funds to retire the old bonds when they come due.

_____ 13. A situation in which the purchaser must pay for certain quantities of goods whether or not the purchaser actually takes delivery of the goods.

_____ 14. Portions of the principal amount come due on a succession of maturity dates.

_____ 15. The market interest rate at the time the debt was issued.

_____ 16. This type of bond carries no specific collateral; instead, it is issued on the general credit of the business.

_____ 17. When allocated over the life of the bond, interest expense is decreased.

Matching. From the classifications of accounting liabilities listed below, select the classification which is most closely associated with each of the liabilities accountings that follows and place the letter for that classification it the space provided.

a. Contingent Obligations
b. Obligations with Fixed Payment Dates and Amounts
c. Obligations with Fixed Payment Amounts but Estimated Payment Dates.
d. Obligations for Which the Firm Must Estimate both Timing and Amount of Payment.
e. Obligations Arising From Advances from Customer on Unexecuted Contracts and Agreements.
f. Obligations under Mutually Unexecuted Contracts.

_____ 1. Warranties Payable.
_____ 2. Purchase Commitments.
_____ 3. Notes Payable.
_____ 4. Unsettled Lawsuits.
_____ 5. Salaries Payable.
_____ 6. Bonds Payable.
_____ 7. Accounts Payable.
_____ 8. Employment Commitments.
_____ 9. Rental Fees Received in Advance.
_____ 10. Interest Payable.
_____ 11. Subscription Fees Received in Advance.
_____ 12. Taxes Payable.

Multiple Choice. Choose the best answer for each of the following questions and enter the identifying letter in the space provided.

_____ 1. Which of the following would be an example of a partially executed contract?

   a. A company sold a 1-year subscription to its publication and received the subscription price in cash.
   b. A customer purchased merchandise on account.
   c. A company issued 10-years bonds for cash.
   d. A company borrowed money from a bank to purchase a delivery van.

_____ 2. Graham Inc., issued bonds on 1/1, Year 1, which mature in 10 years. The bonds were issued at a premium (more than par). Over the 10-year term of the bond issue, Graham, Inc., will record

   a. Increasing amounts of interest expense each year.
   b. Decreasing amounts of interest expense each year.
   c. An unchanging amount of interest expense each year.
   d. The question cannot be answered with the information given.

3. On January 2, Year 1, Yellowstone Company purchased land and gave in exchange a $100,000 noninterest-bearing note that is due in 5 years. Using a 10 percent imputed interest rate, the land and the note payable were both recorded at $62,100. Assuming that Yellowstone recognizes interest under the effective-interest method, interest expense for Year 2 would be:

   a. $7,580.
   b. $6,210.
   c. $6,831.
   d. $10,000.

4. Refer to the previous question. At what amount would the note payable be reported on the 12/31, Year 2 balance sheet?

   a. $100,000.
   b. $ 62,100.
   c. $ 75,141.
   d. None of the above.

5. On 1/1, Year 1, the Colorado Company purchased machinery that had a cash price of $19,720. Colorado gave a $30,000 note that is due in 3 years. The implicit interest rate is 15 percent. What amount of interest expense would Colorado report in its Year 2 Income Statement?

   a. $3,426.
   b. $3,402.
   c. $2,958.
   d. $3,240.

6. Refer to the previous question. At what amount would the $30,000 note be carried on Colorado's 12/31 Year 1, balance sheet?

   a. $22,678.
   b. $23,146.
   c. $23,122.
   d. $30,000.

7. On July 1, Year 1, Willa sold to Leigh an acre of land in exchange for Leigh's $8,000 noninterest-bearing note due in 3 years. The fair market value of the land is determined to be $6,200. What is the present value of Leigh's obligation to Willa on July 1, Year 1?

   a. $6,200.
   b. $6,500.
   c. $8,000.
   d. None of the above.

8. Frisco Company gives a 3-year warranty with its product. At the end of its first year of business, the company reported sales of $920,000 and warranty expense of $27,600. On its 12/31, Year 1, balance sheet, the company reported $24,800 on its Estimated Warranty Liability account. During Year 2, sales totaled $1,300,000 and the company incurred parts and labor costs of $39,500 for warranty work performed. The company used the same warranty expense percentage for both years. The warranty expense for Year 2 and the balance in the Estimated Warranty Liability account at 12/31, Year 2, are, respectively:

a. $39,500; $63,800.
b. $39,500; $14,700.
c. $27,600; $52,400.
d. $39,000; $24,300.

9. White, Inc., issued bonds on 1/1, Year 1, which mature in 10 years. The $500,000 bonds, which pay 8 percent interest annually on 12/31, were issued at a time when the market interest rate was 10 percent. The bonds were issued for $438,550. What amount of bond interest expense would White report in Year 2?

a. $50,000.
b. $40,000
c. $43,855.
d. $44,241.

10. The account, Premium (more than par) on Bonds, should be shown on the balance sheet as a(an):

a. Contra account to Bonds Payable.
b. Current liability.
c. Adjunct account to Bonds Payable.
d. None of the above.

11. The Fuller Corporation issued 10 percent, 10-year bonds several years ago when the market interest rate was 8 percent. The market interest rate is now 12 percent and Fuller purchases its own bonds in the market and retires them. Fuller would report

a. A gain on the transaction.
b. A loss on the transaction.
c. Neither a gain nor a loss.
d. Cannot be determined from the information given.

12. On March 1, Year 1, Richardson issued $500,000, 9 percent bonds, which mature on January 1, Year 10. The bonds pay interest semiannually on January 1 and July 1. The bonds were sold on March 1 and cash of $507,500 was received. Which of the following statements is correct?

a. The bonds sold at par.
b. The bonds sold at a discount (less than par).
c. The bonds sold at a premium (more than par).
d. No conclusion about the selling price of the bonds can be determined from the information given.

_____ 13. Huffman issued an 8 percent bond when the market interest rate was also 8 percent. The Huffman bonds should have sold

   a.   At a discount (less than par).
   b.   At par.
   c.   At a premium (more than par).
   d.   Cannot be determined with information given.

_____ 14. On July 1, Year 1, Borders, Inc., which publishes a weekly news magazine, sold 8,000 2-year subscriptions for $10 each. On its income statement for the year ending December 31, Year 1, what amount from the July 1 transaction should be reported as revenue?

   a. $ 5,000.
   b. $10,000.
   c. $20,000.
   d. $40,000.

_____ 15. The balance in the Estimated Warranty Liability account at the end of the period

   a.   Represents the costs incurred for repairs made.
   b.   Represents the estimated cost of repairs to be made under warranties in effect at that time.
   c.   Should be identical to the balance in the Warranty Expense account.
   d.   Should be closed to Retained Earnings so that warranty costs and revenues will be matched.

_____ 16. Smith Corporation guarantees its product against defects for one year. In what year should the corporation report the warranty expense?

   a.   In the year that the product is sold.
   b.   In the year that the product becomes defective and is repaired or replaced.
   c.   The cost of the warranty is included in the product's selling price, and therefore warranty expense is never recorded.
   d.   None of the above.

_____ 17. If bonds are issued at a premium (more than par) and interest expense is recognized under the effective-interest method

   a.   The amount of premium (more than par) amortized each year will increase.
   b.   The amount of the liability reported on the balance sheet will increase each year.
   c.   The amount of interest expense reported on the income statement will increase each year.
   d.   All of the above are true statements.

_____ 18. The Carlson Corporation issued a 10 percent, 10-year, $500,000 bond at a time when the market interest rate was 15 percent. The bond was issued for $374,550. The Carlson bond pays interest annually on December 31. On December 31 of the current year the bond liability is carried on the balance sheet at $396,019. How many years has the bond issue been outstanding?

    a.   2 years.
    b.   3 years.
    c.   4 years.
    d.   None of the above.

_____ 19. Pritz Corporation sold 10-year, 10 percent coupon bonds, face amount $500,000 on January 1, Year 1, for 97 percent of their face value. Over the bonds' 10-year life, how much interest expense, in total, will Pritz report in its income statements?

    a. $485,000.
    b. $500,000.
    c. $515,000.
    d. $1,000,000

_____ 20. Rose, Inc., issued bonds on 1/1, Year 1, which mature in 10 years. The $500,000 bonds, which pay 12 percent interest annually on 12/31, were issued at a time when the market interest rate was 11 percent. The bonds were issued for $529,450. At the end of Year 1, how much of the premium (more than par) should be amortized?

    a. $1,761.
    b. $2,945.
    c. $3,535.
    d. $4,420.

_____ 21. Walter Company reported a balance of $170,000 in its Liability for Advance Ticket Sales account on its 12/31, Year 1, balance sheet. During Year 2, the company collected $692,000 from customers for additional advance ticket sales. On its income statement for the year ending 12/31, Year 2, the company reported $810,000 on its Revenues From Advanced Ticket Sales account. What balance would Walter report in its Liability for Advanced Ticket Sales account on its 12/31, Year 2, balance sheet?

    a. $118,000.
    b. $288,000.
    c. $522,000.
    d. $ 52,000.

_____ 22. Christian Co. issued 10-year, 10 percent bonds, face amount $500,000 on 1/1, Year 1, when the market rate was 12 percent. On its Year 1 income statement, Christian reports bond interest expense of $53,220. For what amount were the bonds issued on 1/1, Year 1?

    a. $443,500.
    b. $467,800.
    c. $450,000.
    d. $400,000.

23. These bonds can be exchanged for a specific number of shares of common stock.

    a. Mortgage Bonds.
    b. Debenture Bonds.
    c. Convertible Bonds.
    d. Collateral Trust Bonds.

24. On October 1, Year 1, Johnson Company issued $5 million, 12 percent bonds at par. The bonds pay interest semiannually on January 1 and July 1. For the year ending December 31, Year 1, Johnson would report how much interest expense from this bond issue on its income statement?

    a. $600,000.
    b. $300,000.
    c. $150,000.
    d. Interest expense on this bond issue for Year 1 cannot be determined from the information given.

25. Which of the following accounts would usually be classified as a long-term liability?

    a. Warranty Liability.
    b. Premium (more than par) on Bonds Payable.
    c. Magazine Subscription Fees Received in Advance.
    d. Federal Withholding Taxes Payable.

26. Regina Corporation issued a 7 percent, $500,000 bond issue at a price to yield the market interest rate of 8 percent. The bond pays interest semiannually. How much cash would be paid by Regina at the first interest payment date?

    a. $17,500.
    b. $20,000.
    c. $35,000.
    d. $40,000.

27. When a bond issue is sold, the proceeds from the sale of the bonds equal

    a. The present value of the maturity amount.
    b. The present value of all the future interest payments during the life of the bond issue.
    c. The sum of a and b above.
    d. None of the above.

28. On its 12/31, Year 1 Balance Sheet, St. Charles reported an Estimated Warranty Liability of $43,000. The company estimates warranty expense to be 4 percent of sales. During Year 2, sales totaled $900,000 and warranty repair expenditures totaling $23,000 were incurred. At what amount should St. Charles report the Estimated Warranty Liability on its 12/31, Year 2 Balance Sheet?

    a. $20,000.
    b. $36,000.
    c. $79,000.
    d. $56,000.

_____ 29. Which of the following is an example of an executory contract?

     a.   Purchase commitments.
     b.   Estimated Warranty Liability.
     c.   Rental fees received in advance.
     d.   None of the above is an example of an executory contract.

_____ 30. The Clamma Corporation issued a 10 percent $500,000 bond on April 1, Year 1 at par. Interest is paid semiannually on July 1 and January 1. On its Year 1 Income Statement, Clamma would report Interest Expense of

     a. $50,000.
     b. $25,000.
     c. $37,500.
     d. $33,335.

_____ 31. Hudson Company had sales of personal computers totaling $150,000 for the year ending 12/31, Year 1. Hudson provides free warranty service for 18 months after the sale and estimates warranty costs to be 6 percent of sales. For the year, expenditures made for warranty repairs totaled $1,500. What should be the balance in the warranty liability account on the 12/31, Year 1, Balance Sheet?

     a. $1,500.
     b. $7,500.
     c. $9,000.
     d.   None of the above.

_____ 32. The Ashcraft Company issued $400,000 par-value bonds several years ago. On January 1, Year 8, the bond premium (more than par) account has a balance of $24,000 when $100,000 of the bonds are called at 104. What is the amount of the gain or loss on the retirement of the bonds?

     a. $1,000 gain.
     b. $2,000 gain.
     c. $4,000 gain.
     d. $4,000 loss.

_____ 33. Refer to the previous question. The balance in the bond premium (more than par) account on January 1, Year 8, after the retirement of the $100,000 of bonds would be:

     a. $ -0-.
     b. $12,000.
     c. $18,000.
     d.   None of the above.

34. Lang, Inc., issued bonds on 1/1, Year 1, which mature in 10 years. The $500,000 bonds, which pay 9 percent interest annually on 12/31, were issued at a time when the market interest rate was 11 percent. The bonds were issued for $441,100. At the end of Year 1, after adjusting entries have been recorded, the Discount (less than par) on Bonds Payable account would have a balance of

    a. $58,900.
    b. $53,010.
    c. $55,379.
    d. $62,420.

35. The Lanier Corporation sold a $5 million bond issue at 103 percent of its par value. If the company recognizes interest expense by the effective interest method

    a. Interest expense on the bond issue will increase each year.
    b. Interest expense on the bond issue will decrease each year.
    c. Interest expense on the bond issue will be the same amount each year.
    d. None of the above.

36. A bond that is issued on the general credit of the business is commonly known as a

    a. Mortgage bond.
    b. Collateral trust bond.
    c. Debenture bond.
    d. None of the above.

37. Long-term liabilities are reported on a company's balance sheet at the present value of all promised payments using

    a. The current market interest rate.
    b. A rate of 10 percent.
    c. The market interest rate at the time the liability was incurred.
    d. The prime interest rate.

38. Bird Company issued a $500,000 bond on July 1, Year 1. The 10-year bond pays interest annually on June 30. On 12/31, Year 1, Bird carries the bond on its Balance Sheet at $482,250 and reports Interest Payable of $25,000 as a current liability. What is the bond's interest rate?

    a. 10 percent.
    b. 5 percent.
    c. 9 percent.
    d. Cannot be determined from the information given.

_____ 39. The Herring Company issued bonds on 1/1, Year 1, which mature in 10 years. The $500,000 bonds, which pay 12 percent interest annually on 12/31, were issued at a time when the market interest rate was 10 percent. The bonds were issued for $561,450. At what amount would the long-term liability be reported on 12/31, Year 2?

    a. $548,660.
    b. $555,305.
    c. $557,595.
    d. $553,354.

_____ 40. On 1/1, Year 1, Rogers borrowed $300,000 from Green Mountain Bank. The note calls for five annual installment payments of $81,300 to be paid each year on 12/31. The effective interest rate is 11 percent. How much of the first installment (made on 12/31, Year 1) is payment on the principal amount borrowed?

    a. $60,000.
    b. $81,300.
    c. $33,000.
    d. $48,300.

_____ 41. If the Williams Company issued bonds due in 10 years at a discount (less than par), this indicates that

    a.   The market rate of interest exceeded the bond's interest rate at the time the bonds were issued.
    b.   The bond's interest rate exceeded the market rate at the time the bonds were issued.
    c.   The bond's interest rate equaled the market rate of interest at the time the bonds were issued.
    d.   None of the above.

_____ 42. If bonds are issued at a discount (less than par), the net long-term liability reported on the balance sheet

    a.   Increases each year during the life of the bond issue.
    b.   Decreases each year during the life of the bond issue.
    c.   Remains at the maturity value throughout the life of the bond issue.
    d.   Remains at the issue price throughout the life of the bond issue.

_____ 43. Johns, Inc., issued bonds on 1/1, Year 1, which mature in 10 years. The $500,000 bonds, which pay 15 percent interest annually on 12/31, were issued at a time when the market interest rate was 12 percent. The bonds were issued for $584,750. Over the 10-year life of the bonds, how much interest expense will Johns report?

    a. $750,000.
    b. $834,750.
    c. $665,250.
    d. $660,000.

Exercises

1. On January 2, Year 1, Lander Company purchased machinery and gave in exchange a $180,000 noninterest-bearing note due in 3 years. Assuming that a 14 percent interest rate has been imputed for this transaction, the present value of the note on January 2, Year 1, is $121,500. Lander recognizes interest expense under the effective-interest method.

   Record the appropriate entries for the note from January 2, Year 1, until the note is paid upon maturity on January 2, Year 4.

2. The May Company provides a warranty on its product for one year after sale. Warranty costs are estimated to be 3 percent of the selling price. In Year 3, the company had sales of $900,000, which were subject to the warranty. During January, Year 4 $13,800 in parts were used to make repairs covered under the warranty.

   Prepare entries for Year 3 and Year 4 for the sale and related warranty transactions.

3. The Taylor Company issued $800,000 of 10 percent, 10-year bonds for $708,240 on January 1, Year 1. Interest is paid semiannually on July 1 and January 1.

Prepare Year 1 entries relative to the bond issue, assuming (a) that the bonds were sold to yield the market interest rate of 12 percent, (b) that interest expense is recognized on an effective-interest basis, and (c) a Premium or Discount on Bond Payable is used to record the difference between par and the issue price.

4. The Casady Company issued $1,000,000 of 9 percent, 10-year bonds for $1,067,955 on January 1, Year 1. Interest is paid semiannually on July 1 and January 1.

Prepare Year 1 entries relative to the bond issue, assuming (a) the bonds were sold to yield the market interest rate of 8 percent, (b) that interest expense is recognized on an effective-interest basis, and (c) a Premium or Discount on Bonds Payable is used to record the difference between par and the issue price.

5. On January 1, Year 1, Rodney Wainwright purchased equipment that had a cash price of $142,356. In lieu of paying cash, Wainwright gave a 3-year noninterest-bearing note with a face amount of $200,000. The implicit interest rate is 12% per year.

   a. What is the cost of the equipment?

   b. What amount of interest expense would Wainwright report for the first year?

   c. What is the carrying value of the obligation at the end of the second year?

   d. What amount of interest expense would Wainwright report for the third year?

6. On January 1, Year 1, Ramon Company financed the purchase of some land with a 5-year note which calls for payments of $50,000 every 6 months with the first payment due on July 1, Year 1. Fill in the 12 blanks on the amortization schedule below:

Period	Loan Balance at Start of Period	Interest Expense	Payment	Principal Reduction	Liability at End of Period
1/1/1					320,884
7/1/1	_____	_____	_____	_____	_____
1/1/2	299,764	26,979	_____	_____	_____
7/1/2	276,743	_____	_____	_____	_____

7. On July 1, Year 1, Espana Company issued a 10-year $2,000,000 bond which pays interest semiannually on January 1 and July 1. Fill in the 12 blanks on the amortization schedule below:

Period	Liability at Start of Period	Effective Interest	Coupon Interest	Change in Book Value of Liability	Liability at End of Period
0					2,406,900
1	_____	_____	110,000	13,724	_____
2	_____	_____	_____	_____	2,378,903
3	_____	_____	_____	_____	_____

8. Rhonda Company borrowed money and signed a note for $400,000 which is due in 8 years. Fill in the 10 blanks on the amortization schedule below:

Period	Loan Balance at Start of Period	Interest Expense	Change in Book Value of Note	Liability at End of Period
0				216,000
1	_____	17,280	_____	233,280
2	_____	_____	_____	_____
3	_____	_____	_____	_____

9. Campbell Company has outstanding on December 31, Year 5, $2,000,000 of 4 percent bonds that mature on December 31, Year 10. The bonds, which were sold on January 1, Year 1, have an unamortized discount of $60,000 on December 31, Year 5, the last interest payment date. On January 1, Year 6, Campbell purchased $500,000 of its bonds in the open market for $410,000 and retired the bonds.

Prepare the January 1, Year 6, entry to record the retirement of the bonds.

10. On its 12/31, Year 5, balance sheet, Lallance Company reported the following under long-term liabilities:

7 percent Bonds Payable	$1,000,000	
Less: Discount on Bonds Payable	100,661	$899,339

The bond pays interest annually on 12/31.

On its income statement for the year ending 12/31, Year 5, Lallance reported Bond Interest Expense of $80,037.

a. What was the market interest rate when the bonds were issued?

b. What amount of bond discount would be amortized in Year 6?

Answers to Questions and Exercises

True/False

1.	F	9.	F	17.	T	25.	T	33.	F
2.	T	10.	T	18.	T	26.	T	34.	T
3.	T	11.	T	19.	F	27.	T	35.	T
4.	F	12.	T	20.	T	28.	T	36.	T
5.	T	13.	F	21.	T	29.	F	37.	F
6.	F	14.	F	22.	F	30.	F	38.	T
7.	T	15.	T	23.	T	31.	F	39.	F
8.	F	16.	F	24.	T	32.	T	40.	T

Matching

1.	o	4.	h	7.	b	10.	i	13.	p	16.	c
2.	e	5.	k	8.	a	11.	j	14.	n	17.	l
3.	f	6.	q	9.	d	12.	m	15.	g		

Matching II

1.	d	3.	b	5.	c	7.	c	9.	e	11.	e
2.	f	4.	a	6.	b	8.	f	10.	b	12.	c

Multiple Choice

1.	a	10.	c	19.	c	28.	d	37.	c
2.	b	11.	a	20.	a	29.	a	38.	a
3.	c	12.	a	21.	d	30.	c	39.	d
4.	c	13.	b	22.	a	31.	b	40.	d
5.	b	14.	c	23.	c	32.	b	41.	a
6.	a	15.	b	24.	c	33.	c	42.	a
7.	a	16.	a	25.	b	34.	c	43.	c
8.	d	17.	a	26.	a	35.	b		
9.	d	18.	b	27.	c	36.	c		

Exercises

			Dr.	Cr.
1.	1/2 Year 1	Machinery	121,500	
		Note Payable		121,500
		To record purchase of machine in exchange for a noninterest-bearing note.		
	12/31 Year 1	Interest Expense	17,010	
		Note Payable		17,010
		To record interest expense for Year 1. Interest = .14 x $121,500 = $17,010.		
	12/31 Year 2	Interest Expense	19,391	
		Note Payable		19,391
		To record interest expense for Year 2. Interest = .14 x ($121,500 + $17,010) = $19,391		
	12/31 Year 3	Interest Expense	22,099	
		Note Payable		22,099
		To record interest expense for Year 3. Interest = $180,000 - $121,500 - $17,010 - $19,391 = $22,099.		
	1/2 Year 4	Note Payable	180,000	
		Cash		180,000
		To record payment of note at maturity.		

			Dr.	Cr.
2.	Year 3	Cash (or Accounts Receivable)	900,000	
		Warranty Expense	27,000	
		Sales		900,000
		Estimated Warranty Liability		27,000
		To record sales and warranty liability.		
	Year 4	Estimated Warranty Liability	13,800	
		Parts Inventory		13,800
		To record parts used in performing warranty work.		

			Dr.	Cr.
3.	1/1 Year 1	Cash	708,240	
		Discount on Bonds Payable	91,760	
		Bonds Payable		800,000
		To record sale of bonds at a discount.		
	7/1 Year 1	Interest Expense	42,494	
		Discount on Bonds Payable		2,494
		Cash		40,000
		To record interest expense and amortization of discount. Interest expense: $708,240 X .06 = $42,494		
	12/31 Year 1	Interest Expense	42,644	
		Discount on Bonds Payable		2,644
		Interest Payable		40,000
		To record interest expense and amortization of discount. Interest expense: ($708,240 + 2,494) X .06 = $42,644.		

			Dr.	Cr.
4.	1/1 Year 1	Cash	1,067,955	
		Bonds Payable		1,000,000
		Premium on Bonds Payable		67,955
		To record sale of bonds at a premium		
	7/1 Year 2	Interest Expense	42,718	
		Premium on Bonds Payable	2,282	
		Cash		45,000
		To record interest expense and amortization of premium. Interest expense: $1,067,955 x .04 = $42,718.		
	12/31 Year 1	Interest Expense	42,627	
		Premium on Bonds Payable	2,373	
		Interest Payable		45,000
		To record interest expense and amortization of premium. Interest expense: ($1,067,955 - $2,282) x .04 = $42,627		

5. a. $142,356
   b. $17,083 ($142,356 X .12)
   c. $178,572 ($142,356 + $17,083 + $19,133)
   d. $21,429 ($178,572 x .12)

6.

Period	Loan Balance at Start of Period	Interest Expense	Payment	Principal Reduction	Liability at End of Period
1/1/1					320,884
7/1/1	320,884	28,880	50,000	21,120	299,764
1/1/2	299,764	26,979	50,000	23,021	276,743
7/1/2	276,743	24,907	50,000	25,093	251,650

7.

Period	Liability at Start of Period	Effective Interest	Coupon Interest	Change in Book Value of Liability	Liability at End of Period
0					2,406,900
1	2,406,900	96,276	110,000	13,724	2,393,176
2	2,393,176	95,727	110,000	14,273	2,378,903
3	2,378,903	95,156	110,000	14,844	2,364,059

8.

Period	Loan Balance at Start of Period	Interest Expense	Change in Book Value of Note	Liability at End of Period
0				216,000
1	216,000	17,280	17,280	233,280
2	233,280	18,662	18,662	251,942
3	251,942	20,155	20,155	272,097

9.

		Dr.	Cr.
1/1 Year 6	Bonds Payable	500,000	
	Gain on Retirement of Bonds		75,000
	Discount on Bonds Payable		15,000
	Cash		410,000
	To record retirement of bonds.		

Principal amount of bonds	$2,000,000
Less: unamortized discount	60,000
Book value, Jan. 1, Year 6	$1,940,000
25% of bonds reacquired	.25
Book Value of bonds reacquired	$ 485,000
Reacquisition price	410,000
Gain on retirement	$ 75,000

10. a.

Bond interest expense for Year 5		$ 80,037
Less: Contractual interest paid in		
Year 5 ($1,000,000 x .07)		70,000
Bond discount amortized in Year 5		$ 10,037
Book value of bond issue on 12/31, Year 5		$ 899,339
Less: discount amortized in Year 5		10,037
Book value of bond issue on 12/31, Year 4		$ 889,302

$$\frac{\text{Bond interest expense for Year 5}}{\text{Book value of bond issue on 12/31, Year 4}} = \text{Interest rate}$$

$$\frac{\$ 80,037}{\$889,302} = 9\%$$

b.

Bond interest expense for Year 6		$ 80,941
($899,339 x .09)		
Contractual interest paid		70,000
($1,000,000 x .07)		
Bond discount amortized		
in Year 6		$ 10,941

Liabilities: Off-Balance Sheet Financing, Leases, Deferred Income Taxes, And Retirement Benefits

Chapter Highlights

1. In the last decade accounting has considered four controversial topics related to liabilities: off-balance sheet financing, leases, deferred taxes, and retirement benefits.

2. The rationale for off-balance sheet financing is to obtain funds without recording a liability. The objective is to show fewer liabilities on the balance sheet and improve the debt ratios that analysts use to assess the financial risk of a firm.

3. Reasons cited for off-balance sheet financing include (a) the cost of borrowing is lowered and (b) the violation of debt covenants is avoided.

4. To be an accounting liability, a firm must incur an obligation for a past or current benefit received--the event or transaction must already have happened. If the firm will receive the benefit in the future, accounting treats the obligation as an executory contract and typically does not recognize a liability. Similarly, certain contingent obligations, not meeting the criteria for a loss contingency, also keep liabilities from being recognized on the balance sheet. Off-balance sheet financing emphasizes that mutual performance will occur in the future and therefore a liability is not recorded.

5. Firms create innovative financing schemes to keep debt off the balance sheet. Leasing assets, using purchase commitments to obtain loans and selling accounts receivable or inventory are transactions, which may result in keeping debt off the balance sheet. When the entity needing financing enjoys the economic benefits and bears the economic risk of the transaction, a liability is usually recognized on the balance sheet. When the entity providing the financing enjoys the economic benefits and bears the economic risk, the debt does not appear as a liability on the balance sheet of the firm needing financing. As a result of off-balance sheet financing, ratios (such as the debt-equity ratio) will appear more favorable, which may favorably affect future credit ratings and future borrowing costs. Statement users should consider required GAAP disclosures related to off-balance shee liabilities when assessing risk of a firm.

6. There are two approaches to accounting for leases: the operating lease method and the capital lease method. In an operating lease, the lessor transfers only the rights to use the property to the lessee for specified periods of time. At the end of the lease period, the property is returned to the lessor. The lessee merely records annual rent expense when the lease payment is made. Under the capital lease method, the lease is judged to be a form of borrowing to purchase the property. This treatment recognizes the signing of the lease as the acquisition of a long-term asset, called a leasehold, and the incurring of a long-term liability for lease payments. The lessee must amortize the leased asset over its useful life and must recognize each lease payment as part payment of interest on the liability and part reduction of the liability itself.

7. For the lessee, one difference between the operating lease method and the capital lease method is the timing of the expense recognition. Another difference is that the capital lease method recognizes both the asset (leasehold) and the liability on the balance sheet. Most lessees prefer to use the operating lease method because the reported income is higher in the earlier years of the lease than it would be under the capital lease method. Also, with an operating lease, the asset and related liability are not shown on the lessee's balance sheet. When a journal entry debits an asset account and credits a liability account, the debt-equity ratio increases which makes the company appear more risky. Therefore, most managers prefer not to show an asset and a related liability on the balance sheet. However, most analysts think that the capital lease method provides higher quality measures of financial position.

8. A firm must account for a lease as a capital lease if the lease meets any one of four conditions. A lease is a capital lease (a) if it transfers ownership to the lessee at the end of the lease term, (b) if transfer of ownership at the end of the lease term seems likely because the lessee has a "bargain purchase" option, (c) if it extends for at least 75 percent of the asset's life, or (d) if the present value of the contractual minimum lease payments equals or exceeds 90 percent of the fair market value of the asset at the time the lessee signs the lease.

9. The four criteria attempt to identify whether the lessor or lessee enjoys the economic benefit and bears the economic risk of the leased asset. For example, if the leased asset becomes the property of the lessee at the end of the lease period, then the lessee enjoys all of the economic benefits of the asset and incurs all risks of ownership.

10. A bargain purchase option gives the lessee the right to purchase the asset for a price less than the predicted fair market value of the asset when the option is exercised.

11. Generally, the lessor uses the same criteria, as does the lessee for classifying a lease as a capital lease or an operating lease. When the lessor and lessee sign a capital lease, the lessor recognizes revenue in an amount equal to the present value of all future lease payments and recognizes expenses in an amount equal to the book value of the leased asset. The lessor records the lease receivable at the present value of the future cash flows. Lessors tend to prefer the capital lease method because it enables them to recognize income on the "sale" of the asset on the date the lease is signed.

12. The rules for classifying a lease as operating or capital for income tax purposes differ from the FASB rules discussed for financial reporting. Leases sometime appear as operating leases for tax purposes and capital leases for financial reporting, or vice versa.

13. The amount that a firm reports as book income usually differs from the amount of taxable income appearing on the income tax return. The difference arises because of permanent differences and temporary differences.

14. Permanent differences result from book income including revenues or expenses that taxable income never includes. Temporary differences result from book income including revenues or expenses in a different accounting period than when they appear in taxable income.

15. Income taxes _payable_ are based on taxable income which excludes permanent differences and uses the accounting methods a firm selects for income tax purposes.

16. Income tax _expense_ could be based on taxable income and equal income taxes actually payable each period. Or, income tax _expense_ could be equal to income taxes actually payable each period plus the income taxes a firm expects to pay (or minus the income taxes a firm expects to save) in the future when temporary differences reverse. Generally accepted accounting principles require firms to follow the second approach. Thus, income tax expense includes income taxes payable currently plus income taxes deferred because of temporary differences.

17. Generally accepted accounting principles require that the measurement of the deferred portion of income tax expense use a balance sheet approach. Using this basis, firms (a) identify temporary differences between the book basis and tax basis of assets and liabilities at the beginning and end of the year and (b) multiply these temporary differences by the income tax rate applicable to the period when the firm expects the temporary differences to reverse. The change in the deferred tax account on the balance sheet between the beginning and end of the year equals the deferred portion of income tax expense.

18. Temporary differences might create deferred tax assets or deferred tax liabilities. Deferred tax accounts (assets or liabilities) can change each period because of:

    (a)   Temporary differences originating or reversing during the current period,
    (b)   Changes in income tax rates expected to apply in future periods when temporary differences reverse,
    (c)   Changes in the valuation allowance for deferred tax assets.

19. The FASB rules require a more complex procedure than is discussed here. However, in summary, income tax expense each period equals (a) income taxes currently payable on taxable income plus (b) the credit change in the deferred tax asset and the deferred tax liability (or minus the debit change in the deferred tax asset and the deferred tax liability) between the beginning and end of the period.

20. Notes on the financial statements provide additional information regarding a firm's income tax expense. Firms report four items of information: (a) components of income before taxes, which indicates the amount of book income before income taxes that a firm derives from domestic and foreign operations; (b) components of income tax expense, which indicates the amount of income taxes currently payable and the amount deferred because of temporary differences; (c) a reconciliation from statutory to effective tax rates, which indicates why the effective tax rate differs from the statutory tax rate, and (d) components of deferred tax assets and liabilities, which discloses the types of temporary differences that result in the deferred tax asset and the deferred tax liability on the balance sheet each period.

21. The accounting for deferred income taxes has been the subject of much criticism. The economic benefit of deferring tax payments and the economic cost of temporary differences that require immediate cash net flow are ignored. Another criticism is that deferred taxes are neither an asset nor a liability. A third criticism is that, unlike all other long-term liabilities, which are reported on the balance sheet at the present value of future cash payments, deferred tax liabilities are reported as undiscounted amounts.

22. Most employers provide retirement benefits to their employees. Typical benefits include pensions, health insurance, and life insurance. The employer's cost of these retirement benefits is an expense in measuring net income. The accounting issue is whether firms should recognize the expense during the years while employees render services or later, when they receive the benefits during retirement. The matching convention of accrual accounting requires that firms recognize the expense during the employee's working years because those labor services generate revenues.

23. Under a pension plan, an employer promises to make payments to employees after they retire. The employer sets up a pension plan, specifying the eligibility of employees, the types of promises to employees, the method of funding, and the pension plan administrator.

24. The pension plan set up by the employer may be a defined contribution plan or a defined benefit plan. In a defined contribution plan, the amounts to be contributed to the pension plan by the employer are defined, but the benefits to be received by retired employees are not defined (they depend on investment performance). Under a defined benefit plan, the amounts to be paid to an employee upon retirement are based on a formula that usually takes into account the employee's length of service and average earnings. The employer must contribute sufficient amounts to the pension plan so that those contributions plus earnings from investments made with those contributions will be sufficient to pay the specified benefit.

25. The employer computes pension expense each period and transfers cash to a separate pension fund according to some formula. If cumulative pension expenses exceed cumulative pension funding, a pension liability appears on the employer's balance sheet. If cumulative pension funding exceeds cumulative pension expense, a pension asset appears on the employer's balance sheet. Additionally, the FASB requires firms to report a pension liability on the balance sheet if the present value of pension commitments to employees exceeds the assets in the pension fund.

216

26. The employer's pension expense for a defined contribution plan is the amount contributed to the pension fund. Pension expense measurement for a defined benefit plan is too detailed for discussion in this text.

27. The pension plan receives cash each period from the employer and invests the cash to generate income. Also, the pension plan pays cash to retired employees each period. The assets in the pension plan do not appear on the balance sheet of the employer.

28. The pension plan computes the amount of the pension liability each period. The pension liability for a defined contribution plan equals the assets in the pension plan. The pension liability for a defined benefit plan is the present value of the expected amounts payable to employees and is based on the pension benefit formula underlying the pension plan.

29. Health care, insurance, and other benefits are similar in concept to pension benefits. The present value of these commitments, called health-care benefits obligation, represents an economic obligation of the employer. The FASB requires firms to recognize expenses for employers' health care and similar benefits and liabilities for their underfunded obligations to pay for these benefits. Firms may recognize the full liability in one year or recognize it piecemeal over several years.

30. Internationally most industrialized countries maintain a distinction between operating leases and capital leases. While different than US GAAP most countries use criteria to identify the entity enjoying the rewards and bearing the risk of the asset. Generally countries that allow firms to select different methods of accounting for financial and tax reporting require deferred tax accounting. Disclosures about retirement benefits in most countries contain less detail than in the US.

31. When firms account for leases as operating leases, the amount reported as rent revenue or rent expense usually equals the lessee's cash payment. In the statement of cash flows, no adjustment is needed to net income in deriving cash flows from operations.

32. A lease accounted for as a capital lease is an investing and a financing activity that does not affect cash. As the leased asset is depreciated, depreciation expense is added to net income in deriving cash flows from operations. The portion of the lease payment representing interest expense requires no adjustment to net income in deriving cash flows from operations. The portion of the lease payment representing repayment of the lease liability is a financing activity which uses cash.

33. When income tax expense exceeds income tax paid in cash, the difference is added back to net income in deriving cash flows from operations. When income taxes paid in cash exceed income tax expense, the difference is subtracted from net income in deriving cash flows from operations.

34. If pension expense exceeds pension funding, the difference is added back to net income in deriving cash flows from operations. If pension expense is less than pension funding, the difference is subtracted from net income in deriving cash flows from operations. When pension expenses equals pension funding, there is no adjustment to net income in deriving cash flow from operations.

Questions and Exercises

True/False. For each of the following statements, place a T or F in the space provided to indicate whether the statement is true or false.

_____ 1. The concept of temporary differences implies that income taxes which are postponed come due later. In reality, the notion of temporary differences later reversing is questionable.

_____ 2. Income tax expense refers to an amount on the income statement while the amount of income taxes payable results from a tax return computation.

_____ 3. The capital lease method permits a company's management to recognize expenses later rather than sooner for financial reporting and results in a lower debt-equity ratio for the company.

_____ 4. The recognition of a lease asset and obligation on the books of the lessee will increase the lessee's debt-equity ratio.

_____ 5. For an employer with a defined contribution plan, pension expense is the amount contributed to the pension fund.

_____ 6. Generally accepted accounting principles require that income tax expense used in financial reporting be based on actual taxes payable.

_____ 7. A capital lease would be recorded if the present value of the lease payments equals or exceeds 90 percent of the leased asset's fair market value.

_____ 8. In a defined-contribution plan, the benefits to be received by retired employees are not defined.

_____ 9. Like other long-term liabilities, deferred income taxes are reported on the balance sheet at the present value of future cash payments.

_____ 10. Deferred income taxes result from permanent differences between book income and taxable income.

_____ 11. If the lease term extends for at least 75 percent of the leased asset's life, the lease should be accounted for as an operating lease.

_____ 12. Under the capital lease method, the lessee merely records annual rent expense when the lease payment is made.

_____ 13. Lessors prefer to account for a lease as an operating lease because it enables the recognition of income from the "sale" of the leased asset.

_____ 14. A visitor in Florida who rents a car for 2 weeks rents the auto under an operating lease arrangement.

_____ 15. If an employer's cumulative pension expenses exceed the employer's cumulative pension funding, the employer will report a pension asset on its balance sheet.

218

_____ 16. If a pension plan is funded, cash is set aside to pay the future liability.

_____ 17. A liability is usually recognized on the balance sheet if the entity needing financing enjoys the economic benefits and bears the economic risk of the transaction.

_____ 18. When the lessor and the lessee sign a capital lease, the lessor recognizes revenue in an amount equal to the book value of the leased asset.

_____ 19. The amounts to be contributed to the pension plan by the employer are defined in a defined-benefit plan.

_____ 20. In computing pension expense for a defined benefit plan, pension expense is increased by the expected return on pension investments.

_____ 21. Many firms prefer the operating lease method because the reported income is higher in the earlier years of the lease than it would be under the capital lease method.

_____ 22. Income tax expense equals income taxes payable currently plus (minus) credit (debit) changes in deferred tax accounts.

_____ 23. The existence of a bargain purchase option in a noncancellable lease would require that the lease be accounted for as a capital lease.

_____ 24. A temporary difference that will require income tax allocation between periods will result when a company reports interest revenue on an investment in tax-exempt municipal bonds.

_____ 25. A transaction, in which income from credit sales is recognized in the year of sale for book purposes and is recognized in the year cash is collected for tax purposes, creates a temporary difference that requires income tax allocation.

_____ 26. Off-balance sheet financing is preferred by lessees because the leased asset and corresponding obligation is left off the balance sheet.

_____ 27. In an operating lease, the lessor transfers the rights to use the property to the lessee for a specified period of time.

_____ 28. If a lease is considered to be in substance an installment purchase of property, then the property and the unpaid obligation should be accounted for under the operating lease method.

_____ 29. A deferred tax asset arises when a firm recognizes an expense earlier for financial reporting than for tax reporting.

_____ 30. A company's effective tax rate equals it's income tax expense divided by book income before income taxes.

_____ 31. The reason a company's effective tax rate differs from the statutory income tax rate is due solely to permanent differences (for example, municipal bond interest is not taxable).

_____ 32.   Pension expense for a defined benefit plan is not affected by any expected return on pension investments.

Matching. From the list of terms below, select the term which is most closely associated with each of the descriptive phrases or statements that follows and place the letter for that term in the space provided.

a. Bargain Purchase Option

b. Capital Lease Method

c. Debt-Equity Ratio

d. Deferred Tax Asset

e. Deferred Tax Liability

f. Defined Benefit Plan

g. Defined Contribution Plan

h. Income Tax Expense

i. Income Tax Payable

j. Lessee

k. Lessor

l. Off-Balance Sheet Financing

m. Operating Lease Method

n. Pension Expense

o. Permanent Differences

p. Temporary Differences

_____ 1.   This treatment recognizes the signing of a lease as the simultaneous acquisition of a long-term asset and the incurring of a long-term liability.

_____ 2.   Under a defined contribution plan this equals the amount contributed for the period.

_____ 3.   This amount results from a computation on the tax return.

_____ 4.   Differences between book income and taxable income that never reverse.

_____ 5.   Most managements prefer not to show an asset and a related liability on the balance sheet because of the increase in this computation which makes the company appear more risky.

_____ 6.   This equals the income taxes actually payable each period plus the income taxes a firm expects to pay (or minus the income taxes a firm expects to save) in the future when temporary differences reverse.

_____ 7.   The amounts to be paid to an employee upon retirement are based on a formula that usually takes into account the employee's length of service and average earnings.

_____ 8.   The amounts to be contributed to the pension plan by the employer are defined but the benefits to be received by retired employees are not defined.

_____ 9.   Landlord.

_____ 10.   Results in more favorable debt-equity ratios and may favorably affect future credit ratings and future borrowing costs.

_____ 11.   Tenant.

_____ 12.   These result when revenues and expenses for book purposes are reported in a different period than for tax purposes.

_____ 13.   This results when temporary differences that will result in future taxable income are multiplied by the enacted income tax rate expected to apply in the future period of the taxable income.

_____ 14.   Gives the lessee the right to purchase the asset for a price less than the predicted fair market value of the asset when the option is exercised.

_____ 15.   This results when temporary differences that give rise to future tax deductions are multiplied by the enacted income tax rate expected to apply in the future periods of the deduction.

_____ 16.   Under this method, the owner, or lessor, merely sells the rights to use the property to the lessee for specified periods of time.

Multiple Choice. Choose the best answer for each of the following questions and enter the identifying letter in the space provided.

The following information relates to questions 1-5. Vermont Company reports income tax expense of $224,000 on its income statement for the year ending December 31, Year 4. Included in Year 4's income was interest revenue of $40,000 from some tax exempt municipal bonds that the company owns. Additionally, in computing its income tax expense of $224,000, the company had a temporary difference of $80,000, which will result in a future tax deduction. It is assumed that a tax rate of 30 percent will apply to the future tax deduction. The tax rate for Year 4 (the company's first year of operations) is 40 percent.

_____ 1. What amount would Vermont Company report as current income tax payable on its Year 4 balance sheet?

   a. $224,000.
   b. $248,000.
   c. $208,000.
   d.   None of the above.

_____ 2. For the current year, how would Vermont Company report the tax effect of the temporary difference on its balance sheet?

   a.   A Deferred Tax Asset of $24,000 would be reported on its balance sheet.
   b.   A Deferred Tax Liability of $24,000 would be reported on its balance sheet.
   c.   A Deferred Tax Asset of $32,000 would be reported on its balance sheet.
   d.   A Deferred Tax Liability of $32,000 would be reported on its balance sheet.

_____ 3. What is Vermont Company's taxable income for Year 4?

     a. $560,000.
     b. $620,000.
     c. $520,000.
     d.   None of the above.

_____ 4. For the current year, how would Vermont Company report the tax effect of the permanent difference on its balance sheet?

     a.   A Deferred Tax Asset of $16,000 would be reported on its balance sheet.
     b.   A Deferred Tax Liability of $16,000 would be reported on its balance sheet.
     c.   Nothing is reported on the balance sheet because a permanent difference has no effect on deferred taxes.
     d.   None of the above.

_____ 5. What is Vermont Company's effective tax rate for Year 4?

     a. $224,000/$580,000 = .386.
     b. $224,000/$660,000 = .339.
     c. $224,000/$620,000 = .361.
     d.   None of the above.

_____ 6. On January 1, Year 1, Wyoming Company leased a building and recorded the leasehold asset and the liability at $210,620, which is the present value of five end-of-year payments of $50,000 each discounted at 6 percent. The asset has a useful life of five years and a zero salvage value. On December 31, Year 1, when the first lease payment is made. Wyoming would record interest expense of

     a. $ -0-.
     b. $ 7,876.
     c. $39,380.
     d.   None of the above.

_____ 7. Refer to the previous question. Assuming straight-line amortization, on December 31, Year 1, Wyoming would report the book value of the leasehold asset on its balance sheet in the amount of

     a. $250,000.
     b. $168,496.
     c. $210,620.
     d. $160,620.

_____ 8. Arizona Company purchased a machine early in Year 1. For book purposes, Arizona uses straight-line depreciation. For tax purposes, MACRS is followed. Excess depreciation for tax purposes in Year 1 was $36,000. Assuming a tax rate of 30 percent will apply in the future period of taxable income, determine the amount of income taxes deferred in Year 1.

     a. $36,000.
     b. $25,200.
     c. $10,800.
     d.   None of the above.

_____ 9. Refer to the previous question. For Year 2, excess depreciation for tax purposes was $18,000. Assuming that a tax rate of 30 percent will apply in the future period of taxable income, determine the balance in the deferred tax liability account at end of Year 2.

   a. $16,200.
   b. $30,600.
   c. $23,400.
   d. $ 5,400.

_____10. Refer to the two previous questions. In Year 2, Arizona reported a current liability for income taxes of $39,000. What amount of income tax expense did Arizona report on its Year 2 Income Statement?

   a. $39,000.
   b. $44,400.
   c. $33,600.
   d. $49,800.

_____11. Estes Park Company reported book income of $96,000 and taxable income of $120,000 (the $24,000 difference is attributed to warranty expenses). The statutory tax rate is 30 percent and the company reports a current liability for income taxes payable of $36,000 on its Year 1 Balance Sheet. In its Income Statement the company reports income tax expense at an effective rate of 37.5 percent. What amount of Income Tax Expense did Estes Park report for Year 1?

   a. $36,000.
   b. $21,600.
   c. $17,280.
   d. $33,750.

_____12. Refer to the previous question. The difference between the statutory tax rate and the effective tax rate is due to

   a.   A temporary difference that resulted in book income exceeding taxable income.
   b.   A temporary difference that resulted in taxable income exceeding book income.
   c.   A permanent difference resulting in book income exceeding taxable income.
   d.   A permanent difference resulting in taxable income exceeding book income.

_____13. On 1/1, Year 1, Lake Powell Co. leased equipment under a capital lease that calls for five payments of $25,000 each at the end of each year. The first payment is due on 12/31, Year 1. Using 12 percent interest, the present value of the lease liability is $90,000 on 1/1, Year 1. How much of the first payment of $25,000 is interest expense?

   a. $10,800.
   b. $ 7,000.
   c. $15,000.
   d. $10,000.

_____14. Refer to the previous question. At what amount would Lake Powell Co. report the lease liability on its 12/31, Year 1 Balance Sheet?

    a. $ 79,200.
    b. $ 83,000.
    c. $100,000.
    d. $ 75,800.

_____15. In computing its income tax expense for the current year (its first year of operations), Nevada Corporation had an $18,000 temporary difference (accelerated depreciation for tax purposes.) It is assumed that a tax rate of 35 percent will apply to the future period of taxable income. The company's income for tax purposes is $282,000 and the current tax rate is 40 percent. What amount would Nevada Corp. report as income tax expense for the current year?

    a. $119,100.
    b. $120,000.
    c. $105,600.
    d. $106,500.

_____16. Refer to the previous question. For the current year, how would Nevada Corp report the tax effect of the temporary difference on its balance sheet?

    a.   A Deferred Tax Asset of $7,200 would be reported on its balance sheet.
    b.   A Deferred Tax Liability of $7,200 would be reported on its balance sheet.
    c.   A Deferred Tax Asset of $6,300 would be reported on its balance sheet.
    d.   A Deferred Tax Liability of $6,300 would be reported on its balance sheet.

_____17. Cripple Creek reported a current liability for income tax payable of $180,000 on its 12/31, Year 2, balance sheet. During the year, the corporation's Deferred Tax Liability account increased by $54,000 based on a tax rate of 40 percent applying to the future period of taxable income. The tax rate for Year 2 was 30 percent. What was Cripple Creek's book income for Year 2?

    a. $600,000.
    b. $735,000.
    c. $780,000.
    d. $585,000.

_____18. Refer to the previous question. Regarding Cripple Creek's operations in Year 2.

    a.   Book income exceeded taxable income.
    b.   Taxable income exceeded book income.
    c.   Book income equaled taxable income.
    d.   The difference between book income and taxable income is due to a permanent difference.

_____19. Teton Corporation reported book income of $720,000 for Year 1. Included in the computation of the $720,000 was Warranty Expense of $80,000. For tax purposes warranty costs are not deductible until incurred. Actual expenditures for warranty costs during Year 1 totaled $48,000. The tax rate for Year 1 is 30 percent. What amount should Teton report as a current liability for Income Tax Payable on its 12/31, Year 1, balance sheet?

    a. $192,000.
    b. $201,600.
    c. $216,000.
    d. $225,600.

_____20. Refer to the previous question. Regarding Teton's operations in Year 1,

    a.   Book income exceeded taxable income.
    b.   Taxable income exceeded book income.
    c.   Book income equaled taxable income.
    d.   The difference between book income and taxable income is due to a permanent difference.

_____21. On 1/1, Year 1, Utah Company leased some equipment from Dixie Tool Supply under an operating lease for 4 years. Lease payments of $20,000 are payable at the end of each year. The first payment is due on 12/31, Year 1. Using an interest rate of 11 percent, the present value of the four payments is $62,000 on 1/1, Year 1. What expenses would Utah report on its Year 1 Income Statement related to this lease?

    a.   Interest Expense of $6,820 and Depreciation Expense of $15,500.
    b.   Rent Expense of $20,000.
    c.   Interest Expense of $4,500 and Depreciation Expense of $15,500.
    d.   Interest Expense of $6,820 and Depreciation Expense of $20,000.

_____22. Generally, the accounting treatment for leases favored by lessors and lessees is

    a.   Both generally prefer operating leases.
    b.   Both generally prefer capital leases.
    c.   Lessors prefer capital leases while lessees prefer operating leases.
    d.   Lessors prefer operating leases while lessees prefer capital leases.

_____23. This method of recording leases recognizes the signing of the lease as the acquisition of a long-term asset and the incurring of a long-term liability for lease payments.

    a.   Operating lease method.
    b.   Capital lease method.
    c.   Rental lease method.
    d.   None of the above.

_____24. Lessees prefer operating leases for several reasons. Which of the following is such a reason?

   a.   Capital leases result in an increased debt-equity ratio.
   b.   Capital leases result in earlier recognition of expenses.
   c.   Operating leases result in the nonrecognition of lease assets and lease liabilities.
   d.   All of the above are reasons for lessees preferring operating leases.

_____25. Cheyenne Company included in its book income $75,000 of interest on municipal bonds. The company reported a current liability of $270,000 for income tax payable on its Balance Sheet. The tax rate is 30 percent. What net income will Cheyenne report on its Income Statement?

   a. $705,000.
   b. $900,000.
   c. $975,000.
   d. $630,000.

_____26. A lease must be accounted for as a capital lease if it meets any one of four conditions. Which of the following is not one of the conditions?

   a.   The lease contains a bargain purchase option.
   b.   The lease transfers ownership of property to lessee.
   c.   The lease term is 90 percent or more of the estimated economic life of the leased property.
   d.   All of the above are conditions that (if any one is met) would cause the lease to be capitalized.

_____27. In which of the following situations would the lessee enjoy the economic benefits and bear the economic risk of leasing an asset?

   a.   An asset with an economic life of 10 years is leased for 4 years.
   b.   The lease agreement contains a bargain purchase option.
   c.   At the end of the lease term, the lessee returns the leased asset to the lessor.
   d.   The present value of the lease payments is $70,000 and the fair market value of the leased asset is $95,000.

_____28. Under this method of recording leases, the lessee must amortize the leasehold over its useful life and must recognize each lease payment as part payment of interest and part principal.

   a.   Operating lease method.
   b.   Capital lease method.
   c.   Rental lease method.
   d.   None of the above.

_____29. Which of the following is not a criticism of the accounting for deferred income taxes?

    a.   Payment of deferred taxes may be deferred indefinitely.
    b.   The amount on the balance sheet for deferred income taxes is not an obligation.
    c.   Deferred taxes result in the effective tax rate being different than the statutory tax rate.
    d.   The amount on the balance sheet for deferred income taxes is an undiscounted amount.

_____30. An employee is likely to prefer this type of pension plan because it reduces the employee's risk in planning for retirement.

    a.   Nonvesting plan.
    b.   Defined contribution plan.
    c.   Nonfunded plan.
    d.   Defined benefit plan.

_____31. Which of the following statements is not descriptive of a defined contribution pension plan?

    a.   This plan defines the employer's contribution to the plan.
    b.   The amounts to be received by employees depend on the investment performance of the pension plan.
    c.   Pension benefits received during retirement are based on wages earned and number of years of employment.
    d.   The employer's pension expense equals the amount contributed to the pension fund.

_____32. Which of the following is not a perceived advantage of off-balance sheet financing?

    a.   The debt-equity ratio will be higher.
    b.   Future credit ratings might be higher.
    c.   Future borrowing costs might be lower.
    d.   All of the above are perceived advantages of off-balance sheet financing.

_____33. An entry such as the one that follows indicates that the lessee has accounted for the lease in what manner?

```
Interest Expense                              xx
Liability-Present Value of Lease Obligation   xx
  Cash                                              xx
```

    a.   Sales type lease.
    b.   Operating lease.
    c.   Capital lease.
    d.   None of the above.

_____34. Which of the following is not an example of a temporary difference and which, therefore, would not result in a deferred income tax account being debited or credited?

    a. A company uses straight-line depreciation for book purposes and ACRS for tax purposes.
    b. Estimated warranty costs are expensed in the year of sale but warranty costs are deducted for tax purposes in the year when repairs are made.
    c. In its financial reports, a company reports interest revenue earned on tax-exempt municipal bonds held as assets.
    d. For book purposes, a company uses the percentage-of-completion basis but uses the completed contract basis for tax purposes.

_____35. On 1/1, Year 1 the Colorado Springs Medical Clinic leased some diagnostic equipment under a capital lease for 6 years. Using 10 percent interest, the present value of the lease liability was $244,000 on 1/1, Year 1. After the first lease payment is made on 12/31, Year 1, the clinic reports a lease liability of $212,400. What is the amount of each lease payment?

    a. $46,936.
    b. $31,600.
    c. $56,000.
    d. $40,664.

_____36. Montana Corporation's reported book income is $600,000 and income for tax purposes is $570,000. The $30,000 difference is caused by the use of MACRS for tax purposes. Assuming that the current tax rate is 35 percent and that a tax rate of 40 percent will apply to the future period of taxable income, determine the amount of taxes currently payable.

    a. $210,000.
    b. $ 12,000.
    c. $199,500.
    d. $211,500.

Exercises

1. On January 1, Year 1, Phoenix Company leased some equipment for 3 years. The lease calls for the first annual payment to be made on December 31, Year 1.

    a. Fill in the 13 blanks on the lease amortization schedule below:

Year	Lease Liability Beginning of Year	Interest Expense for Year	Payment	Reduction of Obligation	Lease Liability End of Year
0	_____	_____	_____	_____	270,000
1	_____	21,600	_____	_____	_____
2	_____	_____	104,772	_____	_____
3	_____	_____	_____	_____	_____

    b. If Phoenix treated the lease as a capital lease and amortized the leased asset on a straight-line basis over the 3-year lease term, how much expense, in total, would the company report each year relating to the lease transaction? If the lease were treated as an operating lease, how much expense would the company report each year?

2. On its 12/31, Year 3, balance sheet, the Maricopa Corporation reports a deferred tax asset of $170,000 and a deferred tax liability of $106,000.

    For Years 4 and 5, Maricopa Corporation's income statement and balance sheet reported the following:

	Year 4	Year 5
Taxable Income	$1,800,000	$1,500,000
Total Deferred Tax Assets	208,000	242,000
Total Deferred Tax Liabilities	130,000	190,000

    The tax rate for Years 3-5 was 40 percent.

    Prepare entries for Year 4 and Year 5 to record income taxes for each of the 2 years.

3. On January 2, Year 1, the LaVeta Company leased a machine for 4 years from Specialty Products Co. Annual rentals of $37,500 are to be paid at the end of each calendar year. The present value on January 2, Year 1, of the four lease payments, discounted at 8 percent, is $124,200. The asset's useful life is 4 years, and its salvage value is zero.

    Prepare all Year 1 entries relative to the lease of the machine if LaVeta records the lease by the capital lease method. Also, prepare the Year 2 entry for the lease payment.

4. Refer to Exercise 3 above. Prepare all Year 1 entries relative to the lease of the machine on the books of Specialty Products Co. Assume that Specialty Products manufactured the machine at a cost of $112,500 and that the company treats the lease as a capital lease. Also, prepare the Year 2 entry for the receipt of the lease payment.

5. The Jackson Hole Company reports the book basis and tax basis of its asset and liabilities for Years 1-4 as follows:

Date	Book Basis	Tax Basis	Temporary Difference
12/31, Year 1			
Assets	$ 300,000	$ 180,000	$120,000
Liabilities	150,000	150,000	--
12/31, Year 2			
Assets	570,000	390,000	180,000
Liabilities	220,000	220,000	--
12/31, Year 3			
Assets	795,000	630,000	165,000
Liabilities	187,500	187,500	--
12/31, Year 4			
Assets	1,005,000	915,000	90,000
Liabilities	210,000	210,000	--

Assume that the company's taxable income is $375,000 in each of the 4 years and that the tax rate is 35 percent for each of the 4 years.

a. Compute the amount of income tax expense for Year 1 - 4.

b. Record the appropriate entries for income tax allocation at the end of each of the four years.

c. What is the balance in the deferred tax liability account at 12/31, Year 4?

d. The statutory tax rate in each of the 4 years is 35 percent. Compute the effective tax rate for each of the 4 years. Compare the effective tax rate and the statutory tax rate for each year.

6. The North Rim Company reported pretax income of $500,000 at the end of its first year in business. Included in the computation of pretax income were the following two items:
    1. interest earned on municipal bonds totaled $60,000
    2. depreciation expense totaled $100,000.

In computing taxable income, the interest earned on municipal bonds is not taxable. Depreciation for tax purposes totaled $150,000. The statutory tax rate is 40 percent.

a. Compute the company's taxable income.

b. Record the year end entry for tax expense and taxes payable.

c. Compute the company's effective tax rate for the year and compare it to the statutory tax rate.

7. Durango Company reported pretax income of $800,000 at the end of its first year in business. Included in the computation of pretax income were the following two items:
   1. interest earned on municipal bonds totaled $100,000
   2. warranty expense totaled $64,000.

   In computing taxable income, the interest earned on municipal bonds is not taxable. None of the warranty expense is deductible for tax purposes during this first year. It is expected that warranty expenses will be deductible for tax purposes in Years 2 and 3 when the tax rate is expected to be 35 percent. The tax rate for Year 1 is 40 percent.

   a. Compute the company's taxable income.

   b. Record the year end entry for tax expense and taxes payable.

c. Compute the company's effective tax rate for the year and compare it to the statutory tax rate.

8. Camelrock Corporation reported the following relating to a lease transaction on its 12/31 Year 4 balance sheet (the company entered into the lease transaction on 1/1 Year 4):

Leased Asset	$143,900
Less: Accumulated Amortization	
on leased asset	23,983
	$119,917
Liability-Present Value of	
Lease Obligation	$126,168

Assuming (1) that the lease is being amortized on a straight line basis over the term of the lease, (2) that the effective interest rate for the lease transaction is 12 percent, and (3) that lease payments occur at 12/31 of each year, compute

a. the term of the lease

b. the interest expense for Year 4

c. the amount of each lease payment

d. the total of amortization expense and interest expense for Year 5

e. the balance of the lease liability on 12/31 Year 5

Answers to Questions and Exercises

True/False

1.	T	6.	F	11.	F	16.	T	21.	T	26.	T	31.	F
2.	T	7.	T	12.	F	17.	T	22.	T	27.	T	32.	F
3.	F	8.	T	13.	F	18.	F	23.	T	28.	F		
4.	T	9.	F	14.	T	19.	F	24.	F	29.	T		
5.	T	10.	F	15.	F	20.	F	25.	T	30.	T		

Matching

1.	b	4.	o	7.	f	10.	l	13.	e	16.	m
2.	n	5.	c	8.	g	11.	j	14.	a		
3.	i	6.	h	9.	k	12.	p	15.	d		

Multiple Choice

1.	b	8.	c	15.	a	22.	c	29.	c	36.	c
2.	a	9.	a	16.	d	23.	b	30.	d		
3.	b	10.	b	17.	b	24.	d	31.	c		
4.	c	11.	a	18.	a	25.	c	32.	a		
5.	a	12.	b	19.	d	26.	c	33.	c		
6.	d	13.	a	20.	b	27.	b	34.	c		
7.	b	14.	d	21.	b	28.	b	35.	c		

Exercises

1. a.

Year	Lease Liability Beginning of Year	Interest Expense for Year	Payment	Reduction of Obligation	Lease Liability End of Year
0					270,000
1	270,000	21,600	104,772	83,172	186,828
2	186,828	14,946	104,772	89,826	97,002
3	97,002	7,770	104,772	97,002	0

b. Annual Expenses:

	Capital Lease				Operating Lease	
Year	Straight-Line Amortization	Interest Expense	Total Expense		Year	Rent Expense
1	90,000	21,600	111,600		1	104,772
2	90,000	14,946	104,946		2	104,772
3	90,000	7,770	97,770		3	104,772

2.

			Dr.	Cr.
12/31 Year 4	Income Tax Expense		706,000	
	Deferred Tax Asset		38,000	
		Deferred Tax Liability		24,000
		Income Tax Payable		720,000
	To record Year 4 taxes.			
12/31 Year 5	Income Tax Expense		626,000	
	Deferred Tax Asset		34,000	
		Deferred Tax Liability		60,000
		Income Tax Payable		600,000
	To record Year 5 taxes.			

3.

			Dr.	Cr.
1/2 Year 1	Asset-Machine Leasehold		124,200	
		Liability-Present Value of Lease Obligation		124,200
	To record leasehold asset and liability.			
12/31 Year 1	Amortization Expense		31,050	
		Asset-Machine Leasehold		31,050
	To record amortization of asset leasehold. Amortization = $124,200 ÷ 4 = $31,050.			

12/31 Year 1	Interest Expense	9,936	
	Liability-Present Value of		
	Lease Obligation	27,564	
	Cash		37,500
	To record payment of interest		
	and principal.		
	Interest = .08 x $124,200 =		
	$9,936.		
12/31 Year 2	Interest Expense	7,731	
	Liability-Present Value of		
	Lease Obligation	29,769	
	Cash		37,500
	To record payment of		
	interest and principal.		
	Interest = .08 ($124,200 - $27,564)		
	= $7,731.		

4.

1/2 Year 1	Lease Receivable	124,200	
	Sales Revenue		124,200
	To record the sale of a		
	machine.		
	Cost of Goods Sold	112,500	
	Inventory		112,500
	To record the cost of the		
	machine sold.		
12/31 Year 1	Cash	37,500	
	Interest Revenue		9,936
	Lease Receivable		27,564
	To record receipt of first		
	lease payment.		
12/31 Year 2	Cash	37,500	
	Interest Revenue		7,731
	Lease Receivable		29,769
	To record receipt of second		
	lease payment.		

5.

a. Year 1

Income Tax Payable: .35 x $375,000	$131,250
Increase in Deferred Tax Liability: .35 x $120,000	42,000
Income Tax Expense	$173,250

Year 2

Income Tax Payable: .35 x $375,000	$131,250
Increase in Deferred Tax Liability: .35 ($180,000 - $120,000)	21,000
Income Tax Expense	$152,250

Year 3

Income Tax Payable: .35 x $375,000	$131,250
Decrease in Deferred Tax Liability: .35 ($165,000 - $180,000)	(5,250)
Income Tax Expense	$126,000

<u>Year 4</u>
```
Income Tax Payable: .35 x $375,000                               $131,250
Decrease in Deferred Tax Liability: .35 ($90,000 - $165,000)      (26,250)
Income Tax Expense                                               $105,000
```

b.

			Dr.	Cr.
12/31 Year 1	Income Tax Expense		173,250	
	Income Tax Payable			131,250
	Deferred Tax Liability			42,000
	To record income taxes for Year 1.			
12/31 Year 2	Income Tax Expense		152,250	
	Income Tax Payable			131,250
	Deferred Tax Liability			21,000
	To record income taxes for Year 2.			
12/31 Year 3	Income Tax Expense		126,000	
	Deferred Tax Liability		5,250	
	Income Tax Payable			131,250
	To record income taxes for Year 3.			
12/31 Year 4	Interest Tax Expense		105,000	
	Deferred Tax Liability		26,250	
	Income Tax Payable			131,250
	To record income taxes for Year 4.			

c.

```
                     Deferred Tax Liability
                              $42,000   (12/31 Year 1)
                              $21,000   (12/31 Year 2)
(12/31 Year 3) $ 5,250
(12/31 Year 4) $26,250
                              Balance   $31,500
```

d.

	Year 1	Year 2	Year 3	Year 4
Taxable Income	$375,000	$375,000	$375,000	$375,000
Temporary Difference	120,000	60,000	(15,000)	(75,000)
Book Income Before Income Tax Expense	$495,000	$435,000	$360,000	$300,000

Effective Tax Rate = $\dfrac{\text{Income Tax Expense}}{\text{Income Before Taxes}}$

Year 1 $\dfrac{\$173,250}{\$495,000}$ = 35%

Year 2 $\dfrac{\$152,250}{\$435,000}$ = 35%

Year 3 $\dfrac{\$126,000}{\$360,000}$ = 35%

Year 4 $\dfrac{\$105,000}{\$300,000}$ = 35%

The statutory tax rate and the effective tax rate are both 35 percent in all four years because there were no permanent differences and because there were no differences in the tax rate over the four year period.

6.

a.

Pretax income	$500,000
Less: Municipal bond interest-not taxable	(60,000)
Less: Excess depreciation for tax purposes	(50,000)
Taxable income	$390,000

b.

	Dr.	Cr.
12/31 Year 1 Income Tax Expense	176,000	
Deferred Tax Liability		20,000
Income Tax Payable		156,000

To record income tax expense and income tax liabilities.
Income Tax Payable = .40 ($390,000)
Deferred Tax Liability = .40 ($50,000)

c.   Effective Tax Rate = $\dfrac{\text{Income Tax Expense}}{\text{Income Before Taxes}}$

$$= \dfrac{\$176,000}{\$500,000}$$

$$= 35.2\%$$

The difference in the statutory tax rate of 40 percent and the effective tax rate of 35.2 percent is due to the permanent difference (the municipal bond interest is not taxable).

7.

a.

Pretax income	$800,000
Less: Municipal bond interest-not taxable	(100,000)
Plus: Warranty expenses not deductible in Year 1 for tax purposes	64,000
Taxable income	$764,000

	Dr.	Cr.
b. Income Tax Expense	283,200	
Deferred Tax Asset	22,400	
Income Tax Payable		305,600

b.
  To record income tax expense,
deferred tax asset, and
income tax payable.
Income Tax Payable = .40 ($764,000)
Deferred Tax Asset = .35 ($64,000)

c.
$$\text{Effective Tax Rate} = \frac{\text{Income Tax Expense}}{\text{Income Before Taxes}}$$

$$= \frac{\$283,200}{\$800,000} = 35.4\%$$

The difference in the statutory tax rate of 40 percent and the effective tax rate of 35.4 percent is due to the permanent difference (the municipal bond interest is not taxable) and the expected change in the tax rate for Years 2 and 3 when the warranty expenses will be deductible for tax purposes.

8. a. Leased Asset $\frac{\$143,900}{23,983}$ = 6 years
        Amortization for Year

b. Interest Expense = $17,268 ($143,900 x .12)

c.
Liability at 1/1 Year 4	$143,900
Liability at 12/3 Year 4	126,168
Reduction of Liability	$ 17,732
Plus: Interest Expense	17,268
Amount of each lease payment	$ 35,000

d.
Year 5 amortization expense ($143,900/6)	$ 23,983
Year 5 interest expense ($126,168 x .12)	15,140
Year 5 expense	$ 39,123

e.
Liability balance on 12/31 Year 4	$126,168
Plus: Year 5 Interest expense	15,140
Less: Year 5 lease payment	(35,000)
Liability balance on 12/31 Year 5	$106,308

Chapter 11

Marketable Securities, Derivatives, and Investments

Chapter Highlights

1. For a variety of reasons, corporations often acquire the securities (bonds, preferred stock, common stock) of other entities. For example, a business may invest (in the short term) some of its excess cash in income-yielding securities such as bonds or stocks. A business may also invest in securities intending to hold them for a longer period.

2. The accounting for investments in securities depends on the expected holding period and the purpose of the investment.

3. The expected holding period determines where investments in securities appear in the balance sheet. Securities that firms expect to sell within the next year appear as "Marketable Securities" in the Current Asset section of the balance sheet. Securities that firms expect to hold for more than one year from the date of the balance sheet appear in "Investments in Securities," which firms include in a separate section of the balance sheet between Current Assets and Property, Plant and Equipment. When a company owns sufficient number of shares to control the other company, it would prepare consolidated financial statements, consolidating both companies' assets and liabilities on the balance sheet.

4. The purpose of the investment in securities and the percentage of voting stock that one corporation own of another determine the accounting for the investment. Three types of investments can be identified: (1) minority, passive investments, (2) minority, active investments, and (3) majority, active investments.

5. Minority, passive investments are bonds or shares of capital stock of another corporation viewed as a worthwhile expenditure and are acquired for the anticipated interest, dividends and capital gains (increases in the market price of the shares). The percentage of shares owned is not so large (less than 20 percent of the voting stock) that the acquiring company can control or exert significant influence over the other company. The owner may intend to hold these shares for relatively short time spans and classify them as current assets, called, marketable securities, or for an indefinite time and classify them as investments.

6. Minority, active investments are shares of another corporation acquired so that the acquiring corporation can exert significant influence over the other company's activities. Generally accepted accounting principles view investments of 20 percent to 50 percent of the voting stock of another company as minority, active investments "unless evidence indicates that significant influence cannot be exercised." Minority, active investments appear under investments on the balance sheet.

7. Majority, active investments are shares of another corporation acquired so that the acquiring corporation can control the other company both at the broad policy-making level and at the day-to-day operations level. Ownership of more than 50 percent of the voting stock of another company implies ability to control, unless there is evidence to the contrary.

8. Securities, classified as minority, passive investments, when acquired are initially recorded at acquisition cost, which includes the purchase price, plus any commissions, taxes and other costs incurred. Dividends on equity securities become revenue when declared. Interest on debt securities becomes revenue when earned.

9. Generally accepted accounting principles require firms to classify minority, passive investments into three categories: (a) debt securities for which a firm has a positive intent and ability to hold to maturity; (b) debt and equity securities, as well as derivatives, held as trading securities; and (c) debt and equity securities, as well as derivatives held as securities available for sale. This classification scheme is relevant for valuation of securities subsequent to acquisition. This classification scheme is applicable to securities held as current assets (Marketable Securities) and some long-term investments.

10. Debt securities for which a firm has a positive intent and ability to hold to maturity appear in the balance sheet at amortized acquisition cost. The acquisition cost of debt securities may differ from their maturity value. The difference between acquisition cost and maturity value is amortized over the life of the debt security as an adjustment to interest revenue.

11. Trading securities are reported on the balance sheet at market value because (a) active securities markets provide objective measures of market values, and (b) market values provide financial statement users with the most relevant information for assessing the success of a firm's trading activities over time.

12. Decreases in the market value of trading securities and increases in the market value of trading securities are reported in the account, Unrealized Holding Loss or Unrealized Holding Gain on Trading Securities, on the income statement.

13. Debt and equity securities held as securities available for sale, trade in active securities markets and have easily measurable market values. Securities, which a firm intends to sell within one year, appear in Marketable Securities in the current assets section of the balance sheet. All others appear as a noncurrent asset, Investment in Securities, on the balance sheet. Securities available for sale are reported on the balance sheet at market value. Dividends or interest earned on securities available for sale are reported as income each period. Any unrealized holding loss or holding gain each period does not affect income immediately but instead decreases or increases a separate shareholders' equity account, Unrealized Holding Loss or Unrealized Holding Gain on Securities Available for Sale (Accumulated Other Comprehensive Income, typically appearing between Additional Paid-In Capital and Retained Earnings). Holding gains and losses on securities available for sale affect net income only when the securities are sold and are reported as Realized Gain or Realized Loss on Sale of Securities Available for Sale.

14. When securities are transferred from one of the three categories to another one, the firm transfers the security at its market value at the time of the transfer.

15. Firms can purchase financial instruments to lessen the risks of economic losses from changes in interest rate, foreign exchange rates, and commodity prices. The term used for these financial instruments is a derivative. A derivative is a financial instrument that obtains its value from some other financial item. Changes in the value of the derivative instrument offset changes in the value of an asset or liability or changes in future cash flow, thereby neutralizing, at least reducing, the economic loss.

16. For example, in accounting and finance, frequently an entity purchases (or sells) a derivative contract, such as an interest rate swap. An interest rate swap is a derivative that typically obligates one party and counterparty to exchange the difference between fixed and floating rate interest payments on otherwise similar loans. The term counterparty refers to the opposite party in a legal contract.

17. Some elements of a derivative include: a. Derivatives have one or more underlyings. An underlying is a variable such as a specified interest rate, commodity price, or foreign exchange rate. b. A derivative has one or more notional amounts. A notional amount is a number of currency unites, bushels, shares, or other units specified in the contract. c. A derivative often requires no initial investments. The firm usually acquires a derivative by exchanging promises with a counter party (e.g. commercial or investment bank). d. Derivatives typically require, or permit, net settlement.

18. A firm must recognize derivatives in its balance sheet as assets or liabilities, depending on the rights and obligations under the contract. Firms must revalue the derivatives to market value each period. The revaluation amount, in addition to increasing or decreasing the derivative asset or liability, also affects either a) net come immediately or b) other comprehensive income immediately and net income later. Other Comprehensive Income is a temporary shareholders' equity account that reports changes during an accounting period in the recorded amounts of certain assets and liabilities, such as derivatives.

19. Generally accepted accounting principles classify derivatives as a) speculative investments, b) fair value hedges, or c) cash flow hedges. Firms must choose to designate a derivative as either a fair value or cash flow hedge (depending on the strategy and purpose of acquiring a particular derivative) or account for the derivative as a speculative investment.

20. A firm must report changes in the market value of a speculative investment as a gain or loss in current earnings.

21. When a firm acquires a derivative and attempts to reduce risks involving fluctuations in a market value, the FASB classifies the transaction as a fair-value hedge. The derivative appears on the balance sheet at its fair value. The FASB requires the firm to show in income each period the change in the fair value of a derivative that qualifies as a fair-value hedge. The firm will also record at fair value the asset or liability it is hedging so under most circumstances the net effect on both net assets and net income will be zero. If the firm does not acquire a perfect hedge, the firm will report in income and net cost of the unsuccessful hedge or the net benefit of the over-successful hedge.

22. When a firm acquires a derivative and attempts to reduce the risk in future streams of cash flows (inflows or outflows) the FASB classifies the transaction as a cash-flow hedge. A firm will show the cash-flow hedge at its fair value on the balance sheet, but will not report the matching gain or loss in net earnings of the period. The gain or loss will appear as part of comprehensive income (discussed in Chapter 12) and will appear on the balance sheet in owners' equity but does not affect retained earnings. This unrealized gain or loss on changes in the fair value of the cash-flow hedge remain on the balance sheet in a separate shareholders' equity account to later match against any loss or gain on the cash-flow commitment when it settles.

23. In the following discussion the acquiring firm will be referred to as Company P, for purchaser or parent. Company S, for seller or subsidiary, will be used to refer to the firm whose shares are acquired or owned.

24. Generally accepted accounting principles require the use of the equity method for minority, active investments (Company P owns 20 percent or more of the voting stock of Company S, but not more than 50 percent). Under the equity method, the purchase of stock is recorded at acquisition cost. However, Company P treats as income each period its proportionate share of the periodic earnings of Company S. The entry to record this income is a debit to the account, Investment in Stock of S, and a credit to Equity in Earnings of Affiliate (Increase in Shareholders' Equity - Retained Earnings). Dividends paid by Company S to Company P are treated by Company P as a reduction in its investment in Company S. The entry to record dividends received is a debit to Cash and a credit to Investment in Stock of S.

25. One complication using the equity method arises when the acquisition cost of P's shares exceeds P's proportionate share of the book value of the net assets (assets minus liabilities), or stockholders' equity, of S at the date of acquisition. P may pay an amount that differs from the book value of S's recorded net assets because the market values of the net assets differ from their book values or because of unrecorded assets (for example, goodwill) or unrecorded liabilities (for example, an unsettled lawsuit). GAAP previously required firms to write off this excess acquisition cost over a period not to exceed 40 years. Beginning in 2001, firms need no longer amortize this excess to the extent it relates to goodwill. Firms may also discontinue amortizing goodwill from investments made prior to 2001. Firms must still amortize the excess as to the extent it relates to other assets and liabilities.

26. Under the equity method the amount shown in the noncurrent section of the balance sheet for Investment in Stock of S will generally be equal to the acquisition cost of the shares plus Company P's share of Company S's undistributed earnings since the date the shares were acquired. On the income statement, Company P shows its share of Company S's net income as revenue each period.

27. Control of one corporation (Company S) by another (Company P) is assured when Company P owns more than 50 percent of Company S's voting stock. Company P can control both broad policy-making and day-to-day operations. The corporation exercising control through stock ownership is the parent, and the one subject to control is the subsidiary. Generally accepted accounting principles require majority, active investments (over 50 percent) to be reported by the preparation of consolidated statements. Consolidated statements are designed to report the financial position and operations of two or more legally distinct entities as if they were a single, centrally controlled economic entity.

28. When one company controls another, the controlling company could bring the legal existence of the controlled company to an end. However, some important reasons for continued existence of subsidiary companies are (a) to reduce financial risk of one segment (subsidiary) becoming insolvent, (b) to meet more effectively the requirements of state corporation and tax legislation, (c) to expand or diversify with a minimum of capital investment, and (d) to sell an unwanted operation with a minimum of administrative, legal and other costs.

29. Generally, consolidated financial statements provide more useful information than would separate financial statements of the parent and each subsidiary or than would be provided using the equity method. The parent, because of its voting interest, can control the use of all of the subsidiary's assets. Consolidation of the individual assets and equities of both the parent and the subsidiary provides a more realistic picture of the operations and financial position of the single economic entity. Consolidated financial statements are generally prepared when the following two criteria are met: (1) the parent owns more than 50 percent of the voting stock of the subsidiary; and (2) there are no important restrictions on the ability of the parent to exercise control of the subsidiary. However, the FASB requires the consolidation of certain entities where one company (P) may be the primary beneficiary of the outcomes of another entity even if ownership is less than 50 percent.

30. State laws typically require each legally separate corporation to maintain its own set of books. The consolidation of these financial statements basically involves summing the amounts for various financial statement items across the separate company statements. Consolidated financial statements reflect the transactions between the consolidated group of entities and others outside the entity. Thus, adjustments to these summations must be made to eliminate double counting resulting from intercompany transactions. The eliminations typically appear on a consolidation work sheet and not on the books of any of the legal entities being consolidated.

31. For example, a parent may lend money to its subsidiary. If the separate balance sheets were added together, then the funds would be counted twice - once as the notes receivable on the parent's books and again as cash or other assets on the subsidiary's books. Therefore, an entry is made to eliminate the receivable of the parent and the payable of the subsidiary in preparing consolidated statements.

32. Another example of an elimination entry to avoid double counting relates to the parent's investment account. If the assets of the parent (including the investment account) were added to the assets of the subsidiary, there would be double counting of the subsidiary's assets. At the same time the sources of financing would be counted twice if the shareholders equity accounts of Company S were added to those of Company P. Therefore, an eliminating entry removes the investment account of the parent and, correspondingly, shareholders' equity items of the subsidiary. In addition Company P's account, Equity in Earnings of Company S, must be eliminated to avoid the double counting of Company S's revenues and expenses.

33. A consolidated income statement is little more than the sum of the income statements of the parent and the subsidiaries. Intercompany transactions such as sales and purchases are eliminated in order to avoid double counting. Thus, the consolidated income statement attempts to show sales, expenses, and net income figures that report the results of operations of the group of companies in their dealings with the outside world.

34. The amount of consolidated net income for a period is the same as the amount that would be reported if the parent company used the equity method of accounting for the intercorporate investment. That is, consolidated net income is equal to parent company's net income plus parent's share of subsidiary's net income minus profit (or plus loss) on intercompany transactions. However, under the equity method for an unconsolidated subsidiary, the parent's share of subsidiary's net income (adjusted for intercompany transactions) appears on a single line, Equity in Earnings of Unconsolidated Subsidiary. The consolidation process combines the individual revenues and expenses of the subsidiary (adjusted for intercompany transactions) with those of the parent, and eliminates the account Equity in Earnings of Unconsolidated Subsidiary, shown on the parent's books.

35. When a parent company owns less than 100 percent of the subsidiary, the minority stockholders continue to have a proportionate interest in the shareholders' equity of the subsidiary as shown in its separate corporate records. The amount of minority interest appearing in the balance sheet results from multiplying the common stockholders' equity of the subsidiary by the minority's percentage of ownership. Typically the minority interest appears among the equities on the consolidated balance sheet between the liabilities and shareholders' equity.

36. The amount of the minority interest in the subsidiary's net income shown on the consolidated income statement is generally the result of multiplying the subsidiary's net income by the minority's percentage of ownership. The consolidated income statement allocates the portion applicable to the parent company and the portion of the subsidiary's income applicable to the minority interest. Typically, the minority interest in the subsidiary's net income appears as a deduction in calculating consolidated net income.

37. Consolidated statements, because of limitations, do not replace financial statements of individual corporations. For example creditors must rely on resources of the one corporation to which they loaned funds although that corporation may be consolidated by a parent corporation. A corporation can declare dividends only from its own retained earnings. When a parent owns less than 100 percent of the shares, minority shareholder can judge the dividend constraints, both legal and financial, only by inspecting the subsidiary's statements.

38. Most countries outside the United States account for minority, passive investments using a lower-of-cost-or-market method, instead of the market value method. In recent years the accounting for active investments have become similar to practices in the United States: the equity method for minority, active investments and consolidation for majority investments.

39. The various methods of accounting for long-term investments in corporate securities have effects on the statement of cash flows. When a firm uses the market value method dividend revenues generally produce cash. Therefore, calculating cash flow from operations normally requires no adjustment for this component of income. Changes in the Investment account and the Unrealized Holding Gain or Loss account applying the market method do not appear in the statement of cash flows for securities available for sale. In contrast, holding gains and losses on trading securities do appear in income but do not affect cash flow, so they do require an adjustment to net income in deriving cash flow from operations if the firm uses the indirect method. However, under the equity method, equity in investee's undistributed earnings is subtracted from net income to derive cash provided from operations of investor.

Questions and Exercises

True/False. For each of the following statements, place a T or F in the space provided to indicate whether the statement is true or false.

_____ 1. Debt and equity securities, which a firm intends to sell within one year, are reported as current assets on the balance sheet.

_____ 2. The consolidation method of reporting investments in stocks may be used under the same percentage of ownership as the equity method.

_____ 3. Goodwill never appears on the consolidated balance sheet after a business combination.

_____ 4. If a company is appropriately using the market value method of accounting for long-term investments (available for sale) in corporate securities, a decline in market value below cost results in a loss to be recognized on the current period income statement.

_____ 5. Consolidated financial statements reflect only transactions between the group of consolidated companies and other entities.

_____ 6. Minority interest in net income is a deduction in determining the consolidated net income.

_____ 7. A derivative can be an asset not a liability.

_____ 8. To fully disclose consolidated assets, both the parent's Investment in Subsidiary account and individual assets and liabilities of the subsidiary are presented in the consolidated balance sheet.

_____ 9. Companies with minority, passive investments, classified as investments, could report a balance in Unrealized Holding Loss on Investments in Securities as a negative amount in the shareholders' equity section of the balance sheet.

_____ 10. Under the equity method, the investor company treats as income (or revenue) each period its proportionate share of the periodic earnings of the investee company.

_____ 11. Dividends paid to the owner of common shares in an investment accounted for by the equity method are treated as a reduction of the investment account.

_____ 12. When a stockholder owns more than 50 percent of the voting stock of another company, the stockholder is called the majority investor or the parent.

_____ 13. A minority investor owns less than 50 percent of the voting shares of another corporation.

_____ 14. Generally accepted accounting principles require that the equity method be used when a company owns 20 to 50 percent of the voting stock of another company.

_____ 15. The realized gain or loss on the sale of "securities available for sale" is the difference between the sales price and the original cost of the security.

_____ 16. When the market value of an investment in trading securities is less than its cost, the decrease is reported as "Unrealized Holding Loss on Trading Securities (Inc. St.)" on the firm's income statement.

_____ 17. When the market value of an investment in securities available for sale is less than its cost, the holding loss is reported in a shareholders' equity account.

_____ 18. The entries to eliminate intercompany transactions are made on the books of the parent company only.

_____ 19. Generally accepted accounting principles require the parent to combine, or consolidate, the financial statements of majority-owned companies with those of the parent.

_____ 20. A firm's minority, passive investment appears in the firm's balance sheet between the liabilities and shareholders' equity.

_____ 21. Under the market value method the investor firm does not recognize dividends received as income but as a return of investment.

_____ 22. The amount of the minority interest shown on the balance sheet is generally the result of multiplying the common stockholders' equity of the subsidiary by the minority's percentage of ownership.

_____ 23. Dividends can legally be declared only from retained earnings of one corporation.

_____ 24. Subsidiary companies are those which have equal ownership in the common shares of a third corporation.

_____ 25. Most published financial statements report minority interest as a reduction in the cost of the asset, Investment in Stock.

_____ 26. The market value method is used by most countries in a parallel fashion to US firms.

_____ 27. Companies using the market value method for securities available for sale normally require no adjustment to net income when calculating cash flow from operations.

_____ 28. When the market value of an investment in securities available for sale is more than cost, the increase is reported as "Unrealized Holding Gain on Securities Available For Sale(SE)" on the firm's income statement.

_____ 29. A company is required to use the market value method to account for its investments in securities of another company regardless of its percentage of ownership.

_____ 30. Holding gains and losses on securities available for sale affect net income only when the securities are sold.

_____ 31. When securities are transferred from one category to another one, the firm transfers the security at it market value at the time of the transfer.

_____ 32. When the equity method is used, cash from operations in the statement of cash flows is increased by the amount of dividend received.

_____ 33. Goodwill is the excess of the cost of an acquisition over the current market value of the net identifiable assets acquired.

_____ 34. Goodwill must be amortized over a period not to exceed 40 years.

_____ 35. The FASB requires that firms show all derivatives on the balance sheet at their fair market value at the end of the period.

_____ 36. When a firm acquires a derivative and attempts to reduce risks involving fluctuations in a market value, the FASB classifies the transaction as a cash-flow hedge.

_____ 37. The derivative appears on the balance sheet at their cost except in unusual circumstances.

_____ 38. The FASB requires the firm to show in income each period the change in the fair value of a derivative that qualifies as a fair-value hedge.

_____ 39. When a firm acquires a derivative and attempts to reduce the risk in future streams of cash flows (inflows or outflows) the FASB classifies the transaction as a cash-flow hedge.

_____ 40. A firm will show the cash-flow hedge at its fair value on the balance sheet, and will report the matching gain or loss in net earnings of the period.

_____ 41. The gain or loss of the fair value changes of a cash-flow hedge will appear as part of comprehensive income and will appear on the balance sheet in owners' equity but does not affect retained earnings.

_____ 42. When a firm acquires a derivative instrument, but does not use it to hedge some fair value or cash flow, then it must report changes in the market value of that derivative in net income.

_____ 43. The gains or losses on derivatives that do not attempt to hedge are not reported in income.

_____ 44. An interest rate swap is a derivative that typically obligates one party and counterparty to exchange the difference between fixed and floating rate interest payments on otherwise similar loans.

Matching. From the list of terms below, select that term which is most closely associated with each of the descriptive phrases or statements that follows and place the letter for that term in the space provided.

a.	Cash Flow Hedge	l.	Market Value Method
b.	Consolidated Financial Statements	m.	Minority, Active Investment
c.	Consolidation Policy	n.	Minority, Passive Investment
d.	Debt Securities Held to Maturity	o.	Minority Interest
e.	Derivative Instrument	p.	Parent
f.	Equity Method	q.	Securities Available for Sale
g.	Goodwill	r.	Subsidiary
h.	Fair-Value Hedge	s.	Trading Securities
i.	Intercompany Transactions	t.	Unrealized Holding Gain or Loss on Securities Available for Sale (SE)
j.	Interest Rate Swaps	u.	Unrealized Holding Gain or Loss on Trading Securities (Inc. St.)
k.	Majority, Active Investment		

_____ 1. A derivative that typically obligates one party and counterparty to exchange the difference between fixed and floating rate interest payments on otherwise similar loans.

_____ 2. An investment where the stockholder owns greater than 50 percent of the voting stock of another company.

_____ 3. A derivative acquired to reduce the risk in future streams of cash flows.

_____ 4. Under this method the investor's share of ownership is between 20 and 50 percent.

_____ 5. The majority investor who owns more than 50 percent of the voting stock of another company.

_____ 6. Statements combining the results of operations, financial position, and statement of cash flows of a parent company and its subsidiaries as if the companies were one economic entity.

_____ 7. A parent discloses a statement about this policy in the summary of significant accounting principles, a required part of the financial statement notes.

_____ 8. These would be eliminated in preparing consolidated statements.

_____ 9. An investment where the percentage of the ownership of voting shares in between 20 percent and 50 percent.

_____ 10. The equity of minority stockholders shown in a consolidated balance sheet.

_____ 11. The excess of the cost of the acquisition over the current market value of the net assets acquired.

_____ 12. Companies use this method to account for long-term investments where their ownership is less than twenty percent of the outstanding voting common stock.

_____ 13. The corporation which is subject to control by a parent corporation.

_____ 14. An investment where the percentage of the other corporation's shares owned is not so large that the acquiring company can control or exert significant influence over the other company.

_____ 15. This account is a shareholder's equity account.

_____ 16. These securities appear in the balance sheet at amortized acquisition cost.

_____ 17. Increases and decreases in the market value of these securities are reported as unrealized holding gains and losses on the income statement.

_____ 18. Increases and decreases in the market value of these securities do not affect income until the securities are sold.

_____ 19. This account is reported as a gain or a loss on the income statement.

_____ 20. A derivative acquired to reduce risks involving fluctuations in a market value.

_____ 21. A financial instrument designed to help firms cope with various kinds of risk.

Multiple Choice. Choose the best answer for each of the following questions and enter the identifying letter in the space provided.

_____ 1. A derivative:

      1. Can be an asset.
      b. Can be a liability.
      c. Is presented on the balance sheet at their fair market value at the end of the period.
      d. All of the above.

The following information relates to Questions 2-6. Fatigue Company has three securities in its portfolio of securities available for sale:

		Market Value	
Security	Cost	12/31, Year 1	12/31, Year 2
Beauty	$ 78,000	$ 93,600	$100,100
Cole	$117,000	$120,900	--
Sells	$ 58,500	$ 53,300	$ 50,700

The Cole stock was sold in Year 2 for $127,400.

_____ 2. Which of the following statements is true?

      a. On its 12/31, Year 1, balance sheet, Fatigue would report the Beauty stock at its cost of $78,000.
      b. On its income statement for the year ending 12/31, Year 1, Fatigue would report an unrealized holding gain on the Beauty stock of $15,600.
      c. On its 12/31, Year 1, balance sheet, Fatigue would report an unrealized holding gain on the Beauty stock of $15,600 in a shareholders' equity account.
      d. Statements "a" and "b" are true.

_____ 3. Which of the following statements is true?

      a. On its 12/31, Year 2, balance sheet, Fatigue would report the Beauty stock at its market value of $100,100.
      b. On its income statement for the year ending 12/31, Year 2, Fatigue would report an unrealized holding gain on the Beauty stock of $6,500.
      c. On its 12/31, Year 2, balance sheet, Fatigue would report an unrealized holding gain on the Beauty stock of $22,100 in a shareholders' equity account.
      d. Statements "a" and "c" are true.

_____ 4. What would Fatigue report on its income statement for the year ending 12/31, Year 2, relative to the sale of the Cole stock in Year 2?

      a. A realized gain of $6,500.
      b. A realized gain of $6,500 and an unrealized gain of $3,900.
      c. A realized gain of $10,400.
      d. An unrealized gain of $10,400.

_____ 5. Which of the following statements is true?

    a. On its 12/31, Year 1, balance sheet, Fatigue would report the Sells stock at its cost of $58,500.

    b. On its income statement for the year ending 12/31, Year 1, Fatigue would report an unrealized holding loss of $5,200.

    c. On its income statement for the year ending 12/31, Year 2, Fatigue would report an unrealized holding loss of $2,600.

    d. None of the above statements is true.

_____ 6. Assume that on 12/31, Year 2, Fatigue reclassifies the Sells stock to a "trading security" status. At what amount would the Sells stock be reported in Fatigue's trading security portfolio?

    a. $58,500.

    b. $53,300.

    c. $50,700.

    d. None of the above.

_____ 7. The following are true statements describing the effects of Investments in Securities on the statement of cash flows except

    a. When a company uses the market value method for securities available for sale calculating cash flow from operations normally required no adjustment to net income.

    b. Unrealized Holding Loss for securities available for sale is usually added back to net income in calculating cash flow from operations.

    c. When a firm uses the equity method and received dividends less than its share of infested's earnings, normally there is a subtraction from net income in calculating cash flow from operations.

    d. Two of the above statements are true.

_____ 8. Generally work sheet procedures to prepare consolidated statements include the following steps

    a. Elimination of the parent company's investment account.

    b. Elimination of intercompany receivables and payables.

    c. Elimination of intercompany sales and purchases.

    d. All of the above.

_____ 9. Majority investments are generally reported by

    a. Preparation of consolidated statements.

    b. Application of the equity method.

    c. One-line presentations on the balance sheet (as an Investment).

    d. Application of the market value method.

_____ 10. One important reason for continued legal existence of subsidiary companies is

   a. To reduce the financial risk of one segment becoming insolvent.
   b. To meet more effectively the requirements of state corporation and tax legislation.
   c. To expand with a minimum of capital investment.
   d. All of the above.

_____ 11. The entry to record a decline in value at year end in a company's marketable equity securities held as long-term investments is

   a. Debit Investment in Securities credit Unrealized Holding Loss on Investment in Securities.
   b. Debit Unrealized Holding Loss on Investment in Securities credit Investments in Securities.
   c. Debit Realized Loss on Valuation of Marketable Investments, credit Investment in Securities.
   d. Debit Realized Gain on Valuation of Marketable Equity Investments, credit Investment in Securities.

_____ 12. The market value method is used to account for

   a. Minority, passive investments.
   b. Minority, active investments.
   c. Majority, active investments.
   d. None of the above.

_____ 13. The ownership percentage of voting stock of minority, active investments is usually

   a. Zero to 20 percent.
   b. 20 to 50 percent.
   c. Over 50 percent.
   d. 100 percent.

_____ 14. This method is required by generally accepted accounting principles for accounting for investment in common stock of 20 percent to 50 percent.
   a. Market Value method.
   b. Equity method.
   c. Consolidation method.
   d. All of the above are acceptable.

_____ 15. Which of the following account titles is not associated with the use of the market value method?

   a. Unrealized Holding Loss on Investments in Securities.
   b. Unrealized Holding Gain on Investments in Securities.
   c. Equity in Earnings of Affiliate.
   d. Investment in Securities.

_____ 16. Under the equity method, as the invested company declares dividends the investor company would

   a. Increase the investment account.
   b. Decrease the investment account.
   c. Increase the revenue account.
   d. Decrease the revenue account.

_____ 17. All of the following statements are true except

   a. Consolidated net income is the same amount as that which results when the parent uses the equity method for an unconsolidated subsidiary.
   b. Consolidated retained earnings is the same amount as that which results when the parent uses the equity method for an unconsolidated subsidiary.
   c. The consolidation process eliminates the account, Equity in Earnings of Subsidiary.
   d. All of the above are true.

_____ 18. The eliminations to remove intercompany transactions are typically made on

   a. Separate books for the consolidated entity.
   b. Company P's books.
   c. A consolidated work sheet.
   d. Company S's books.

_____ 19. Financial statements generally are consolidated for parent and subsidiary companies for

   a. Minority, passive investments.
   b.   Minority, active investments.
   c. Majority, active investments.
   d. None of the above.

_____ 20. Consolidated financial statements are generally prepared when the following characteristic is present

   a. The parent owns more than 50 percent of the voting stock of the subsidiary.
   b. The parent owns 100 percent of the voting stock of a real estate subsidiary.
   c. The parent owns 100 percent of the voting stock of a finance subsidiary.
   d. All of the above.

_____ 21. All of the following accounts would be eliminated in the preparation of consolidated financial statements except

   a. Common Stock (Company P).
   b. Common Stock (Company S).
   c. Investment in stock of Company S (Company P).
   d. All of the above.

22. All of the following accounts would be eliminated in the preparation of consolidated financial statements except

a. Equity in Earnings of Company S (Company P).
b. Accounts Receivable (Intercompany).
c. Sales (Intercompany).
d. Dividends Declared (Company P).

23. Elimination entry for the parent company's Investment account would typically include debits to the following except

a. Common Stock (Company S).
b. Retained Earnings (Company S).
c. Equity of Earnings of Company S (Company P).
d. Investments in Stock of Company S (Company P).

24. Lake State Bank often purchases and sells debt and equity securities for their short-term profit potential. The bank should account for these securities as:

a. Held to maturity securities.
b. Trading securities.
c. Available for sale securities.
d. Investment in securities.

25. The equity method is used to account for

a. Minority, passive investments.
b. Minority, active investments.
c. Majority, active investments.
d. All of the above.

26. Benson Co. acquired common stock of the Earl Co. to develop a long-term relationship with Earl which is a major supplier of the raw material used to manufacture Benson's product. How would Benson report these securities on its balance sheet?

a. At acquisition cost and classified as a current asset, Marketable Securities.
b. At acquisition cost and classified as a noncurrent asset, Investments in Securities.
c. At market value and classified as a current asset, Marketable Securities.
d. At market value and classified as a noncurrent asset, Investment in Securities.

27. The Arcadia State Bank actively trades in debt securities with the intent of earning profits from short-term differences in market prices. How should the bank report the debt securities on its balance sheet?

a. At acquisition cost.
b. At market value.
c. At amortized acquisition cost.
d. None of the above.

_____ 28. How should debt securities, which a firm intends to hold to maturity be reported on the balance sheet?

a. At acquisition cost.
b. At market value.
c. At amortized acquisition cost.
d. None of the above.

_____ 29. A 4-month, 6 percent, $28,500 note is received by the Cassidy Co. during Year 1. How much interest will Cassidy earn if it holds the note to maturity?

a. $570.
b. $428.
c. $-0-
d. $1,710.

_____ 30. Petrov Company purchased some debt securities in Year 2 with the intent of selling the securities when the company needs the cash in its operations. Under generally accepted accounting principles, this investment would fall under which of the following categories?

a. Debt securities, which the firm intends to hold to maturity.
b. Debt and equity securities held as trading securities.
c. Debt and equity securities held as securities available for sale.
d. None of the above.

_____ 31. Garden Co. acquired marketable securities in Year 1 at a cost of $90,000. The securities can be readily converted into cash and Garden intends to convert the securities into cash when it needs cash. How would Garden report this investment on its Year 1 balance sheet?

a. As a current asset, Marketable Securities.
b. As a current asset, Investment in Securities.
c. As a noncurrent asset, Marketable Securities.
d. As a noncurrent asset, Investment in Securities.

_____ 32. Eros Landscaping, Inc. purchased some LaPalme Co. stock for $56,000 on January 1, Year 1. At 12/31, Year 1, the market value of the LaPalme stock was $48,000. On 7/1, Year 2, Eros sold all of the LaPalme stock for $45,000. Eros accounted for the investment as a trading security. On its 12/31, Year 2 income statement, what would Eros report regarding the investment in the LaPalme Co. stock?

a. Realized loss on trading security of $11,000.
b. Unrealized loss on trading securities of $8,000.
c. Realized loss on trading securities of $3,000.
d. Unrealized loss on trading securities of $3,000.

_____ 33. J. Williams Company purchased securities at a cost of $220,000 on April 16. Additionally the company paid a 5 percent commission ($11,000) on the purchase, a 6 percent tax ($13,200), and a transfer fee of $3,000. At what amount should the company record the acquisition cost of the securities?

a. $220,000.
b. $247,200.
c. $244,200.
d. $234,000.

_____ 34. When a firm acquires a derivative and attempts to reduce risks involving fluctuations in a market value:

1. The FASB classifies the transaction as a fair-value hedge.
2. The FASB classifies the transaction as a cash-flow hedge.
3. The FASB requires the derivative to be recorded and continued to be reported at the cost of acquiring.
4. All of the above.

_____ 35. A cash-flow hedge is:

1. When a firm acquires a derivative and attempts to reduce risks involving fluctuations in a market value.
2. When a firm acquires a derivative and attempts to reduce the risk in future steams of cash flows.
3. Required to be recorded and continued to be reported at the cost of acquiring.
4. All of the above.

_____ 36. The FASB requires the firm to show in income each period the change in the fair value of a derivative:

1. That attempts to reduce the risk in future steams of cash flows.
2. That does not attempt to hedge fair value or cash flow.
3. Both a and b above.
4. Neither a or b above.

_____ 37. This unrealized gain or loss on changes in the fair value remain on the balance sheet in a separate shareholders' equity account for a:

a. Fair-value hedge.
b. A derivative that is not used to hedge some fair value or cash flow.
c. Cash-flow hedge.
d. None of the above.

Exercises

1. Ian Craig Co. purchased 20,000 shares of Earl-Bush Co. stock on January 17, Year 1, at $12 per share. At year end December 31, Year 1, the market value for the Earl-Bush Co. shares was $14 per share. On February 17, Year 2, a $.10 per share dividend was received on the Earl-Bush Co. stock. On July 11, Year 2, 2,500 shares of Earl-Bush Co. stock were sold for $13 per share. At the end of Year 2, the market value for the Earl-Bush Co. stock was $17 per share.

   a. Use proper journal form to record all original entries and year-end adjusting entries for Ian Craig that would be needed for Year 1 and Year 2. Assume that Ian Craig Co. actively trades securities with the objective of generating profits from short-term differences in market prices.

   b. What would Ian Craig Co. report on its income statements for Year 1 and Year 2 relating to its investment in marketable securities?

2. Refer to Exercise 1. Now assume that Ian Craig Co. acquired these securities for an operating purpose instead of for their short-term profit potential.

   a. Record in proper journal form all original entries and year-end adjusting entries that would be needed for Year 1 and Year 2.

b. What would Ian Craig Co. report on its income statements for Year 1 and Year 2 relating to its investment in marketable securities?

3. DeWitt Corporation reported the following items on its 12/31, Year 2 balance sheet:

Current Assets

Marketable Securities $510,000

Stockholder's Equity

Unrealized Holding Loss on
  Securities Available for Sale   82,000

In a footnote to the balance sheet, it was noted that the "Unrealized Holding Loss" account had been increased by $35,000 in Year 2.

Answer the following questions:

a. What is the cost of the marketable securities?

b. What was the market value of the marketable securities on 12/31, Year 1?

4. Demry Corporation reported the following item on its 12/31, Year 2 balance sheet:

Current Assets

    Marketable Securities $390,000

The marketable securities consist of 10,000 shares of Gibb Corporation stock which Demry purchased during Year 1.

On its income statement for the year ending 12/31, Year 2, the company reported an "Unrealized Holding Gain on Trading Securities" of $64,000.

On its income statement for the year ending 12/31, Year 1, the company had reported an "Unrealized Holding Loss on Trading Securities" of $28,000.

Answer the following questions:

a. What is the cost of the marketable securities?

b. What was the market value of the marketable securities on 12/31, Year 1?

5. Prepare general journal entries for each of the following transactions on the books of Mills Corporation.

a. Purchases common shares of Grogg Co. (available for sale) for $100,000. Assume this investment represents 15 percent of the outstanding common stock of Grogg Co.

b. At Mills' year end, Grogg Co. shares have a market value of $103,000 and Grogg Co. announces net income of $50,000.

c. Grogg Co. declared and paid dividends of $20,000.

d. Mills sold the Grogg shares for $102,000.

6. Prepare journals entries for transactions a. through d. in 5. above except, assume the investment represents 25 percent (rather than 15 percent as indicated in a.) of the outstanding common stock of Grogg Co.

7. Prepare general journal entries for each of the following transactions on the books of the Clio Corporation.

January 18, Year 1: Purchased 10 percent of the outstanding shares of Franklin Enterprises (available for sale) for $40,000. (Use the market value method.)

February 12, Year 1: Purchased 30 percent of the outstanding shares of Merritt Company for $75,000. (Use the equity method.)

December 31, Year 1: Franklin Enterprises reported $10,000 of net income and Merritt Company reported $5,000 of net income. Franklin Enterprises shares are currently valued at $35,000. (Apply market value method for Franklin Enterprises and the equity method for Merritt Company.)

January 15, Year 2:   Franklin Enterprises declared and distributed
                         cash dividends totaling $5,000.

January 18, Year 2:   Merritt Company declared and distributed $3,000
                         in cash dividends.

January 19, Year 2:   Clio Corporation sold one-half of its interest in
                         Franklin Enterprises for $18,000.

January 20, Year 2:   Clio Corporation sold 10 percent of its interest
                         in Merritt Company for $8,000.

December 31, Year 2:   The remaining Franklin Enterprises shares are
                         currently valued at $19,000. (Apply market value
                         method.)

8. Company P acquired 100 percent of the outstanding shares of Company S for $500,000 cash on January 1, Year 1. At the time of acquisition, the book value of the shareholders' equity of Company S was $500,000, comprising the following account balances:

Common Stock $200,000

Retained Earnings 300,000

Total Stockholders' Equity $500,000

During Year 1, Company S reported net income of $50,000. At December 31, Year 1 $5,000 of Company S's accounts receivable represent amounts payable by Company P. During Year 1 Company P sold merchandise to Company S for $15,000. None of that merchandise remains in Company S's inventory at year end. Assuming Company P properly applied the equity method of accounting for its investment in Company S, prepare elimination entries in general journal form for the preparation of the December 31, Year 1 financial statements for the following:

a. Elimination of the parent company's investment account.

b. Elimination of intercompany receivables and payable.

c. Elimination of intercompany sales and purchases.

9. George Company issued 8 percent, fixed-rate, semiannual coupon bonds on January 1 at par for $8 million. It simultaneously entered into an interest rate swap with Penny Bank under which George will pay the bank at the end of each six-month period if interest rates exceed 8 percent and the bank will pay George if interest rates are below 8 percent. If the market rate is r on the date of the payment, then the bank will pay George an amount equal to ½ x (.08-r) x $8,000,000; the one-half factor results from the semiannual timing of the payments. The market interest rate is 8 percent at the time of issue. Interest rates decrease to 7 percent by the end of the first six-months period, increasing the market value of the bonds to $9 million and in increasing the market value of the interest rate swap by $.9 million. By the end of the year, interest rates rise to 7 ½ percent and the market value of the bond decreases to $8.5 million. The market value of the interest rate swap decreases by $.45 million during the period July 1 through December 31.

Record journal entries for the following dates:

a) January 1, at the time of bond issue.

b) June 30, at the time of the first debt service payment.

c) December 31, at the time of the second debt service payments.

d) Is this a fair-value hedge or cash-flow hedge? Has the hedge fulfilled its purpose?

Answers to Questions and Exercises

True/False

1.	T	9.	T	17.	T	25.	F	33.	T	41.	T
2.	F	10.	T	18.	F	26.	F	34.	F	42.	T
3.	F	11.	T	19.	T	27.	T	35.	T	43.	F
4.	F	12.	T	20.	F	28.	F	36.	F	44.	T
5.	T	13.	T	21.	F	29.	F	37.	F		
6.	T	14.	T	22.	T	30.	T	38.	T		
7.	F	15.	T	23.	T	31.	T	39.	T		
8.	F	16.	T	24.	F	32.	T	40.	F		

Matching

1.	j	5.	p	9.	m	13.	r	17.	s	21.	e
2.	k	6.	b	10.	o	14.	n	18.	q		
3.	a	7.	c	11.	g	15.	t	19.	u		
4.	f	8.	i	12.	l	16.	d	20.	h		

Multiple Choice

1.	d	8.	d	15.	c	22.	d	29.	a	36.	b
2.	c	9.	a	16.	b	23.	d	30.	c	37.	c
3.	d	10.	d	17.	d	24.	b	31.	a		
4.	c	11.	b	18.	c	25.	b	32.	c		
5.	d	12.	a	19.	c	26.	d	33.	b		
6.	c	13.	b	20.	d	27.	b	34.	a		
7.	b	14.	b	21.	a	28.	c	35.	b		

Exercises

1.

	Dr.	Cr.
a. 1/17, Year 1: Marketable Securities	240,000	
Cash		240,000
Purchase of 20,000 shares of Earl-Bush Co. stock for $12 per share.		
12/31, Year 1: Marketable Securities	40,000	
Unrealized Holding Gain on Trading Securities (Inc. St.)		40,000
To revalue trading securities to market value and recognize an unrealized holding gain of $40,000 (20,000 x $2 = $40,000).		
2/17, Year 2: Cash	2,000	
Dividend Income		2,000
Receipt of $.10 per share dividend on Earl-Bush stock.		

```
7/11, Year 2: Cash                                    32,500
              Realized Loss on
                Sale of Trading Securities             2,500
                Marketable Securities                                35,000
              Sold 2,500 shares of Earl-Bush Co.
              stock for $13 per share.

12/31, Year 2: Marketable Securities                  52,500
               Unrealized Holding
                 Gain on Trading Securities (Inc. St.)              52,500
               To revalue trading securities
               to market value and recognize
               an unrealized holding gain of
               $52,500 (17,500 x $3 = $52,500).
```

b.   Year 1 income statement:
      Unrealized Holding Gain on Trading Securities $40,000

      Year 2 income statement:
      Dividend Income $ 2,000
      Realized Loss on Sale of Trading Securities   2,500
      Unrealized Holding Gain on Trading Securities   52,500

2.

		Dr.	Cr.

a.   1/17, Year 1: Marketable Securities   240,000
                    Cash   240,000
                    Purchase of 20,000 shares of
                    Earl-Bush Co. stock for $12
                    per share.

      12/31, Year 1: Marketable Securities   40,000
                     Unrealized Holding Gain
                       on Securities Available
                       for Sale (SE)   40,000
                     To revalue Earl-Bush Co. stock
                     to market value (20,000 x $2 =
                     $40,000).

      2/17, Year 2: Cash   2,000
                    Dividend Income   2,000
                    Receipt of a $.10 per share
                    dividend on Earl-Bush Co. stock.

      7/11, Year 2: Cash   32,500
                    Realized Gain on Sale of
                      Securities Available for Sale   2,500
                      Marketable Securities   30,000
                    Sold 2,500 shares of Earl-Bush
                    Co. stock for $13 per share.

```
7/11, Year 2: Unrealized Holding Gain on
               Securities Available for Sale (SE)  5,000
               Marketable Securities                              5,000
             The 2,500 shares sold had risen in
             value and the firm had recorded an
             unrealized holding gain and an
             increase in the value of the
             securities of $5,000 ($2 per share
             x 2,500 shares) at 12/31, Year 1.
             This entry eliminates both the
             unrealized holding gain and the
             increase in the marketable
             securities for the 2,500 shares sold.

12/31, Year 2: Marketable Securities              52,500
               Unrealized Holding
               Gain on Securities
               Available for Sale (SE)                           52,500
             To revalue Earl-Bush Co.
             stock to market value
             (17,500 x $3 = $52,500.
```

b.   Year 1 income statement:
       Nothing would be reported on Ian Craig's Year 1 income statement
       relating to the investment in marketable securities. The
       Unrealized Holding Gain on Securities Available for Sale account
       is reported in the balance sheet as a shareholders' equity item.

       Year 2 income statement:

Dividend Income	$ 2,000
Realized Gain on Sale of Securities Available for Sale	2,500

3.

a.

Market value of securities, 12/31, Year 2	$510,000
Balance in "Unrealized Holding Loss" on 12/31, Year 2	82,000
Cost of marketable securities	$592,000

b.

Balance in "Unrealized Holding Loss" on 12/31, Year 2	$ 82,000
Increase in account during Year 2	(35,000)
Balance in account on 12/31, Year 1	$ 47,000
Cost of marketable securities	$592,000
Balance in "Unrealized Holding Loss" on 12/31, Year 1	(47,000)
Market value of securities on 12/31, Year 1	$545,000

4.

a.

"Unrealized Holding Gain" reported in Year 2	$ 64,000
"Unrealized Holding Loss" reported in Year 1	(28,000)
Net increase in market value over 2 years	$ 36,000
Market value of securities on 12/31, Year 2	$390,000
Net increase in market value over 2 years	(36,000)
Cost of marketable securities	$354,000

b. Cost of marketable securities $354,000
"Unrealized Holding Loss" reported in Year 1 (28,000)
Market value of securities on 12/31, Year 1 $326,000

5.

		Dr.	Cr.
a.	Investment in Grogg Co.	100,000	
	Cash		100,000
	Purchased 15% of Grogg Co.		
b.	Investment in Grogg Co.	3,000	
	Unrealized Holding Gain on Investments in Securities (S/E)		3,000
	Recognized the increase in market value of Grogg Co. stock.		
c.	Cash	3,000	
	Dividend Revenue		3,000
	Recognized the receipt of 15% of Grogg Co. dividends.		
d.	Cash	102,000	
	Investment in Grogg Co.		100,000
	Realized Gain on Sale of Securities		2,000
	Sold Grogg Co. Common Stock.		
	Unrealized Holding Gain on Investments in Securities (S/E)	3,000	
	Investment in Grogg Co.		3,000
	Eliminates the balance in the Unrealized Holding Gain account.		

6.

		Dr.	Cr.
a.	Investment in Grogg Co.	100,000	
	Cash		100,000
	Purchased 25% of Grogg Co.		
b.	Investment in Grogg Co.	12,500	
	Equity in Earnings of Affiliate		12,500
	Recognized 25% of Grogg Co. earnings under the equity method.		
c.	Cash	5,000	
	Investment in Grogg Co.		5,000
	Receipt of 25% of Grogg Co. dividends.		
d.	Cash	102,000	
	Realized Loss of Sale of Investment	5,500	
	Investment in Grogg Co.		107,500 *
	Sale of equity investment		

* 107,500 = 100,000 + 12,500 - 5,000

270

7.

	Dr.	Cr.
January 18, Year 1:		
Investment in Franklin Enterprises	40,000	
Cash		40,000
Purchased 10% of outstanding shares (market value method).		
February 12, Year 1:		
Investment in Merritt Company	75,000	
Cash		75,000
Purchased 30% of outstanding shares (equity method).		
December 31, Year 1:		
Investment in Merritt Company	1,500	
Equity in Earnings of Affiliate		1,500
Recognized 30% of Merritt Company income.		
Unrealized Holding Loss on Investments in Securities (S/E)	5,000	
Investment in Franklin Enterprise		5,000
Recognized decline in market value of Franklin shares.		
January 15, Year 2:		
Cash	500	
Dividend Revenue		500
Received Franklin Enterprises dividends.		
January 18, Year 2:		
Cash	900	
Investment in Merritt Company		900
Received Merritt Company dividends.		
January 19, Year 2:		
Cash	18,000	
Realized Loss on Sale of Investments	2,000	
Investment in Franklin Enterprises		17,500
Unrealized Holding Loss on on Investments in Securities (S/E)		2,500
Sold one-half interest in Franklin Enterprises.		
January 20, Year 2:		
Cash	8,000	
Investment in Merritt Company		7,560 *
Gain on Sale of Investment in Stock		440
Sold 10% interest of Merritt Company.		
*($75,000 + 1,500 - 900) x 10%.		
December 31, Year 2:		
Investment in Franklin Enterprises	1,500	
Unrealized Holding Loss on Investments in Securities (S/E)		1,500
Adjusted remaining shares of Franklin Enterprises to reflect market value.		

8. a.

	Dr.	Cr.
Common Stocks (Company S)	200,000	
Retained Earnings, January 1, Year 1 (Company S)	300,000	
Equity in Earnings of Company S (Company P)	50,000	
Investment in Company S (Company P)		550,000

To eliminate the parent company
investment account and subsidiary's
shareholders' equity accounts.
($550,000 = $500,000 + $50,000).

		Dr.	Cr.
b.	Accounts Payable	5,000	
	Accounts Receivable		5,000

To eliminate intercompany accounts
receivables and payables on
consolidated work sheet.

		Dr.	Cr.
c.	Sales Revenue	15,000	
	Cost of Goods Sold		15,000

To eliminate intercompany sales and
purchases on consolidated work sheet.

9.

	Dr.	Cr.

a. January 1

	Dr.	Cr.
Cash	8,000,000	
Bonds Payable		8,000,000

(The interest swap has a zero market value
on January 1 since the interest rate is
8 percent on this date.)

b. June 30

	Dr.	Cr.
Interest Expense (8,000,000 x 8% x ½)	320,000	
Cash		320,000
Cash (1/2 x [8%-7%] x8,000,000)	40,000	
Interest Expense		40,000
Loss on Revaluation of Bonds (9,000,000-8,000,000)	1,000,000	
Bonds Payable		1,000,000
Derivative Financial Asset	900,000	
Gain on Derivative Financial Asset		900,000

c.   December 31

       Interest Expense (8,000,000x8%x 1/2)   320,000
         Cash   320,000

       Cash (1/2 x [.8%-7.5%]x8,000,000)   20,000
         Interest Expense   20,000

       Bonds Payable (9,000,000-8,500,000)   500,000
         Gain on Revaluation of Bonds   500,000

       Loss on Derivative Financial Asset   450,000
         Derivative Financial Asset   450,000

d.   The interest rate swap represents a fair-value hedge. It has reduced risk of interest rate fluctuation, thus the gain or loss associated with the market value changes of the bonds. The loss has been reduced to $50,000 (1,000,000-900,000-500,000+450,000) by the hedge. Otherwise, the loss on the fair market value of the bonds would have been $500,000. A perfect hedge would have resulted in the losses and gains exactly offsetting each other.

Chapter 12

Shareholders' Equity: Capital Contributions, Distributions, and Earnings

Chapter Highlights

1. Both creditors and owners provide the funds to finance a corporation's assets and therefore have a claim on those assets. When owners provide funds, the source of these funds appear on the balance sheet as owners' equity, or in the context of corporations, as shareholders' equity. Changes in assets and liabilities often cause shareholders' equity to change. Changes in shareholders' equity result from three types of transactions, capital contributions, distributions, and earnings transactions. This chapter discusses reporting, or disclosing, these three types of shareholders' equity changes in the financial statements.

2. The corporation is a widely used form of business organization in the United States for at least three reasons:
    a. The corporate form provides the owner, or shareholder, with limited liability. The assets of the individual owners are not subject to the claims of the corporation's creditors. Comparatively, creditors of partnerships and sole proprietorships have a claim on both the owners' business and _personal_ assets to settle firms' debts.
    b. The corporate form facilitates raising owners' capital by the sale of shares of capital stock to the general public.
    c. Transfers of ownership interest may take place relatively easily because owners can sell individual shares to others without interfering with the ongoing management of the business.

3. Corporations have a separate legal existence. Individuals or other entities make capital contributions under a contract between themselves and the corporation. Because those who contribute capital funds are usually issued certificates for shares of stock, they are known as stockholders or shareholders. State laws, articles of incorporation or charter (an agreement between the firm and the state in which the business is incorporated), the corporation bylaws, and the stock contract govern the rights and obligations of shareholders. Corporate charters often authorize the issue of more than one class of stock, each representing ownership in the corporation. Most shares issued are either common or preferred. Each class of shares appears separately on the balance sheet, with a short description of the major features of the shares.

4. Preferred shares are granted special privileges. These privileges or rights vary from issue to issue. Generally, preferred shares have a senior claim on the assets in the event of bankruptcy relative to common shareholders. Preferred shareholders usually are entitled to dividends at a certain rate which must be paid by the firm prior to paying dividends to common shareholders. Preferred shares may be cumulative, callable, or convertible. If preferred shares are cumulative, then all current and previously postponed preferred dividends must be paid before dividends can be distributed to common shareholders. The corporation may reacquire callable preferred stock at a specified price, which may vary according to a predetermined time schedule. Convertible preferred shares may be exchanged by their owner into a specified amount of common shares at specified times. Some preferred stock issues carry mandatory redemption features requiring the issuing firm to repurchase the shares from their holders, paying a specified dollar amount at a specified future time.

5. Firms may or may not issue preferred stock. All firms must issue common shares. Common shares, frequently the only voting shares, have a residual claim on earnings and assets after commitments to creditors and preferred shareholders have been satisfied.

6. Shares of stock often have a par or stated value per share specified in the articles of incorporation and printed on the face of the stock certificates. Par value of common shares has little economic significance, but it is separated for legal reasons from other contributed capital amounts on the balance sheet. The issue price of a share of stock depends on its market value, not its par value. Accountants separate amounts equal to par value received from issuing stock from amounts received that exceed the par value. The par value rarely denotes the worth of the shares except perhaps at the date of issue.

7. When shares of stock are issued, the corporation credits the Capital Stock account (either Preferred Stock or Common Stock) with the par value or stated value of the shares issued. When shares are issued for amounts greater than par (or stated) value, the corporation credits the excess to an account called Additional Paid-In Capital. Other titles for this account include Capital Contributed in Excess of Par (Stated) Value and Premium on Capital Stock.

8. Corporations give various individuals or entities the right, or option, to acquire common shares at a price that is less than the market price of the shares at the time they exercise the option.

9. Under a stock option plan employees may purchase, at some time within a specified number of years in the future, shares in their company at a specified price, usually the market price of the stock on the day the option is granted. Stock options have market value resulting from two elements: a) the benefit realized at exercise date because the market price of the stock exceeds the exercise price, and b) the time value associated with the length of the period during which the holder can exercise the option. GAAP allow two methods of accounting for employee stock options, the market value method and a method not recording the market value of the option but disclosing in notes the market value of the options. However, standard setters recently have issued standards that would require financial statement recognition (market value-option pricing model) beginning in 2005.

10. Under the market method, the fair value of the option is amortized over the benefit period by debiting an expense (reduction of retained earnings) and crediting a shareholders' equity account, Common Stock Options. When the stock option is exercised, the firm debits cash for the proceeds, debits Common Stock Options and credits Common Stock and Additional Paid-in Capital for an excess of the value of the options plus the cash proceeds over the par value of the shares issued.

11. The alternative method recognizes the market value of the options in financial statement disclosures only. If on the date of the grant of the option the exercise price is equal to or exceeds the fair market price, then generally accepted accounting treatment results in no entry being made. When the options are exercised an entry is made to treat the transaction simply as an issue of stock at the option price. The expiration of an option without being exercised requires no entry. If the exercise price is less than the market price of the stock on the grant date, then compensation expense may have to be recognized under some circumstances.

12. Corporations may grant opportunities to buy shares of stock through stock rights and stock warrants. Stock rights are similar to stock options. Corporations grant stock options to employees as a form of compensation. Firms issue stock rights to current stockholders. The rights usually trade in public markets. Firms grant rights without cost to stockholders therefore no journal entry is required at the issuance date. When the rights are exercised, the entry is like the one to record the issue of new shares at the price paid.

13. On the other hand, firms issue stock warrants to the general investing public for cash. The warrants allow the holder to acquire additional shares at a specified amount within a specified period. At the date of the sale of the warrants the entry is a debit to Cash and a credit to Common Stock Warrants (shareholders' equity increase). When the rights are exercised, the firm debits cash for the additional proceeds, debits Common Stock Warrants for the cost of the warrants and makes offsetting credits to Common Stock (for par value) and Additional Paid-In Capital. If the warrants expire without the holders exercising them, the firm debits Common Stock Warrants and credits Additional Paid-in Capital. Firms sometimes attach common stock warrants to a bond or preferred stock. When the accountant can measure objectively the value of the warrant and the value of the associated bond or preferred stock, the accounting allocates the issue price between the two securities.

14. Convertible bonds and convertible preferred stock allow the holder of the bond or preferred stock to convert or "trade in" the bond for shares of common stock. The bond or preferred stock specifies the number of shares to be received when converted into stock, the dates when conversion can occur, and other details. The owner can hold the security as a bond or preferred stock or convert to common stock equity should the company be so successful that its common stock rises in price on the stock market. Although some accountants argue that some of the original proceeds from the issuance of convertible debt or preferred stock should be allocated to the conversion feature, currently firms following generally accepted accounting principles attribute all the proceeds to the debt or preferred stock with an entry which includes a debit to Cash for the proceeds and a credit to either Convertible Bond Payable or Preferred Stock. Upon conversion the usual entry ignores current market prices and merely shows a swap of common stock for bonds or preferred stock at their book value.

An acceptable alternative recognizes the market value of the shares of common stock issued, and a firm records the difference between that market value and the book value of the bonds or preferred stock as a gain or loss (increase or decrease in retained earnings) on conversion.

15. Profitable companies generate additional owners' equity from undistributed earnings. One misconception about net income is that it represents a fund of cash available for distributions or expansion. Although earnings from operations generally involve cash at some stage, the only certain statement that can be made about the effect of retaining earnings is that it results in increased net assets (excess of all assets over all liabilities). Generally a retention of earnings results in an increase in the market price of the firm's common stock.

16. Most publicly held firms distribute a portion of the assets generated by earnings as a dividend to shareholders. The board of directors declares these dividends periodically. The directors, in considering whether or not to declare cash dividends, must conclude both (a) that the declaration of a dividend is legal and (b) that it would be financially expedient. In other words, the directors should carefully examine the statutory restrictions on dividends, the contractual restrictions on dividends, and the corporate financial policy in regard to dividends.

17. State corporation laws generally provide that dividends "may not be paid out of capital" but must be "paid out of earnings." "Capital" is usually defined as the total paid in capital. In some states, dividends may be paid out of current earnings even though there is an accumulated deficit from previous periods. Balance sheet disclosure should provide the user with information to determine any legal restrictions on dividend payment. For example, state statutes can provide that "treasury shares may be acquired only in amounts less than retained earnings."

18. Contracts with bondholders, preferred shareholders, and lessors often place restrictions upon dividend payments and thereby compel the retention of earnings.

19. Some of the reasons why the directors may decide to allow the retained earnings to increase as a matter of corporate financial policy are: (a) the earnings may not reflect corresponding increase of available cash; (b) a restriction of dividends in prosperous years may permit the continued payment of dividends in poor years; (c) a corporation may need funds for expansion of working capital or plant and equipment; (d) the firm may consider the reduction of indebtedness desirable rather than the declaration of all or most of the net income as dividends; and the firm can distribute the funds to shareholders with lower tax burdens for them by using the cash to repurchase shares.

20. Firms may pay dividends in cash, other assets, or shares of its common stock. When cash dividends are declared, the entry is a debit to Retained Earnings and a credit to Dividends Payable. At the date of payment, Dividends Payable is debited and Cash is credited.

21. A distribution of a corporation's assets other than cash to its shareholders is a dividend in kind or a property dividend. The amount debited to Retained Earnings is the fair market value of the assets distributed. Any gain or loss is recognized as part of income for the period.

22. A stock dividend is a distribution of additional shares to stockholders in proportion to their existing holdings without any additional contributions. In the accounts, a stock dividend requires a transfer from retained earnings to the contributed capital accounts. Generally accepted accounting principles require that the amount transferred from retained earnings be equal to the market value of the shares issued. Therefore, the resulting entry generally is a debit to Retained Earnings (for fair market value) and credits to the Common Stock account (for par value) and to the Additional Paid-In Capital account for the excess of fair market value over the par value. Following the stock dividend, a stockholder has additional shares, but the stockholder's proportionate interest in the capital of the corporation and proportionate voting power have not changed.

23. A stock split (or more technically, split-up) is a distribution of additional shares of stock to shareholders in proportion to their existing holdings without additional contributions. Although difficult to distinguish, the primary difference between a stock dividend and a stock split is that in a stock split the par or stated value of all stock in the issued class is reduced proportionately to the additional shares issued. A stock split usually does not require a journal entry. Large stock dividends are generally treated as stock splits. Stock splits (or large stock dividends) usually reduce the market value per share in reverse proportion to the split (or dividend). Management, to keep the market prices per share from rising to an unacceptable price level, has used stock splits.

24. Treasury shares or treasury stock are shares of stock reacquired by the issuing corporation. Firms reacquire their own shares to use in various option arrangements, invest excess cash, to defend against unfriendly takeover bids and to distribute cash to shareholders in a tax-advantaged way. When stock is reacquired, the corporation debits an account, Treasury Shares, with the total amount paid to reacquire the shares. If the corporation reissues the shares, it debits cash for the amount received and credits the Treasury Shares account with the cost of the shares. If the reissue price is greater than the acquisition price, the corporation credits the difference to the Additional Paid-in Capital account to make the entry balance. If the reissue price is less than the amount paid, the debit to make the entry balance is usually to Additional Paid-In Capital, as long as there is a sufficient credit balance in that account. If there is not, the additional balancing debit goes directly to Retained Earnings. Corporations present the Treasury Shares account as a contra account to total stockholders' equity on the balance sheet. A corporation does not report profit or loss on transactions involving its own shares.

25. Firms use assets provided by creditors and owners in operating transactions to generate earnings. Analyst use information about past earnings to project future earnings and often use projected earnings to value the firm, particularly when they use price-earnings ratios.

26. The Retained Earnings account increases (decreases) each period by the amount of net income (net loss) and decreases for dividends declared. The income statement reports revenues from the sale of products to customers and the expenses for the resources used to generate these revenues. Firms sometimes engage in transaction that are peripherally related to their customary revenue generating operations, nonrecurring, or relate to measurements of income of prior periods. The reporting issue for these peripheral transactions is whether they should be reported on the income statement of the current period or added (credited) or deducted (debited) directly in retained earnings, bypassing the income statement. Generally accepted accounting principles usually require disclosures of all items on the income statement before their transfer to retained earnings. Others advocate reporting peripheral transactions directly in retained earnings providing only current periods usual recurring transactions on the income statement.

27. Earnings transactions can be recurring (versus nonrecurring), central to the firm's business (versus peripheral), unrealized (versus realized) gains and losses from changes in the market values of assets and liabilities or adjustments for errors and changes in accounting principles and estimates. The issues related to the type of operating transactions affect the quality of earnings. Firms have incentives to report good earnings news in ways that make it appear recurring and central but to report bad earnings news as nonrecurring and peripheral. In evaluating a firm's profitability, the nature of income items must be considered. Does the income item result from the firm's primary operating activity or from an activity incidental or peripheral to the primary operating activities? Is the income item recurring or nonrecurring? Earnings items of a nonrecurring nature should not affect ongoing assessments of profitability.

28. Accountants distinguish between revenues and expenses on the one hand and gains and losses on the others. Revenues and expenses result from the recurring, primary operating activities of a business. Gains and losses result from either peripheral activities or nonrecurring activities. A second distinction is that revenues and expenses are gross concepts, whereas gains and losses are net concepts.

29. Depending on the nature of a firm's income for the period, the income statement may contain some or all of the following sections or categories: (a) earnings from continuing operations; (b) earnings, gains, and losses from discontinued operations; (c) extraordinary gains and losses.

30. "Earnings from Continuing Operations" reflects the revenues, gains, expenses, and losses from the continuing areas of business activity of a firm and includes income derived from a firm's primary business activities as well as from activities peripherally related to operations.

31. If a firm sells a major division or segment of its business during the year or contemplates such a sale within a short time after the end of an accounting period, any earnings, gains, and losses related to the segment should be disclosed separately and reported below earnings from continuing operations. The separate disclosure in a section titled "Earnings, Gains and Losses from Discontinued Operations" alerts the financial statement reader that the firm does not expect this source of income to continue.

32. Extraordinary gains and losses are presented in a separate section of the income statement and are reported net of their tax effect. For an item to be classified as extraordinary, it must meet both of the following criteria: (a) unusual in nature and (b) infrequent in occurrence.

33. A correction of errors causes the total of retained earnings to change other than transactions reported in the income statement for that period and dividends. A firm records a correction of errors of previous accounting periods by making either a debit or a credit to Retained Earnings. Examples of such errors are miscounting inventories or arithmetic mistakes.

34. A firm that changes its principles, or methods, of accounting during the period must disclose in some cases the effects of the change on beginning Retained Earnings and retroactively restate net income for each prior year reported under the new principle or method.

35. Changes in accounting estimates occur as time passes and new information becomes available. Examples of changes in estimates include the amount to recognize as uncollectible accounts and the useful lives of depreciable assets. The effects of changes in estimates are reported in the income statements of the current and future periods not through retained earnings as a correction of errors.

36. The FASB has increasingly required firms to report certain assets and liabilities at their current market values at the end of each period instead of their historical, or acquisition, costs. When a firm writes assets and liabilities down or up to market value, the question arises as to how it should treat the offsetting debit (loss) or credit (gain). In some cases, GAAP require firms to include the gains and losses, even though not yet realized, in earnings in the period of the revaluation. The FASB has been reluctant, however, to require firms to include all unrealized gains and losses from the revaluation of asset and liabilities in earnings. Unrealized gains and losses have typically appeared on a separate line in the shareholders' equity section of the balance sheet. In 1997, the FASB began requiring firms to disclose unrealized gains and losses that historically bypassed the income statement in a new category called other comprehensive income. Other comprehensive income can be reported in a combined statement of earnings and other comprehensive income, in a separate statement of other comprehensive income, or included in a statement of changes in shareholders' equity.

37. Accountants calculate earnings per share of common stock by dividing net income attributable to common shareholders by the weighted-average number of shares of common stock outstanding during the period. Earnings-per-share calculations become more complicated when a firm has outstanding securities that if exchanged for common stock would decrease earnings per share. Stock options, stock rights, warrants, and convertible bonds all have the potential of reducing earnings per share and must be taken into account in calculating earnings per share.

38. Balance sheet accounts contain information about capital contribution, retained earnings and dividends, accumulated other comprehensive income, and treasury stock activity related to common shareholders' equity. These four components are the equity of the common shareholders. The book value of a common share is the total common stockholders' equity divided by the number of shares outstanding.

39. The annual report to shareholders must explain the changes in all share-holders' equity accounts. The reconciliation of retained earnings may appear in the balance sheet, in a combined statement of earnings and retained earnings, or in a separate statement of shareholders' equity. The reconciliation of Other Comprehensive Income may also appear in a separate statement.

40. The accounting for stockholders' equity in most developed countries closely parallels that in the United States. One major difference is the use of "reserve" accounts. In many other countries the use of the reserve account is to disclose a portion of retained earnings that is either permanently or temporarily not available for future dividends. A second use of reserve accounts relates to revaluations of assets. Accounting regulations in the Great Britain and France permits firms to revalue periodically their plant and other assets.

41. Most transactions (with the exception of net income) affecting shareholders equity accounts appear in the statement of cash flows as financing activities. Example transactions include cash received from the issue of common stock, preferred stock, and stock under options, rights, or warrants arrangements. Cash dividends paid appear as outflows in the financing activities section of the statement of cash flows, significant shareholder equity transactions not involving cash are disclosed in a supplementary schedule or note to the financial statements.

Questions and Exercises

True/False. For each of the following statements, place a T or F in the space provided to indicate whether the statement is true or false.

_____ 1. Preferred stock is frequently the only voting stock of the company.

_____ 2. Common shareholders have the claim to earnings of the corporation after commitments to creditors and preferred shareholders have been satisfied.

_____ 3. Additional Paid-In Capital, Capital Contributed in Excess of Par (Stated) Value, and Premium on Capital Stock are three titles referring to the same type of account.

_____ 4. Premium on Common Stock is amortized in the same manner as Premium on Bonds.

_____ 5. Treasury Stock refers to shares of stock reacquired by the issuing corporation.

_____ 6. Bondholder agreements often place restrictions upon dividend payments.

_____ 7. Stock splits and stock dividends are accounted for in the same manner.

_____ 8. Changes in accounting estimates are reported in income statements of the current and future periods.

———— 9. Accounting regulations permit the use of a reserve account for plant revaluation in the United States, the United Kingdom and France.

———— 10. Changes in shareholders' equity usually are not reported in annual reports but are provided to the SEC.

———— 11. "Earnings from Continuing Operations" includes only income derived from a firm's primary business activities.

———— 12. Earnings per share data should be considered as supplementary and therefore disclosed only at the discretion of management.

———— 13. In assessing the quality of a firm's earnings, one factor to consider is the recurring or nonrecurring nature of various income items.

———— 14. Gains or losses on sale of a segment of a business should not be disclosed in a separate classification on the income statement.

———— 15. For an item to qualify as extraordinary, it must be both unusual in nature and infrequent in occurrence.

———— 16. Comprehensive income is the change in equity (net assets) of an entity during a period from transactions and other events and circumstances from nonowner sources.

———— 17. Accumulated other comprehensive income is the change in equity (net assets) of an entity during a period from transactions and other events and circumstances from nonowner sources.

———— 18. Other comprehensive income refers to items of comprehensive income not themselves part of earnings.

———— 19. State corporation laws generally provide that dividends must be "paid out of earnings."

———— 20. The corporate form provides the owner, or shareholder with unlimited liability.

———— 21. Cumulative preferred stock entitles the holder to receive all current and previously postponed dividends before common stock dividends can be distributed.

———— 22. Many state laws carry mandatory redemption features, requiring the issuing firm to repurchase the shares from their holders.

———— 23. The cost of treasury stock is presented in the Investment section of the balance sheet with other securities owned by the company.

———— 24. The book value of common stock while not equal to fair market value is almost always equal to the par value or stated value of the shares.

———— 25. Stock options and stock rights are similar but stock options are nontransferable while stock rights are traded in the open market.

_____ 26. At the end of an accounting period, a well-managed company will always have an increase in cash at least equal to the net income for the period.

_____ 27. Net assets refers to the excess of all assets over all liabilities.

_____ 28. For most companies the amount and timing of dividend declarations are determined by the shareholders at their annual meeting.

_____ 29. Corporations in most cases pay out dividends equal to net income unless specific restrictions (either legal or financial) are stated in the annual report.

_____ 30. A stock dividend is often referred to as a dividend in kind.

_____ 31. In a stock split the par or stated value of all stock in the issued class is reduced in proportion to the additional shares issued.

_____ 32. Cash received from the issuance of stock to an employee exercising a stock option is reported in the financing section of the statement of cash flows.

_____ 33. Stock rights cannot be traded in the open market since it is an exclusive right for employees.

_____ 34. Stock options, often a part of compensation plans, offer employees the opportunity to purchase, at some time within a specified number of years in the future, shares in their company at a specified price.

_____ 35. Corrections of errors result in either a debit or credit to Retained Earnings.

_____ 36. It is difficult to raise large amounts of funds for corporations because so many shares of relatively small value must be sold.

_____ 37. Par value and stated value have basically the same effect on the recording in the accounts of the issue of capital stock.

_____ 38. Convertibility is generally a feature of common stock allowing the holder to convert shares into preferred stock at some specified time in the future.

Matching.

1. From the list of terms below, select that term which is most closely associated with each of the descriptive phrases or statements that follows and place the letter for that term in the space provided.

    a. Additional Paid-in Capital
    b. Callable Preferred Shares
    c. Common Shares
    d. Comprehensive Income
    e. Contractual Restriction on Dividends
    f. Convertible Bonds
    g. Convertible Preferred Shares
    h. Corporate Bylaws
    i. Corporate Charter
    j. Cumulative Preferred Shares

    k. Net Assets
    l. Par Value
    m. Preferred Shares
    n. Redeemable Preferred Shares
    o. Reserve Accounts
    p. Stock Dividends
    q. Stock Options
    r. Stock Rights
    s. Stock Splits
    t. Stock Warrants
    u. Treasury Shares

_____ 1. Income includes the effects of all transactions changing shareholders' equity (except capital contributions and dividends), even those such as unrealized gains and losses on holdings of investments.

_____ 2. The rules and regulations governing the internal affairs of the corporation.

_____ 3. An example would be a restriction of dividends imposed by an agreement between bondholders and the corporation.

_____ 4. Type of preferred shares which may be reacquired by the corporation at a specified price, which may vary according to a predetermined time schedule.

_____ 5. A nominal value per share specified in the articles of incorporation and printed on the face of the stock certificates.

_____ 6. Class of stock usually entitling the holder to dividends at a certain rate which must be paid before dividends can be declared and paid to common shareholders.

_____ 7. Used in many countries to disclose a portion of retained earnings that is either permanently or temporarily not available for future dividends.

_____ 8. Shares of stock reacquired by the issuing corporation.

_____ 9.   The agreement between the firm and the state in which the business is incorporated.

_____ 10. Type of shares that must receive all current and previously postponed dividends before dividends may be issued to other classes of stock.

_____ 11. Account title used to designate contributed capital by owners paid in excess of par or stated value.

_____ 12. An issue of additional shares of stock to shareholders in proportion to existing holdings without any additional contributions but with a proportional reduction of the par or stated value of all the stock in the issued class.

_____ 13. An issue of an additional number of shares to shareholders in proportion to their existing holdings without any additional contribution and without a change in the par value per share of stock.

_____ 14. The voting class of stock which also has a residual claim to earnings.

_____ 15. Issued to the general public for cash allowing the holder to buy shares of stock in the future at a specified price.

_____ 16. Granted to current stockholders, usually at no cost, allowing the holder to buy shares of stock at a specified price in the future.

_____ 17. Securities with a feature which allows the stockholder to convert the shares into a specified amount of common shares at specified times.

_____ 18. Preferred stock issues which have some characteristics of debt i.e. required repurchase features or repurchase at the option of the holder.

_____ 19. Part of employee compensation plan which under generally accepted accounting principles may in the future require the market value at the date of the grant to be amortized over the periods benefitted.

_____ 20. Type of bonds which may be exchanged for common shares at specified times at the option of its owner.

_____ 21. Excess of all assets over all liabilities of a firm.

2.   Indicate whether each of the following transactions and events should be classified within the statement of earnings and comprehensive income as (a) earnings from continuing operations; (b) earnings, gains, and losses from discontinued operations; (c) extraordinary gains and losses; or (d) other comprehensive income.

_____ 1.   Foreign currency translation adjustments.

_____ 2.   Gain on the sale of the vice-president's company automobile.

_____ 3.   Loss from sale of investment in preferred stock.

_____ 4. President's salary during the year.

_____ 5. Loss on damages from a tidal wave that hit the company's factory in Key West, Florida.

_____ 6. The cost of goods sold during the year.

_____ 7. Loss on factory and equipment in a South American country when confiscated by the government of that country.

_____ 8. Interest received on short-term investments.

_____ 9. Gain on sale of the company's only division for manufacturing sports equipment.

_____ 10. Losses during the year up to the time of sale of the division in (9).

_____ 11. Unrealized holding losses on securities held during the period.

_____ 12. Loss on decline in the market value of several inventory items.

Multiple Choice. Choose the best answer for each of the following questions and enter the identifying letter in the space provided.

The information which follows relates to Questions 1 - 4. Choose the answer to each question from the following four choices:

    a. Primary operating activity, which is recurring.

    b. Primary operating activity, which is nonrecurring.

    c. A recurring activity, which is peripheral to primary operations.

    d. A nonrecurring activity, which is peripheral to primary operations.

_____ 1. A manufacturing firm sold a parcel of land next to one of its warehouses.

_____ 2. A fast food restaurant chain sold a division that operated movie theaters.

_____ 3. A professional soccer team paid a signing bonus to one of its new players.

_____ 4. A Florida hotel chain's properties located on the "Emerald Coast" were destroyed when the area was devastated by an earthquake.

_____ 5. Which of the following is usually sold to the general public for cash?

    a. Stock options.
    b. Stock rights.
    c. Stock warrants.
    d. None of the above.

_____ 6. Which of the following does not generally require a journal entry?

    a. Issue shares in a stock split.
    b. Issue shares in a stock dividend.
    c. Reissue treasury shares.
    d. Issue stock warrants.

_____ 7. Which of the following increases total shareholders' equity?

    a. Issue shares in a stock split.
    b. Issue shares in a stock dividend.
    c. Reissue treasury shares.
    d. None of the above.

_____ 8. Which of the following generally requires a debit to retained earnings?

    a. Stock dividend.
    b. Stock split.
    c. Both (a) and (b) above.
    d. None of the above.

_____ 9. When a corporation reissues treasury shares for a price above their acquisition price the amount above the acquisition price is credited to

    a. Additional Paid-in Capital.
    b. Treasury Stock.
    c. Gain on Sale of Treasury Stock.
    d. Retained Earnings.

_____ 10. The account, Treasury Shares, should be disclosed in the balance sheet as a

    a. Short-term investment.
    b. Contra to total shareholders equity.
    c. Deferred charge.
    d. Stock investment account.

_____ 11. The owners' equity account with a normal debit balance is

    a. Additional Paid-in Capital.
    b. Common Stock.
    c. Retained Earnings.
    d. Treasury Shares.

_____ 12. Accumulated other comprehensive income:

a. Is the change in equity (net assets) of an entity during a period from transactions and other events and circumstances from nonowner sources.
b. Is the balance sheet amount in owners' equity showing the total of all other comprehensive income amounts from all prior periods.
c. Refers to items of comprehensive income not themselves part of earnings.
d. None of the above.

_____ 13. Which of the following items would not appear on an Earnings Statement?

a. Earnings from continuing operations.
b. The effects of a change in accounting principles.
c. Additional paid in capital.
d. An extraordinary loss.

_____ 14. The Orange Bottling Company owned a professional baseball team, which it sold on June 30, Year 1, for a gain of $36 million. This transaction is an example of which of the following?

a. Income from Continuing Operations.
b. Extraordinary gain.
c. Gain from a discontinued operation.
d. A change in accounting principle.

_____ 15. Other comprehensive income can be reported each period by:

a. Including it in a combined statement of earnings and other comprehensive income, in effect appending it to the bottom of the traditional income statement.
b. Including it in a separate statement of other comprehensive income.
c. Including it in a statement of changes in shareholders' equity.
d. All of the above are acceptable.

_____ 16. The following would be included in other comprehensive income:

a. Unrealized holding gains on securities arising during the period.
b. Foreign currency translation adjustments.
c. Unrealized holding losses on securities arising during the period.
d. All of the above.

_____ 17. Comprehensive income:

a. Is the change in equity (net assets) of an entity during a period from transaction and other events and circumstances from nonowner sources.
b. Is the balance sheet amount in owners' equity showing the total of all other comprehensive income amounts from all prior periods.
c. Refers to items of comprehensive income not themselves part of earnings.
d. None of the above.

_____ 18. Other comprehensive income:

a. Is the change in equity (net assets) of an entity during a period from transaction and other events and circumstances from nonowner sources.
b. Is the balance sheet amount in owners' equity showing the total of all other comprehensive income amounts from all prior periods.
c. Refers to items of comprehensive income not themselves part of earnings.
d. None of the above.

_____ 19. The corporate charter (or articles of incorporation) is

a. The contract between the firm and the state in which the business is incorporated.
b. The corporation laws of the state in which incorporation takes place.
c. The bylaws of the corporation.
d. The stock contract.

_____ 20. One feature that is generally not associated with preferred stock is the

a. Cumulative feature.
b. Callable feature.
c. Voting right.
d. Conversion right.

_____ 21. Which of the following enables the holder to become a common stockholder?

a. Callable preferred shares.
b. Redeemable preferred shares.
c. Convertible preferred shares.
d. None of the above.

_____ 22. A corporation usually recognizes a gain or loss when

a. It reissues treasury stock for an amount less than or greater than its par value.
b. It reissues treasury stock for an amount less than or greater than its cost to acquire the stock.
c. It issues stock to employees at a price specified in a stock option plan.
d. None of the above.

_____ 23. When a company issues its capital stock for an amount in excess of the par value the excess amount is credited to

a. Additional Paid-in Capital.
b. Capital Contributed in Excess of Par Value.
c. Premium on Capital Stock.
d. All three account titles in (a), (b), and (c) are acceptable.

_____ 24. The following should be accounted for in current and future income statements

a. The effect on past year's earnings of a change from LIFO to FIFO.
b. Changes in Accounting Estimates.
c. Error corrections.
d. All of the above.

_____ 25. The following should be presented in the statement of cash flows as an inflow from financing activities.

a. Payment of cash dividends.
b. The receipt of cash from the reissue of treasury shares.
c. The purchase of treasury shares using cash.
d. None of the above.

_____ 26. All of the following should be presented in the financing activities section of the statement of cash flows except

a. Issue of common shares for cash.
b. Issue of preferred shares for cash.
c. Sale of investment in stock for cash.
d. Payment of cash dividends.

_____ 27. Income statement prepared under generally accepted accounting principles may contain the following components except

a. Income from extraordinary items.
b. Corrections of errors.
c. Adjustments for changes in accounting principles.
d. Income, gains, and losses from discontinued operations.

_____ 28. The Zerbini Company reported a loss when a foreign government expropriated the assets of Zerbini's division in that country. The foreign government did not compensate Zerbini for the assets taken. This transaction is an example of which of the following:

a. Loss from continuing operations.
b. Extraordinary loss.
c. Loss from a discontinued operation.
d. A change in accounting principle.

_____ 29. On January 1, Year 3, Fettig Company purchased some machinery for $500,000. The machinery had a 10-year life; a salvage value of $50,000; and was depreciated using straight-line depreciation. In Year 6, Fettig decided to switch from straight-line depreciation to the double declining balance method of depreciation. This is an example of which of the following?

a. Extraordinary item.
b. Discontinued operation.
c. Change in accounting principle.
d. Correction of an error.

_____ 30. In assessing the quality of a firm's earnings, one factor to consider is the recurring or nonrecurring nature of various income items. Which of the following items would be considered in predicting a firm's future earnings performance?

a. A loss which resulted from a hurricane.
b. A gain on the sale of a discontinued operation.
c. Losses reported by a fashion merchandising chain that resulted from style changes.
d. A loss which resulted from an expropriation of the firm's assets located in a foreign country.

_____ 31. Which of the following distributions usually does not require a debit to retained earnings?

a. Cash dividend.
b. Dividend in kind.
c. Stock dividend.
d. Stock split.

_____ 32. Which of the following is usually associated with employee compensation plans?

a. Stock options.
b. Stock rights.
c. Stock warrants.
d. None of the above.

_____ 33. Which of the following entries are correct when a company issues convertible bonds?

a. Debit Cash, credit Convertible Bonds Payable.
b. Debit Cash, credit Convertible bonds Payable and Additional Paid-in Capital.
c. Neither entry is correct.
d. Both entries are correct.

_____ 34. Which of the following require direct adjustments to retained earnings?

a. Extraordinary items.
b. Gain or loss from discontinued operations.
c. Error Correction.
d. None of the above.

Exercises

1. Marcks Company reported the following for the year ending December 31, Year 3:

Administrative Expenses	1,950,000
Cost of Goods Sold	15,600,000
Gain on Sale of Division (net of tax)	1,170,000
Loss from Expropriation of Assets by Foreign Government (net of tax)	650,000
Loss from Operations of Division Sold (net of tax)	910,000
Sales	26,000,000
Selling Expenses	3,250,000

The company's "Income from Continuing Operations" is taxed at a 30 percent rate.

Prepare an income statement for Marcks Company for the year ending December 31, Year 3.

2. Prepare journal entries for the following treasury stock transactions of Heather Company.

   a. Reacquired 4,000 shares of $10 par value common stock on September 14 for $28 per share.

   b. Reacquired 5,000 shares of $10 par value common stock on September 15 for $29 per share.

   c. Issued 2,100 shares of treasury stock to employees upon the exercise of stock options (The firm did not use the market value method.) at a price of $31 per share on November 1. Heather Company uses a first-in, first-out assumption on reissues of treasury stock.

   d. Issued 1,800 shares of treasury stock to holders of 900 shares of convertible preferred stock, which had a book value of $52,000 on November 4. Heather uses book value to record conversions of preferred stock.

   e. Sold 600 shares of treasury stock on the open market for $27 per share on December 1.

3. From the following accounts, indicate in the space provided the correct debit and credit entries corresponding to the transactions described. Credit entries should be shown in parentheses. The first is answered as an example.

    a. Additional Paid-in Capital   h. Preferred Stock

    b. Cash   i. Retained Earnings

    c. Common Stock   j. Redeemable Preferred Stock

    d. Common Stock Warrants   k. Treasury Stock

    e. Dividends Payable   l. Stock Options

    f. Inventory   m. Some account not listed

    g. Investments   n. No Formal Journal Entry

<u>b, (c)</u>   1. Issued common stock at par value for cash.

_____   2. A stock dividend is declared and distributed at a time when the market value is above the par value.

_____   3. The board of directors authorize the distribution of a 2 for 1 stock split.

_____   4. Stock warrants to acquire common stock are issued for cash to the public.

_____   5. One-half of the warrants in (4) are submitted for redemption with the appropriate cash (the amount exceeds the par value of the stock).

_____   6. The remaining warrants from (4) expire without having been exercised.

_____   7. Closed Income Summary (credit Balance) to Retained Earnings.

_____   8. The board of directors declared a cash dividend to be distributed in 3 weeks.

_____   9. Cash dividend from (8) is paid.

_____ 10. Preferred stock is issued for cash in excess of the par value of the shares issued.

_____ 11. A stock option is granted to employees when the option price was equal to the market price (The firm uses the market value method.).

_____ 12. The option in (11) above is exercised. The option price is above par value.

_____ 13. Preferred stock is "retired." The price paid to retire is in excess of the original issue price (which was above par value).

294

_____ 14. A declaration and distribution of a dividend in kind, distributing shares of another company held as an investment. The investment cost is equal to its fair market value at the time of the declaration.

_____ 15. Common shares previously issued are reacquired by the corporation, which gives cash in excess of the price for which the shares were initially sold.

_____ 16. One-half of the shares in (11) are reissued at an amount which exceeds one-half the purchase price.

_____ 17. The remaining one-half of the treasury shares are reissued at an amount which is less than one-half the purchase price.

_____ 18. An error was discovered in which the inventory at the end of the previous period was understated by $15,000.

4. Record the following entries in the books of Prince-Williams Corporation.

a. Issued 1,000 shares of common stock for $15 cash per share. The common shares had a $10 par value per share.

b. A 10% common stock dividend was declared and issued. At the time of issuance there were 100,000 shares outstanding, each share was currently trading on the open market for $16 per share.

c. Reacquired 1000 shares of common stock (treasury shares) paying $14,000.

d. Reissued 250 shares obtained in (c) above, receiving $13 per share.

e. Reissued 250 shares obtained in (c) above, receiving $15 per share.

f.	Issued 400 shares of preferred stock for $50 cash per share. The preferred stock had a $40 par value per share.

g.	Reacquired 300 shares of preferred stock (treasury shares) from (f) above paying $52 per share.

h.	Reacquired 100 shares of preferred stock from (f) above paying $52 per share and formally "retired" these shares.

i.	Reissued 200 shares of preferred stock (treasury shares) from (g) above receiving $52 per share.

j.	Retired 100 shares of preferred stock (treasury shares) from (g) above.

k.	Declared a cash dividend to shareholders totaling $200,000.

l.	Granted a common stock option to employees to acquire 3,000 shares at $15 a share, which is the current market price of the stock. (The firm uses the market value method. The market value of the option for these shares is $5,000. Assume all of the employee benefit is attributed to the current period.).

m. Employees exercised stock options in (1) to acquire the 3,000 shares.

n. The firm issues at par $50,000 of 20-year bonds, 12 percent semiannual coupon bonds, each $1,000 bond convertible into 40 shares of the company's $10 par-value common stock. The bonds without the convertible feature would have sold for $47,000.

o. Paid cash dividend declared in (k) above.

p. Declares and distributes a dividend in kind. Prince-Williams owns 1,000 shares of Stephens which had a cost of $10 per share. The shares have a $12 per share fair market value at the time of the dividend. The Stephens shares are distributed as a dividend.

q. Issued stock warrants to the public containing rights to purchase 2,000 common shares for $15 each and received $2,500 cash for the warrants.

r. Issued 500 shares of treasury stock (from transaction (c) above) as the rights for 500 common shares in (q) above were exercises.

s. The rights for 1,000 common shares in (q) above were exercised and common stock issued. The market price was $16.

t. The remaining rights in (q) above expire without being exercised.

u. The firm acquired a truck two years ago. The truck cost $40,000 and had a $5,000 estimated salvage value. The firm had recorded depreciation correctly for the past two years based on an estimated seven-year life using straight-line depreciation. The firm now estimates the total life will be four years. Record depreciation for this year (third year of asset's life) and any required adjustments to depreciation of previous years. Assume the estimated salvage value to remain $5,000.

v. Net income of $300,000 (balance in Income Summary) is closed to Retained Earnings.

Answers to Questions and Exercises

True/False

1. F	9. F	17. F	25. T	33. F
2. T	10. F	18. T	26. F	34. T
3. T	11. F	19. T	27. T	35. T
4. F	12. F	20. F	28. F	36. F
5. T	13. T	21. T	29. F	37. T
6. T	14. F	22. F	30. F	38. F
7. F	15. T	23. F	31. T	
8. T	16. T	24. F	32. T	

Matching

1. d	6. m	11. a	16. r	21. k
2. h	7. o	12. s	17. g	
3. e	8. u	13. p	18. n	
4. b	9. i	14. c	19. q	
5. l	10. j	15. t	20. f	

Matching

1. d	4. a	7. c	10. b
2. a	5. c	8. a	11. d
3. a	6. a	9. b	12. a

Multiple Choice

1. c	8. a	15. d	22. d	29. c
2. b	9. a	16. d	23. d	30. c
3. a	10. b	17. a	24. b	31. d
4. d	11. d	18. c	25. b	32. a
5. c	12. b	19. a	26. c	33. a
6. a	13. c	20. c	27. b	34. c
7. c	14. c	21. c	28. b	

Exercises

1.

Marcks Company
Income Statement
For Year Ending December 31, Year 3

Income (earnings) from Continuing Operations

Sales	$ 26,000,000
Less Cost of Goods Sold	(15,600,000)
Gross Margin	$ 10,400,000
Less Operating Expenses:	
Administrative Expenses	(1,950,000)
Selling Expenses	(3,250,000)
Earnings from Continuing Operations before Taxes	$ 5,200,000
Income Taxes	(1,560,000)
Earnings from Continuing Operations	$ 3,640,000

Earnings, Gains and Losses from Discontinued Operations

Loss from Operations of Division Sold (net of tax)	$(910,000)
Gain on Sale of Division (net of tax)	1,170,000
Earnings from Discontinued Operations	$ 260,000
Earnings Before Extraordinary Items	$ 3,900,000

Extraordinary Gains and Losses

Loss from Expropriation of Assets (net of tax)	($ 650,000)
Net Income (Earnings)	$ 3,250,000

2.

		Dr.	Cr.
a.	Treasury Shares - Common	112,000	
	Cash		112,000
	Reacquired 4,000 shares for $28 per share.		
b.	Treasury Shares - Common	145,000	
	Cash		145,000
	Reacquired 5,000 shares for $29 per share.		
c.	Cash	65,100	
	Treasury Shares - Common Cash		58,800
	Additional Paid-in Capital		6,300
	Issued 2,100 treasury shares of upon the exercise of stock options at $31 per share.		
d.	Preferred Stock	52,000	
	Treasury Shares - Common		50,400
	Additional Paid-in Capital		1,600
	Issued treasury stock for convertible preferred stock.		
e.	Cash	16,200	
	Additional Paid-in Capital	1,100	
	Treasury Shares - Common*		17,300
	To reissue 600 treasury shares.		
	* 100 @ 28 + 500 @ 29		

3.

1.	b,(c)	7.	m(i)	13.	h,a,i,(b)
2.	i,(c),(a)	8.	i,(e)	14.	i,(g)
3.	n	9.	e,(b)	15.	k,(b)
4.	b,(d)	10.	b,(h),(a)	16.	b,(k),(a)
5.	b,d,(c),(a)	11.	m,l	17.	b,i,(k), or b,a,(k)
6.	d,(a)	12.	b, l,(c),(a)	18.	f,(i)

4.

		Dr.	Cr.
a.	Cash	15,000	
	Common Stock		10,000
	Additional Paid-Capital		5,000
	To issue 1,000 shares of common stock for $15 per share.		
b.	Retained Earnings	160,000	
	Common Stock		100,000
	Additional Paid-in Capital		60,000
	To issue a 10% stock dividend.		
c.	Treasury Shares - Common	14,000	
	Cash		14,000
	To reacquire 1000 shares of common stock.		
d.	Cash	3,250	
	Additional Paid-in Capital*	250	
	Treasury Shares - Common		3,500
	To reissue 250 treasury shares. *Debit to Retained Earnings would be appropriate if balance insufficient in Additional Paid-in Capital.		
e.	Cash	3,750	
	Treasury Shares - Common		3,500
	Additional Paid-in Capital		250
	To reissue 250 treasury shares.		
f.	Cash	20,000	
	Preferred Stock		16,000
	Additional Paid-in Capital		4,000
	To issue 400 shares of preferred stock for $50 per share.		
g.	Treasury Shares - Preferred	15,600	
	Cash		15,600
	To reacquire 300 shares of preferred stock.		
h.	Preferred Stock	4,000	
	Additional Paid-in Capital	1,000	
	Retained Earnings	200	
	Cash		5,200
	To retire 100 shares of preferred stock paying $52 per share.		

4.(cont.)

		Dr.	Cr.
i.	Cash	10,400	
	Treasury Shares - Preferred		10,400
	To rcissue 200 shares of preferred stock.		
j.	Preferred Stock	4,000	
	Additional Paid-in Capital	1,000	
	Retained Earnings	200	
	Treasury Shares - Preferred		5,200
	To retire 100 shares of preferred stock held in treasury.		
k.	Retained Earnings	200,000	
	Dividends Payable		200,000
	To declare $200,000 cash dividend.		
l.	Compensation Expense	5,000	
	Stock Options		5,000
m.	Cash	45,000	
	Stock Options	5,000	
	Common Stock		30,000
	Additional Paid-in Capital		20,000
	To issue 2,000 shares under stock option plan.		
n.	Cash	50,000	
	Convertible Bonds Payable		50,000
	To issue $50,000 par 20-year, 12% semiannual coupon bonds convertible into 40 shares of common stock for each $1,000 bond.		
o.	Dividend Payable	200,000	
	Cash		200,000
	To pay cash dividend.		
p.	Retained Earnings	12,000	
	Investments		10,000
	Gain on Disposition of Investments		2,000
	To issue dividend in kind when shares of investment had a fair market value in excess of cost.		
q.	Cash	2,500	
	Common Stock Warrants		2,500
	To issued stock warrants.		
r.	Cash	7,500	
	Common Stock Warrants	625	
	Treasury Shares - Common		7,000
	Additional Paid-In Capital		1,125
	Treasury shares issued for the exercise of stock warrants for 500 shares.		